MATHEMATICS EXPLAINED
FOR PRIMARY TEACHERS

DEREK HAYLOCK is Senior Lecturer in Education at the University of East Anglia Norwich, where he is Co-Director of Primary Initial Teacher Training and responsible for the Mathematics components of the primary programmes. He has worked for 30 years in teacher education, both initial and in-service, but he also has considerable practical experience of teaching in primary classrooms. His work in mathematics education has taken him to Germany, Belgium, Lesotho, Kenya, Brunei and India. He is co-author (with Anne Cockburn) of *Mathematics in the Lower Primary Years* (Paul Chapman Publishing, 1997), co-author (with Doug McDougall) of *Mathematics Every Elementary Teacher Should Know* (Trifolium Books, Toronto, 1999), co-author (with Marcel D'Eon) of *Helping Low Achievers Succeed at Mathematics* (Trifolium Books, Toronto, 1999) and author of *Teaching Mathematics to Low Attainers 8–12* (Paul Chapman Publishing, 1991). His other publications include six books of Christian drama for young people and a Christmas musical (published by Church House/National Society), and frequent contributions to education journals.

MATHEMATICS EXPLAINED FOR PRIMARY TEACHERS

Second edition

Derek Haylock

P·C·P
Paul Chapman
Publishing

ISBN 0-7619-6950-0 (hbk)
ISBN 0-7619-6951-9 (pbk)
© Derek Haylock 1995, 2001
First published 1995
Second edition 2001
Reprinted 2001, 2002, 2003, 2004 (twice)

Paul Chapman Publishing Ltd
A SAGE Publications Company
1 Oliver's Yard
55 City Road
London EC1Y 1SP

SAGE Publications Inc
2455 Teller Road
Thousand Oaks
California 91320

SAGE Publications India Pvt. Ltd
B-42 Panchsheel Enclave
PO Box 4109
New Delhi 110 017

British Library Cataloguing in Publication data
A catalogue record for this book is available from the British Library

Typeset by Dorwyn Ltd., Rowlands Castle, Hampshire
Printed and bound in Great Britain by
Cromwell Press Limited, Trowbridge, Wiltshire

Contents

Acknowledgements

My thanks and genuine appreciation are due to the many student-teachers and primary-school teachers with whom I have been privileged to work over the years on initial training and in-service courses in teaching mathematics: for their willingness to get to grips with understanding mathematics, for their patience with me as I have tried to find the best ways of explaining mathematical ideas to them, for their honesty in sharing their own insecurities and uncertainties about the subject, and for thereby providing me with the material on which this book is based.

Introduction

Since the first edition of this book there have been some significant changes in primary school mathematics and teacher training in this country. The introduction in 1999 of the National Numeracy Strategy, with its emphasis on more interactive direct teaching of mathematics in primary schools, has underlined the importance of primary teachers themselves being confident with the mathematical ideas and processes they discuss with their pupils. Alongside this there has been the introduction in England of the new National Curriculum (DfEE/QCA, 2000), which reflects the Numeracy Strategy's emphases on the development of mental strategies for calculations and the encouragement of a greater facility with number, number facts, number relationships and number properties. Primary teachers coming to terms with the implications of these initiatives for their own teaching of mathematics should find this second edition of *Mathematics Explained for Primary Teachers* a useful reference book to clarify their own understanding.

For student-teachers we have seen the arrival of the National Curriculum for Initial Teacher Education (DfEE, Circular 4/98) – which includes a detailed and substantial requirement for mathematical knowledge for primary trainees – and a basic skills test in Numeracy that must be passed in order to obtain Qualified Teacher Status. This second edition of *Mathematics Explained for Primary Teachers* takes into account these extra requirements for mathematical knowledge. Substantial additions have been made to the original book in order to ensure that all the areas of mathematics in which primary student-teachers are required to be confident are explained in a straightforward and non-threatening manner.

Mathematics Explained for Primary Teachers is the book that many student-teachers and primary-school teachers have asked to be written. Time and time again when I have been explaining some mathematical ideas to such audiences I have been asked, 'Is there a book which explains all this?' Many people may be surprised that there is a need for such a book as this. But all my experience of working with primary teachers and student-teachers convinces me that there is. Even well-qualified graduates feel insecure and uncertain about much of the mathematics they have to teach, as is demonstrated in Chapter 1 of the book, and appreciate a systematic explanation of even the most elementary mathematical concepts and procedures of the primary curriculum. This insecurity leads to a neglect of the important teaching skill of 'explanation' in much of primary-school mathematics. So the book is written to explain mathematics to primary-school teachers, so that they in turn will have the confidence to provide appropriate, systematic and careful explanation of mathematical ideas and procedures to their pupils, with an emphasis on the development of understanding, rather than mere learning by rote.

After the introductory chapter, each of the subsequent chapters follows the same format. They each start with a reference to the programmes of study for mathematics in the National Curriculum (DfEE/QCA: *Mathematics: the National Curriculum for England*, London, 2000); this consists of an edited quotation taken mainly from Key Stage 2 and occasionally from Key Stage 1. This is just the starting point for the content covered in the chapter, since the mathematical material in the chapter must often go beyond this in order to deepen the teacher's own understanding and confidence appropriately. There follows a summary of the ideas explained in the chapter. Each section of the material in the chapter is then headed by a question of the kind that I am frequently asked by primary teachers and student-teachers, and sets out to answer the question posed. Then there is a set of self-assessment questions, which will enable the reader to reinforce his or her learning from the chapter. I would strongly encourage the reader to engage with these. Answers are provided at the end of the book. Each chapter then concludes with a summary of some teaching implications for dealing with the mathematics in question in the primary classroom.

1

Primary Teachers' Insecurity about Mathematics

One of the best ways for children to learn much of the mathematics in the primary-school curriculum is for a teacher who understands it to explain it to them. Much of the criticism of primary-school teaching of mathematics in recent reports (Ofsted, 1993a; 1993b) suggests that there is too great a reliance on approaches to the organization of pupils' activities which allow insufficient opportunities for teachers to provide this explanation. I have personally been particularly critical of the way in which some teachers rely almost exclusively on a commercial scheme to do the teaching of mathematics (Haylock, 1991). For many children, their only experience of mathematics in primary school is to work individually page by page through the scheme, hardly ever receiving any substantial explanation or teaching, other than at a procedural level when they get stuck on a particular question. I may be old-fashioned, but I do actually believe that teachers are paid to teach. Of course, there is more to learning mathematics than just having a teacher explain something and then following this up with exercises. Using and applying mathematics must always be at the heart of learning the subject. But children need 'explanation' and teachers must organize their lessons and the pupils' activities in ways that give opportunities for them to provide careful, systematic and appropriate explanation of mathematical concepts, procedures and principles to groups of children. That many primary teachers neglect this aspect of teaching may possibly be associated with a prevailing primary ethos, which emphasizes active learning and the needs of the individual pupil. But it is more likely to be a consequence of the insecurity about mathematics which is characteristic of many primary-school teachers and which seems to have been increased by the frequent revisions to the National Curriculum that have been experienced in England and Wales in recent years. This insecurity has made it more likely that teachers will lean heavily on the

1

commercial scheme to do their teaching for them. This book is written, therefore, to encourage teachers to redress the balance in their teaching, and to provide more opportunities to explain mathematical ideas to their pupils. I have set out to provide explanations of all the key mathematical ideas in the National Curriculum for England for Key Stages 1 and 2 (DfEE/QCA, 2000), with the aim of improving primary teachers' own understanding and increasing their personal confidence in talking to their pupils about these ideas.

The background for this book is partly my experience of working with graduates enrolled on a primary one-year initial teacher-training programme. The student-teachers I work with are highly motivated, good-honours graduates, with the subjects of their degree studies ranging across the curriculum. The ages of these student-teachers range from 23 to 40 years, with the mean age about 27. Over a number of years of working with such student-teachers, it has become clear that many of them start their course with a high degree of anxiety about having to teach mathematics. So an invitation was given for any student-teachers who felt particularly worried about mathematics to join a group who would meet for an hour a week throughout their course, to discuss their anxieties and to identify which aspects of the National Curriculum for mathematics appropriate to the age range they would be teaching gave them most concern. A surprisingly large number of student-teachers turned up for these sessions. Discussions with these student-teachers revealed both those aspects of mathematics anxiety which they still carry around with them, derived clearly from their own experiences of learning mathematics at school, and the specific areas of mathematics which they will have to teach for which they have doubts about their own understanding.

The students' comments on their feelings about mathematics can be conveniently categorized under five headings: 1) feelings of anxiety and fear; 2) expectations; 3) teaching and learning styles; 4) the image of mathematics and 5) language. These categories reflect closely the findings of other studies of the responses towards mathematics of adults in general and primary teachers in particular.

Mathematics anxiety in adults

Anxiety about mathematics and feelings of inadequacy in this subject are widespread amongst the adult population in Britain (Buxton, 1981). These phenomena are clearly demonstrated by surveys of adults' attitudes to mathematics (Sewell, 1981; Cockcroft, 1982). Findings indicate that many adults, in relation to mathematical tasks, admit to feelings of anxiety, helplessness, fear, dislike and even guilt. The feeling of guilt is found to be particularly marked amongst those with high academic qualifications, who feel they ought to be more confident in their under-standing of this subject. There is a common feeling that there are proper ways of doing mathematics and that the subject is characterized by questions to which your answers are either right or wrong. Feelings of failure, frustration and anxiety are identified by many adults as having their roots in unsympathetic attitudes of teachers and the expectations of parents. Furthermore, there are widespread confusions about many of the basic mathematical processes of everyday life (ACACE, 1981).

Mathematics anxiety in primary teachers

Research into primary-school teachers' attitudes to mathematics reveals that many of them continue to carry around with them these same kinds of 'baggage' (Briggs and Crook, 1991). There is evidence that many primary teachers still experience feelings of panic and anxiety when faced with un-familiar mathematical tasks (Briggs, 1993), that they are muddled in their thinking about many of the basic mathematical concepts which underpin the material they teach to children, and that they are all too aware of their personal inadequacies in mathematics (Haylock and Cockburn, 1997).

Student-teachers' anxieties

Below I have recounted many of the statements made by the primary student-teachers in my group about their attitudes towards and experi-ences of learning mathematics. In reading these comments it is import-ant to remember that these are students who have come through the system with relative success in mathematics: all must have GCSE grade C, or the equivalent, and can therefore be judged to be in the top 30% for mathematics attainment. Yet this is clearly not how they feel about themselves in relation to this subject.

Feelings of anxiety and fear

When these student-teachers talk freely about their memories of mathe-matics at school, their comments are sprinkled liberally with such words as *frightened*, *terror*, *horrific*, and several recalled having nightmares. These memories were very vivid and still lingered in their attitudes to the subject today as academically successful adults:

> I was very good at geometry, but really frightened of all the rest.

> Maths struck terror in my heart: a real fear that has stayed with me from over twenty years ago.

> I had nightmares about maths. They only went away when I passed my A-level!

> I had nightmares about maths as well: I really did, I'm not joking. Numbers and figures would go flashing through my head. Times tables, for example. I especially had nightmares about maths tests.

> It worried me a great deal. Maths lessons were horrific.

Others recalled feelings of stupidity or frustration at being faced with mathematical tasks:

> I remember that I would always feel stupid. I felt sure that everyone else understood.

> Things used to get hazy and frustrating when I was stuck on a question.

Those of us who teach mathematics must pause and wonder what it is that we do to pupils which produces successful, intelligent students who continue to feel like this about the subject.

Expectations

It seems as though the sources of anxiety for some student-teachers were the expectations of others:

> It was made worse because Dad's best subject was maths.

> My teacher gave me the impression that she thought I was bad at maths. So that's how I was labelled in my mind. When I got my GCE result she said, 'I never thought you'd get an A!' So I thought it must just be a fluke. I still thought I was no good at maths.

But the most common experience cited by these student-teachers was the teacher's expectation that they *should* be able to deal successfully with all the mathematical tasks they were given. They recalled clearly the negative effect on them of the teacher's response to their failure to understand:

> There were few maths teachers who could grasp the idea of people not being mathematical.

> The teacher just didn't understand why I had problems.

> Teachers expect you to be good at maths if you're good at other things. They look at your other subjects and just can't understand why you can't do maths. They say to you, 'You should be able to do this . . .'

I remember when I was 7 I had to do 100 long divisions. The headmaster came in to check on our progress. He picked me up and banged me up and down on my chair, saying, 'Why can't you do it?' After that I wouldn't ask if I couldn't understand something.

Teaching and learning styles

The student-teachers spoke with considerable vigour about their memories of the way mathematics was taught to them, recognizing now, from their adult perspective, that part of the problem was a significant limitation in the teaching style to which they were subjected:

> Surely not everyone can be bad at maths. Is it just that it's really badly taught?

> I remember one teacher who was good because she actually tried to explain things to me.

It was clear that most of the student-teachers in this group felt that they had been encouraged to learn by rote, to learn rules and recipes without understanding. This rote-learning style was then reinforced by apparent success:

> I was quite good at maths at school but I'm frightened of going back to teach it because I think I've probably forgotten most of what we learnt. I have a feeling that all I learnt was just memorized by rote and now it's all gone.

> I could rote learn things, but not understand them.

> I got through the exams by simply learning the rules. I would just look for clues in the question and find the appropriate process.

> I don't think I understood any of it. I got my O-level, but that just tested rote learning.

The limitations of this rote-learning syndrome were sometimes apparent to the students:

> I found you could do simple problems using the recipes, but then they'd throw in a question which was more complex. Then when the recipe I'd learnt didn't work I became angry.

> We would be given a real-life situation but I would find it difficult to separate the maths concepts out of it.

But it seems that some teachers positively discouraged a more appropriate learning style:

> I was made to feel like I was a nuisance for trying to understand.

> Lots of questions were going round in my head but I was too scared to ask them.

> I always tried to avoid asking questions in maths lessons because you were made to feel so stupid if you got it wrong. There must be ways of convincing a child it doesn't matter if they get a question wrong.

The following remark by one student-teacher in this context highlights how the role as a student-teacher serves to focus the feeling of anxiety and inadequacy arising from the rote-learning strategy adopted in the past:

> I have a real fear of teaching young children how to do things in maths as I just learnt rules and recipes. I have this dread of having to explain why we do something.

Image of mathematics

For some students, mathematics had an image of being a difficult subject, so much so that it was socially acceptable not to be any good at it:

> Maths has an image of being hard. You pick this idea up from friends, parents and even teachers.

> My Mum would tell me not to worry, saying, 'It's alright, we're all hopeless at maths!' It was as if it was socially acceptable to be bad at maths.

> Among my friends and family it was OK to be bad at maths, but it's not acceptable in society or employment.

For some, the problem seemed to lie with the feeling that mathematics was different from other subjects in school because the tasks given in mathematics are seen as essentially convergent and uncreative:

> Maths is not to do with the creativity of the individual, so you feel more restricted. All the time you think you've just got to get the right answer. And there is only one right answer.

> There's more scope for failure with maths. It's very obvious when you've failed, because things are either right or wrong, so you feel a fool, or look a fool in front of the others.

Language

A major problem for all the student-teachers was that mathematical language seemed to be too technical, too specific to the subject and not reinforced through their language use in everyday life:

> I find the language of maths difficult, but the handling of numbers is fine.

> Most of the words you use in maths you never use in everyday conversation.

Some words seem to have different meanings in maths, so you get confused.

I was always worried about saying the wrong things in maths lessons, because maths language seems to be so precise. I worry now that I'll say things wrong to children in school and get them confused. You know, like, 'Which is the bigger half?'

When we discussed the actual content of the National Curriculum programmes of study for mathematics, it became clear that the majority of the students' anxieties were related to language. Often they would not recognize mathematical ideas which they actually understood quite well, because they appeared in the National Curriculum in formal mathematical language, which they had either never known or forgotten through neglect. This seemed to be partly because most of this technical mathematical language is not used in normal everyday adult conversation, even amongst intelligent graduates:

I can't remember what prime numbers are . . . Why are they called prime numbers anyway?

Is a product when you multiply two numbers together?

What's the difference between mass and weight?

What is congruence? A mapping? Discrete data? A measure of spread? A quadrant? An inverse? Reflective symmetry? A translation? A transformation?

Even as a 'mathematician', I must confess that it is very rare for any of this kind of technical language to come into my everyday conversation, apart from when I am actually 'doing mathematics'. When this technical language was explained to the students, typical reactions would be:

Oh, is that what they mean? Why don't they say so, then?

Why do they have to dress it up in such complicated language?

Mathematics explained

Recognizing that amongst primary student-teachers and, indeed, amongst many primary-school teachers in general, there is this background of anxiety and confusion, a major task for initial and in-service training is the promotion of positive attitudes towards teaching mathematics in this age range. The evidence from my conversations with student-teachers suggests that to achieve this we need to shift perceptions of teaching mathematics away from the notion of teaching recipes and more towards the development of understanding. And we need to give time to explaining mathematical ideas, to the ironing out of confusions over the content and, particularly, the language of the mathematics National Curriculum.

Some students' comments later in the year highlighted the significance to them of having mathematics explained. The emphasis on explaining and understanding paid off in shifts of attitudes towards the subject:

> It's the first time anyone has actually explained things in maths to me. I feel a lot happier about going into the classroom now.

> The course seems to have reawakened an interest in mathematics for me and exploded the myth that maths was something I had to learn by rote for exams, rather than understand.

> I was really fearful about having to teach maths. That fear has now declined. I feel more confident and more informed about teaching maths now.

These kinds of reactions have prompted me to write this book. It is my hope that by focusing specifically on explaining the language and content of the mathematics that we teach in the primary age range, this book will help other student-teachers – and primary-school teachers in general – to develop this kind of confidence in approaching their teaching of this core subject of the curriculum to children who are at such an important stage in their educational development.

References

ACACE (Advisory Council for Adult and Continuing Education) (1981) *Adults' Mathematical Ability and Performance*, Leicester, ACACE.

Briggs, M. (1993) Bags and baggage revisited, *Mathematics Education Review*, Vol. 2, pp. 16–20.

Briggs, M. and Crook, J. (1991) Bags and baggage, in E. Love and D. Pimm (eds) *Teaching and Learning Mathematics*, London, Hodder & Stoughton.

Buxton, L. (1981) *Do You Panic About Maths?* London, Heinemann.

Cockcroft, W. H. (1982) *Mathematics Counts. Report of the Committee of Inquiry into the Teaching of Mathematics under the Chairmanship of Dr W.H. Cockcroft*, London, HMSO.

DfEE/QCA (Department for Education and Employment/Qualifications and Curriculum Authority) (2000) *Mathematics: The National Curriculum*, London, HMSO.

Haylock, D. (1991) *Teaching Mathematics to Low Attainers, 8–12*, London, Paul Chapman Publishing.

Haylock, D. and Cockburn, A. (1997) *Understanding Mathematics in the Lower Primary Years*, London, Paul Chapman Publishing.

Ofsted (Office for Standards in Education) (1993a) *The Teaching and Learning of Number in Primary Schools*, London, HMSO.

Ofsted (Office for Standards in Education) (1993b) *Curriculum Organisation and Classroom Practice in Primary Schools: A Follow-up Report*, London, HMSO.

Sewell, B. (1981) *Use of Mathematics by Adults in Daily Life*, Leicester, Advisory Council for Adult and Continuing Education.

2

Place Value

Pupils should be taught to: read, write and order whole numbers, recognizing that the position of a digit gives its value; count on or back in tens or hundreds from any two- or three-digit number; multiply and divide any whole number by 10 or 100, then extend to multiplying and dividing by 1000; understand and use decimal notation for tenths and hundredths in context; locate on a number line and order a set of numbers or measurements written in decimal notation; recognize thousandths; convert between centimetres and millimetres or metres, then between millimetres and metres, and metres and kilometres, explaining methods and reasoning.

In this chapter there are explanations of

- the way in which our Hindu-Arabic system of numeration uses the principle of place value;
- some contrasts with numeration systems from other cultures;
- powers of ten;
- multiplication and division by 10, 100 and 1000;
- two ways of demonstrating place value with materials;
- the role of zero as a place-holder;
- the extension of the place-value principle to tenths, hundredths, thousandths;
- the decimal point used as a separator in the contexts of money and measurement; and
- locating numbers written in decimal notation on a number line.

What is meant by 'place value'?

The system of numeration we use today is derived from an ancient Hindu system which was picked up and developed by Arab traders in the ninth and tenth centuries and which spread through Europe. Of course, there have been many other systems developed by various cultures

9

through the centuries, each with their particular features. Comparing some of these with the way we write numbers today enables us to appreciate the power and elegance of the Hindu-Arabic legacy. There is not space here to go into much detail, but the history of different numeration systems is a fascinating topic, with considerable potential for cross-curriculum work in schools, which will repay further study by the reader.

The Egyptian hieroglyphic system, used as long ago as 3000 BC, for example, had separate symbols for ten, a hundred, a thousand, ten thousand, a hundred thousand and a million. The Romans, some three thousand years later, in spite of all their other achievements, were using a numeration system which was still based on the same principle as the Egyptians, but simply had symbols for a few extra numbers, including 5, 50 and 500. Figure 2.1 illustrates how various numerals are written in these systems and, in particular, how the numeral 366 would be constructed. Clearly, the Hindu-Arabic system we use today is far more economic in its use of symbols. The reason for this is that it is based on the highly sophisticated concept of *place value*.

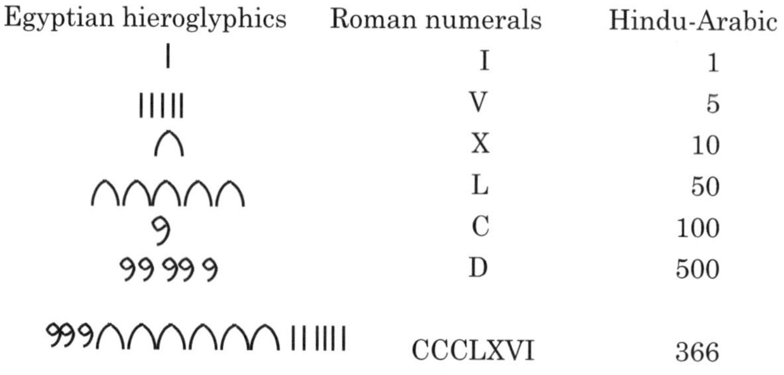

Egyptian hieroglyphics	Roman numerals	Hindu-Arabic
|	I	1
|||||	V	5
∧	X	10
∧∧∧∧∧	L	50
𐦀	C	100
99 99 9	D	500
999∧∧∧∧∧ |||||	CCCLXVI	366

Figure 2.1   Some numbers written in different numeration systems

In the Roman system, for example, to represent three hundreds, three Cs are needed, and each of these symbols represents the same quantity, namely, a hundred. Likewise, in the Egyptian system, three 'scrolls' are needed, each representing a hundred. In the Hindu-Arabic system we do not use a symbol representing a hundred to construct three hundreds: we use a symbol representing three! Just this one symbol is needed to represent three hundreds, and we know that it represents three hundreds, rather than three tens or three ones, because of the place in which it is written. The two sixes in 366, for example, do not stand for the same number: reading from left to right, the first stands for six tens and the second for six ones, because of the places in which they are written.

So, in our Hindu-Arabic place-value system, all numbers can be represented using a finite set of *digits*, namely, 0, 1, 2, 3, 4, 5, 6, 7, 8, 9. Like most numeration systems, no doubt because of the availability of our ten fingers for counting purposes, the system uses ten as a *base*. Larger whole numbers than 9 are constructed using *powers* of the base: ten, a hundred, a thousand, and so on. Of course, these powers of ten are not limited and can continue indefinitely with higher powers. This is how some of these powers are named, written as numerals, constructed from tens, and expressed as powers of ten in symbols and in words:

A million $\quad$ $1\,000\,000$ $= 10 \times 10 \times 10 \times 10 \times 10 \times 10 = 10^6$
(ten to the power six).

A hundred thousand $100\,000$ $= 10 \times 10 \times 10 \times 10 \times 10 \quad = 10^5$
(ten to the power five).

Ten thousand $\quad$ $10\,000$ $= 10 \times 10 \times 10 \times 10 \quad\quad = 10^4$
(ten to the power four).

A thousand $\quad$ 1000 $= 10 \times 10 \times 10 \quad\quad\quad = 10^3$
(ten to the power three).

A hundred $\quad$ 100 $= 10 \times 10 \quad\quad\quad\quad = 10^2$
(ten to the power two).

Ten $\quad$ 10 $= 10 \quad\quad\quad\quad\quad = 10^1$
(ten to the power one).

The place in which a digit is written then represents that number of one of these powers of ten. So, for example, working from right to left, in the numeral 2345 the 5 represents 5 ones, the 4 represents 4 tens, the 3 represents 3 hundreds and the 2 represents 2 thousands. Perversely, we work from right to left in determining the place values, with increasing powers of ten as we move in this direction. But, since we read from left to right, the numeral is read with the largest place value first: 'two thousands, three hundreds, four tens, and five'. Certain conventions of language then transform this into the customary form, 'two thousand, three hundred and forty-five'. So, the numeral 2345 is essentially a clever piece of shorthand, condensing a complicated mathematical expression into four symbols, as follows:

$$(2 \times 10^3) + (3 \times 10^2) + (4 \times 10^1) + 5 = 2345.$$

Notice that each of the powers of ten is equal to ten times the one below: a hundred equals 10 tens, a thousand equals 10 hundreds, and so on. This means that whenever you have accumulated ten in one place this can be exchanged for one in the next place to the left. This principle of being able to 'exchange one of these for ten of those' as you move right to left along the powers of ten, or to 'exchange ten of these for one of those' as you move left to right, is a very significant feature of the place-value system. It is essential for understanding the way in which we count. For example, the next number after 56, 57, 58, 59 . . . is 60, because we fill up the units position with ten ones and these are exchanged for an extra ten in the next column. This principle of exchanging is also fundamental to the ways we do calculations with numbers. It is the principle of 'carrying one' in addition (see Chapter 6). It also means that when necessary we can exchange one in any place for ten in the next lower place, for example, when doing subtraction by decomposition (see Chapter 6).

What are the best ways of explaining place value in concrete terms?

There are two sets of materials which provide particularly effective concrete embodiments of the place-value principle and therefore help us to explain the way our number system works. They are 1) base-ten blocks and 2) 1p, 10p and £1 coins. Figure 2.2 shows how the basic place-value principle of exchanging one for ten is built into these materials, for ones, tens and hundreds. Note that the ones in the base-ten blocks are sometimes referred to as units, the tens as longs and the hundreds as flats. With the blocks, of course, ten of one kind of block do actually make one of the next kind. With the coins it is simply that ten ones are *worth* the same as one ten, and so on.

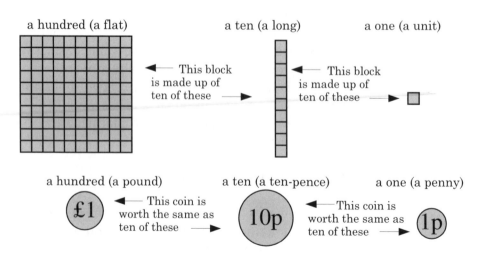

Figure 2.2   Materials for explaining place value

Figure 2.3 shows the number 366 represented with these materials. Notice that with both the blocks and the coins we have 3 hundreds, 6 tens and 6 ones; that the blocks are equivalent to 366 units; and that the coins amount to 366 pence. Representing numbers with these materials enables us to build up images which can help to make sense of the way we do calculations such as addition and subtraction by written methods, as will be seen in Chapter 6.

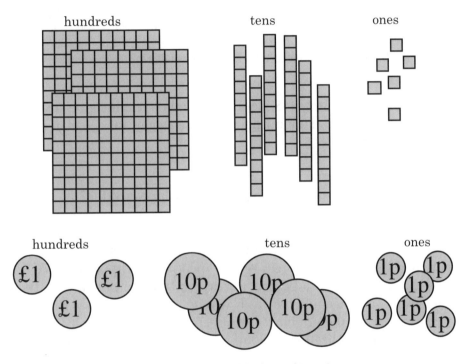

Figure 2.3   The number 366 in base-ten blocks and in coins

Another important image of number is that of the *number-line*. This image is particularly helpful for appreciating where a number is positioned in relation to other numbers. This positional aspect of a number is not so overt in the representation of numbers using base-ten materials. Figure 2.4 shows how the number 366 is located on the number line. The number-line image shows clearly that it comes between 300 and 400; that it comes between 360 and 370; and that it comes between 365 and 367. The significant mental processes involved in locating the position of the number on the number-line are counting in 100s, counting in 10s and counting in 1s. First you count from zero in 100s until you get to 300: 100, 200, 300; then from here in 10s until you get to 360: 310, 320, 330, 340, 350, 360; and then in 1s from here until you get to

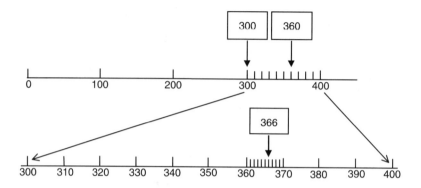

Figure 2.4   The number 366 located on the number-line

366: 361, 362, 363, 364, 365, 366. The number-line image is also particularly significant in supporting mental strategies for calculations, as will be seen in Chapter 5.

What is meant by saying that zero is a place-holder?

The Hindu-Arabic system was not the only one to use a place-value concept. Remarkably, about the same time as the Egyptians, the Babylonians had developed a system which incorporated this principle, although it used sixty as a base as well as ten. But a problem with their system was that you could not easily distinguish between, say, three and three sixties. They did not have a symbol for zero. It is generally thought that the Mayan civilization of South America was the first to develop a numeration system which included both the concept of place value and the consistent use of a symbol for zero. Clearly, there is some rich potential here for the inclusion of a mathematical dimension for pupils studying, for example, the ancient Egyptian and Mayan civilizations.

Figure 2.5 shows 'three hundred and seven' represented in base-ten blocks. Translated into symbols, without the use of a zero, this would easily be confused with thirty-seven: 37. The zero is used therefore to 'hold the place'; that is, to indicate the position of the tens' place, even though there are no tens there: 307. It is worth noting, therefore, that when we see a numeral such as 300, we should not think to ourselves that the 00 means 'hundred'. It is the *position* of the 3 which indicates that it stands for 'three hundred'; the function of the zeros is to make this position clear whilst indicating that there are no tens and no ones. This may seem a little pedantic, but it is the basis of the confusion that leads some children to write, for example, 30045 for 'three hundred and forty-five'.

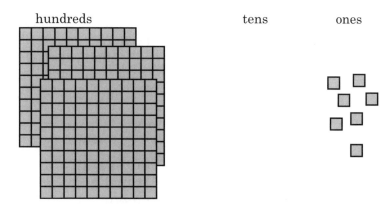

Figure 2.5   Three hundred and seven in base-ten blocks

What's the difference between a 'numeral' and a 'number'?

A numeral is the symbol, or collection of symbols, that we use to represent a number. The number is the concept represented by the numeral. We have seen in Figure 2.1 that the same number (for example, the one we call 'three hundred and sixty-six') can be represented by different numerals, such as 366 and CCCLXVI. Because the Hindu-Arabic system of numeration is now more or less universal, the distinction between the numeral and the number is easily lost.

How does the place-value system work for quantities less than one?

In exactly the same way. Once the principle of being able to 'exchange one of these for ten of those' is established, we can continue with it to the right of the units position, with tenths, hundredths, thousandths, and so on. These positions are usually referred to as *decimal places* and are separated from the units by the *decimal point*. Since a tenth and a hundredth are what you get if you divide a unit into ten and a hundred equal parts respectively, it follows that one unit can be exchanged for ten tenths, and one tenth can be exchanged for ten hundredths. In this way the principle of 'one of these being exchanged for ten of those' continues indefinitely to the right of the decimal point, with the values represented by the places getting progressively smaller by a factor of ten each time.

   A useful way to picture decimals is to explore what happens if we decide that the 'flat' piece in the base-ten blocks represents 'one whole unit'. In this case the 'longs' represent tenths of this unit and the small cubes represent hundredths. Then the collection of blocks shown in Figure 2.3 is made up of 3 units, 6 tenths and 6 hundredths. This quantity is represented by the decimal number 3.66. Similarly the blocks in Figure 2.5 would now represent the decimal number 3.07, that is, 3 units, no tenths and 7 hundredths.

Do you have to explain tenths, hundredths and decimal places when you introduce decimal notation in the contexts of money and measurement?

If we decide to call a pound coin the 'unit', then the collection of coins in Figure 2.3 also represents the number 3.66, since the ten-penny coins are tenths of a pound and the penny coins are hundredths of a pound. This makes sense, since this amount of money written in pounds, rather than in pence, is recorded conventionally as £3.66.

Now in terms of decimal numbers in general, the function of the decimal point is to indicate the transition from units to tenths. Because of this a decimal number such as 3.66 is read as 'three point six six', with the first figure after the point indicating the number of tenths and the next the number of hundredths. It would be confusing to read it as 'three point sixty-six', since this might be taken to mean three units and sixty-six tenths. There is a different convention, however, when using the decimal point in recording money: the amount £3.66 is read as 'three pounds sixty-six'. In this case there is no confusion about what the 'sixty-six' refers to: the context makes clear that it is 'sixty-six pence'. In practice, it is in money notation like this that children first encounter the decimal point. In this form we use the decimal point quite simply as something that separates the pounds from the pennies – so that £3.66 represents simply 3 whole pounds and 66 pence – without any awareness necessarily that the first 6 represents 6 tenths of a pound and the next 6 represents 6 hundredths. It is because the decimal point here is effectively no more than a separator of the pounds from the pennies that we have the convention of always writing two figures after the point when recording amounts of money in pounds. So, for example, we would write £3.20 rather than £3.2, and read it as 'three pounds twenty (meaning twenty pence)'. By contrast, if we were working with pure decimal numbers then we would simply write 3.2, meaning '3 units and 2 tenths'.

Since there are a hundred centimetres (cm) in a metre (m), just like a hundred pence in a pound, the measurement of length in centimetres and metres offers a close parallel to recording money. So, for example, a length of 366 cm can also be written in metres, as 3.66 m. Once again the decimal point is seen simply as something which separates the 3 whole metres from the 66 centimetres. In this context it is helpful to exploit pupils' familiarity with money notation and press the parallel quite strongly, following the same convention of writing two figures after the point when expressing lengths in metres, for example, writing 3.20 m rather than 3.2 m. We can then interpret this simply as three metres and twenty centimetres. I shall explain in Chapter 15 how this convention is very useful when dealing with additions and subtractions involving decimals.

This principle then extends to the measurement of mass (or, colloquially, weight) where, because there are a thousand grams (g) in a kilogram (kg), it is best, at least to begin with, to write a mass measured in kilograms with three figures after the point. For example, 3450 g written in kg is 3.450 kg. The decimal point can then simply be seen as something that separates the 3 whole kilograms from the 450 grams. Similarly, in recording liquid volume and capacity, where there are a thousand millilitres (ml) in a litre, a volume of 2500 ml is also written as 2.500 litres, with the decimal point separating the 2 whole litres from the 500 millilitres.

So, when working with primary-school children, it is not necessary initially to explain about tenths and hundredths when using the decimal point in the context of money, length and other measurement contexts. To begin with we can use it simply as a separator and build up the pupils' confidence in handling the decimal notation in these familiar and meaningful contexts. Later, of course, money and measurement in general will provide fertile contexts for explaining the ideas of tenths, hundredths and thousandths. For example, a decimal number such as 1.35 can be explained in the context of length by laying out in a line 1 metre stick, 3 decimetre rods (tenths of a metre) and 5 centimetre cubes (hundredths of a metre), as shown in Figure 2.6. This can then be connected with the number-line image of numbers, where 1.35 is now represented by a point: the point you get to if you start at zero, count along 1 unit, 3 tenths and then 5 hundredths, as shown in Figure 2.7. Note again how this image enables us to appreciate the position of the number 1.35 in relation to other numbers: for example, it lies between 1 and 2; it lies between 1.3 and 1.4; it lies between 1.34 and 1.36.

Figure 2.6   The decimal number 1.35 shown as a length

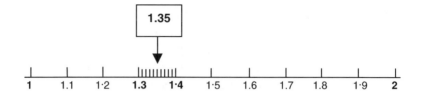

Figure 2.7   The decimal number 1.35 as a point on a number-line

Self-assessment questions

2.1: Arrange these numbers in order from the smallest to the largest, without converting them to Hindu-Arabic numbers: DCXIII, CCLXVII, CLXXX-VIII, DCC, CCC. Now convert them to Hindu-Arabic, repeat the exercise and note any significant differences in the process.

2.2: Add one to four thousand and ninety-nine.

2.3: Write these numbers in Hindu-Arabic numerals, and then write them out in full using powers of ten: a) five hundred and sixteen; b) three thousand and sixty; and c) two million, three hundred and five thousand and four.

2.4: I have 34 one-penny coins, 29 ten-penny coins and 3 pound coins. Apply the principle of 'exchanging ten of these for one of those' to reduce this collection of coins to the smallest number of 1p, 10p and £1 coins.

2.5: Interpret these decimal numbers as collections of base-ten blocks (using a 'flat' to represent a unit) and then arrange them in order from the smallest to the largest: 3.2, 3.05, 3.15, 3.10.

2.6: There are a thousand millimetres (mm) in a metre. How would you write lengths of 3405 mm and 2500 mm in metres?

2.7: How should you write a) 25p in pounds; b) 25 cm in metres; c) 7p in pounds; d) 45 g in kilograms; e) 50 ml in litres; and f) 5 mm in metres?

2.8: Fill in the boxes with single digits: on a number-line, 3.608 lies between □ and □; it lies between □.□ and □.□; it lies between □.□□ and □.□□; it lies between □.□□□ and □.□□□.

Summary of teaching points

1. Incorporate some study of numeration systems into history-focused topics such as Egyptian and Mayan civilizations, highlighting the advantages and significance of the place-value system we use today.

2. Give appropriate credit to the non-European cultures which have contributed so much to the development of numeration.

3. Use coins (1p, 10p and £1) and base-ten blocks to develop pupils' understanding of the place-value system.

4. Use the materials to reinforce especially the principle of 'exchanging one of these for ten of those' as you move right to left along the powers of ten, and 'exchanging ten of these for one of those' as you move left to right.

5. Give particular attention to the function and meaning of zero when writing and explaining numbers to pupils.

6. Articulate the words 'tenths' and 'hundredths' very carefully when explaining decimal numbers; pupils may think you are saying 'tens' and 'hundreds'.

7. Explain decimal numbers by using the flat pieces in the base-ten materials to represent units, the longs to represent tenths and the small cubes to represent hundredths.

8. Children will first encounter the decimal point as a separator in the context of money (pounds and pence) and then length (metres and centimetres), with two figures after the point. They can use the notation in these contexts initially without having any real awareness of figures representing tenths and hundredths.

9. This can then extend to further experience of decimal notation in the contexts of mass (kilograms and grams) and liquid volume and capacity (litres and millilitres), with three figures after the point.

10. Later these contexts can be used to reinforce the explanation of the idea that the figures after the point represent tenths, hundredths and thousandths.

11. Locating both whole numbers and numbers involving decimals as points on the number-line provides pupils with an important image to support their understanding of number, particularly the position of a number in relation to other numbers.

3

Mathematical Modelling

Pupils should be taught to: choose and use suitable number operations to solve a given problem, including word problems involving numbers in 'real life' such as money or measures, and recognize similar problems to which they apply; choose and use an appropriate way to calculate; check that their results are reasonable by thinking about the context of the problem; use a calculator for calculations involving several digits, including decimals; know how to enter and interpret money calculations on a calculator.

In this chapter there are explanations of

- three approaches to calculations: algorithms, adhocorithms and calculators;
- the fundamental process of mathematical modelling;
- the contribution of electronic calculators to this process;
- three different kinds of answers which might be obtained from a calculation done on a calculator; and
- truncation.

What is an algorithm?

There are essentially three ways in which we can do a calculation, such as an addition, a subtraction, a multiplication or a division. For example, consider the problem of finding the cost of 16 items at 25p each. To solve this we may decide to work out 16×25.

One approach to this would be to use an *algorithm*. The word 'algorithm' (derived from the name of the ninth-century Arabian mathematician, Al-Khowarizmi) refers to a step-by-step process for obtaining the solution to a mathematical problem or, in this case, the result of a calculation. In number work we use the word to refer to the formal, paper-and-pencil methods that we might use for doing calculations, which, if the procedures are followed correctly, will always lead to the required result. These would include, for example, subtraction by decomposition and long division. So, solving the problem above using an algorithm might involve, for example, performing the calculation for 16 × 25 as shown in Figure 3.1, using the method known as long multiplication.

$$
\begin{array}{r}
1\,6 \\
\times \;\;2\,5 \\
\hline
3\,2\,0 \\
8\,0 \\
\hline
4\,0\,0 \\
\hline
\end{array}
$$

Figure 3.1   Using an algorithm for 16 × 25

Second, there is a vast array of informal methods for doing calculations, most of which have often not been written down in textbooks or explained by teachers to pupils, but which are actually the methods that most numerate adults employ for the calculations they encounter in everyday life. For example, to solve the problem above, we might make use of the fact that four 25-pences make £1, so 16 of them must be £4. Or we might work out ten 25s (250), four 25s (100) and two 25s (50) and add these up, to get 400. Or we could reason, 'two 25s is 50, so four 25s is 100, so eight 25s is 200, so sixteen 25s is 400'. This kind of approach, in which we make *ad hoc* use of the particular numbers and relationships in the problem in question, I like to call an *adhocorithm*. These informal, *ad hoc* approaches to calculations are at last being recognized as being as equally valid as the formal, algorithmic approaches. They have the advantage that they are based on our own personal level of confidence with numbers and number operations. In Chapters 5, 6, 8 and 9, I discuss various algorithms and adhocorithms for each of the four operations.

Then, third, we could just use a *calculator*.

Isn't it cheating to use a calculator?

Many people are not convinced that there's any mathematics involved in using a calculator. The argument is that all you have to do is to press the buttons and the machine does all the thinking for you. This is a common misconception about calculators. In fact, using a calculator to solve a practical problem involves us in a fundamental mathematical process called *mathematical modelling*. This is nothing to do with making shapes out of card. It's about using and applying mathematics in the real world.

For example, how would you work out how many boxes you need to hold 150 calculators if each box holds just 18 calculators? Personally I would use one of the calculators to work out 150 divided by 18. That gives me the result 8.3333333. That's just a bit more than 8 boxes. So I would actually need 9 boxes. If I only had 8 boxes there would be some calculators which couldn't be fitted in, although the calculator answer doesn't actually tell me how many. The four steps involved in the reasoning here provide essentially an example of the process called mathematical modelling. This process is summarized in Figure 3.2.

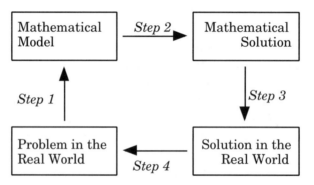

Figure 3.2   The process of mathematical modelling

A problem in the real world is translated into a problem expressed in mathematical symbols. (Strictly, the term 'modelling' is usually used for problems expressed in algebraic symbols, but since the four steps involved are essentially the same, we can adapt the idea and language of modelling and apply them to word-problems being translated into number statements.) So, in this example, we shall say that the real-world problem about buying boxes to hold calculators is *modelled* by the mathematical expression 150 ÷ 18.

The mathematical symbols are then manipulated in some way – this could be by means of a mental or written calculation or, as on this occasion, by pressing keys on a calculator – in order to obtain a mathematical solution, 8.3333333. This must then be interpreted back in the real world – for example, by saying that this means '8 boxes and a bit of a box'. The final step is, of course, to compare the result with the reality of the original situation. In this case, by considering the real situation and recognizing that 8 boxes would leave some calculators not in a box, the appropriate conclusion is that we actually need 9 boxes.

So in this process there are basically four steps:

1. Set up the mathematical model.
2. Obtain the mathematical solution.
3. Interpret the mathematical solution back in the real world.
4. Compare the solution with the reality of the original situation.

There is potentially a fifth step, of course: if the solution does not make sense when compared with the reality of the original problem, then I may have to go round the cycle again, checking each stage of the process to determine what has gone wrong. Now it is important to note that the calculator does only the second of the steps in the process of mathematical modelling. I have done all the others. My contribution is significant mathematics. In a technological age, in which most calcula-tions are done by machines, it surely cannot be disputed that knowing which calculation to do is more important than being able to do the calculation. As will be seen in Chapters 4 and 7, recognizing which operations correspond to various real-world situations (step 1 above) is not always straightforward. These chapters indicate the range of cate-gories of problems which pupils should learn to model with addition, subtraction, multiplication and division.

Is there much to learn about the interpretation of a calculator result?

The interpretation of the calculator result is also far from being an insig-nificant aspect of the process. For example, in the problem above, the interpretation of the result 8.3333333 required a decision about what to do with all the figures after the decimal point.

When we carry out a calculation on a calculator in order to solve a practical problem, particularly those modelled by division, we can get three kinds of answer:

- An exact, appropriate answer.
- An exact but inappropriate answer.
- An answer which has been *truncated*.

In the last two cases, we normally have to round the answer in some way to make it appropriate to the real-world situation (rounding is considered in more detail in Chapter 10). For example, consider these three problems, all with the same identical mathematical structure:

1. How many apples at 15p each can I buy with 90p?
2. How many apples at 24p each can I buy with 90p?
3. How many apples at 21p each can I buy with 90p?

For problem (1) we might enter '90 ÷ 15 =' on to a calculator and obtain the result 6. In this case there is no difficulty in interpreting this result back in the real world. The answer to the problem is indeed exactly 6 apples. The calculator result is both exact and appropriate.

For problem (2) we might enter '90 ÷ 24 =' and obtain the result 3.75. This is the exact answer to the calculation that was entered on the calculator, that is, the solution to the mathematical problem that we used to model the real-world problem, and is correctly interpreted as 3.75 apples. But, since greengrocers sell only whole apples, clearly the answer is not appropriate. In the final step of the modelling process – comparing the solution with reality – the 3.75 apples must be rounded to a whole number of apples. In this case we would conclude that we can actually afford only 3 apples.

For problem (3) we might enter '90 ÷ 21 =' on to the calculator and find that we get the result 4.2857142. This is not an exact answer. Dividing 90 by 21 actually produces a *recurring decimal*, namely, 4.285714285714 . . ., with the 285714 repeating over and over again without ever coming to an end. (This is usually written 4.$\dot{2}$8571$\dot{4}$, with a dot over the first and last of the recurring digits.) Since a simple calculator can display only eight digits, it *truncates* the result, by throwing away all the extra digits. Of course, in this case, the bits that are thrown away are relatively tiny and the error involved in this truncation process is fairly insignificant. We can interpret the result displayed on the calculator as 'about 4.2857142 apples'. But again, when we compare this with the real-world situation, we must recognize the constraints of purchasing fruit and round the answer in some way to give a whole number of apples. The obvious conclusion is that we can afford only 4 apples.

Another problem arises when the calculator result in a money problem gives only one figure after the decimal point. For example, here is a problem in the real world: how much for 24 marker pens at £1.15 each? We might model this with the mathematical expression, 24 × 1.15 (step 1). Handing over the donkey work (step 2) to a calculator gives the result 27.6. Primary children have to be taught how to interpret this (step 3) as £27.60, in order to draw the conclusion (step 4) that the total cost of the 24 marker pens is £27.60.

Self-assessment questions

3.1: How much altogether for three books costing £4.95, £5.90 and £9.95? Use a calculator to answer this question, then identify the steps in the process of mathematical modelling in what you have done.

3.2: What does each person pay if three people share a restaurant bill for £27.90? Use a calculator to answer this question. Is the calculator result a) an exact, appropriate answer; b) an exact but inappropriate answer; or c) an answer which has been truncated? Identify the steps in the process of mathematical modelling in what you have done.

3.3: Repeat Question 3.2 with a bill for £39.70.

3.4: John was given £50 for his birthday and thought he might spend it all on his favourite chocolate bars. They cost 32p each. He wondered how many he might get. What is the mathematical model of this problem? Obtain the mathematical solution, using a calculator. Interpret the mathematical solution back in the real world. Is the calculator result a) an exact, appropriate answer; b) an exact but inappropriate answer; or c) an answer which has been truncated?

3.5: How many months will it take me to save £500 if I save £35 a month? Use a calculator to answer this question. Is the calculator result a) an exact, appropriate answer; b) an exact but inappropriate answer; or c) an answer which has been truncated? Identify the steps in the process of mathematical modelling in what you have done.

Summary of teaching points

1. Recognize the validity of the three ways of doing calculations: algorithms, adhocorithms and calculators.
2. Provide pupils with plenty of opportunities to work through the process of mathematical modelling, emphasizing the four steps in the process.
3. Recognize that all the steps are important and that step 2 (doing the calculation) is no more important than the other three steps.
4. Allow pupils to use a calculator when the calculations associated with a real-life problem are too difficult, so that they can still engage in the modelling process and learn to choose the right operation, to interpret the result and to compare it with reality.
5. Discuss with pupils real-life problems, particularly in the context of money, that produce calculator answers which require different kinds of interpretation, including those with a) an exact, appropriate answer; b) an exact but inappropriate answer; and c) an answer which has been truncated.

6. Explain truncation to primary pupils, but use informal language: 'When the calculator answer has a decimal point and fills up all the available spaces, then there are probably lots more figures to come after the ones we can see. Because the calculator does not have room for these it throws them away. This does not usually matter because they represent very small quantities.'

4

Addition and Subtraction Structures

Pupils should be taught to: understand addition and use related vocabulary; recognize that addition can be done in any order; understand subtraction both as 'take away' and 'difference' and use the related vocabulary; recognize that subtraction is the inverse of addition; develop further their understanding of addition and subtraction; understand why the commutative and associative laws apply to addition; choose and use addition or subtraction to solve problems in 'real life', money or measures of lengths, mass, capacity or time.

In this chapter there are explanations of

- two different structures of real-life problems modelled by addition;
- the situations in which pupils will meet these structures;
- the commutative law of addition;
- four different structures of real-life problems modelled by subtraction; and
- the situations in which pupils will meet these structures.

What are the different kinds of situation that primary pupils might encounter to which the operation of addition applies?

There are two basic categories of real-life problems that are modelled by the mathematical operation we call addition. The problems in each of these categories may vary in terms of their content and context, but essentially they all have the same structure. I refer to the structures in these two categories of problems as

- the aggregation structure; and
- the augmentation structure.

Aggregation refers to a situation in which two or more quantities are combined into a single quantity and the operation of addition is used to determine the total. For example, there are 15 marbles in one circle and 17 in another: how many marbles altogether? This idea of 'how many (or how much) altogether' is the central notion in the aggregation structure (see Figure 4.1).

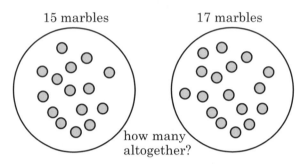

Figure 4.1   Addition as aggregation

Augmentation refers to a situation where a quantity is increased by some amount and the operation of addition is required in order to find the augmented or increased value. For example, the price of a bicycle costing £149 is increased by £25: what is the new price? The important language in augmentation therefore includes phrases like 'increased by' and 'goes up by'. This is the addition structure which lies behind the idea of counting-on along a number line which we might use with young children for experiencing simple additions such as, say, 7 + 5: 'start at 7 and count on 5' (see Figure 4.2).

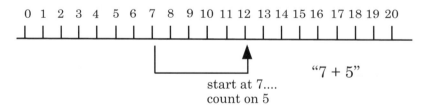

Figure 4.2   Addition as augmentation

It should just be mentioned at this stage that if the number that is added is a negative number, then the addition will not result in an increase, but in a *decrease*. This extension of the augmentation structure to negative numbers is discussed in Chapter 13, which deals with positive and negative integers.

Distinguishing between these two addition structures is not always easy, nor is it necessarily helpful to try to do so. But I find it is useful in teaching to have them in mind to ensure that pupils have opportunities to experience the full range of situations and, most importantly, the associated language which they have to learn to connect with addition.

What are some of the contexts in which pupils will meet addition in the aggregation structure?

First and most simply, pupils will encounter this structure whenever they are putting together two sets of objects into a single set, to find the total number. For example, combining two discrete sets of pupils (for example, 25 boys and 29 girls, how many altogether?); combining two separate piles of counters (for example, 46 red counters, 28 blue counters, how many altogether?).

Second, and, in terms of relevance, most importantly, pupils will encounter the aggregation structure in the context of money. This might be, for example, finding the total cost of two or more purchases, or the total bill for a number of services. The question will be, 'How much altogether?'

Then they also have to recognize addition in situations of aggregation in the contexts of measurements, such as length and distance, mass, capacity and liquid volume, and time. For example, addition would be the operation required to find the total distance for a journey made up of two stages of 48 miles and 63 miles, and also to find the total time for the journey if the first stage takes 65 minutes and the second stage takes 85 minutes.

What are some of the contexts in which pupils will meet addition in the augmentation structure?

The most important and relevant context for this structure is again that of money, particularly the idea of increases in price or cost, wage or salary. The key language that signals the operation of addition is that of 'increasing'. This idea may also be encountered occasionally, but not often, in other measurement contexts, such as length (for example, stretching a length of elastic by so much), mass (for example, putting on so many pounds over Christmas) and time (for example, increasing the length of the lunch break by so many minutes).

What is the commutative law of addition?

It is clear from Figure 4.1 that the problem there could be represented by either 15 + 17 or by 17 + 15. Which set is on the left and which on the right makes no difference to the total number of marbles. The fact that these two additions come to the same result is an example of what is called the *commutative law* of addition. To help remember this technical term, we could note that commuters go both ways on a journey. The commutative property of addition is simply the fact that an addition can go both ways: 17 + 15 = 15 + 17, and so on.

We can state this commutative law formally by the following generalization, which is true whatever the numbers *a* and *b*:

$$a + b = b + a.$$

The significance of this property is twofold. First, it is important to realize that subtraction does *not* have this commutative property. For example, 10 – 5 is not equal to 5 – 10. Second, it is important to make use of commutativity in addition calculations. Particularly when using the idea of counting-on, it is nearly always best to start with the bigger number. For example, it would not be sensible to calculate 3 + 59 by starting at 3 and counting on 59! The obvious thing to do is to use the commutative law mentally to change the addition to 59 + 3, then start at 59 and count on 3.

What are the different kinds of situation that primary pupils might encounter to which the operation of subtraction applies?

There is a daunting range of situations in which we have to learn to recognize that the appropriate operation is subtraction. I find it helpful to categorize these into at least the following four structures:

- the partitioning structure;
- the reduction structure;
- the comparison structure; and
- the inverse-of-addition structure.

It is important for teachers to be aware of this range of structures, to ensure that pupils get the opportunity to learn to apply their number skills to all of them. It helps us to connect these mathematical structures with the operation of subtraction if we ask ourselves the question: What is the calculation I would enter on a calculator in order to solve this problem? In each case the answer will involve using the subtraction key. It is one of the baffling aspects of mathematics that the same symbol, as we shall see particularly with the example of the subtraction symbol, can have so many different meanings.

The *partitioning* structure refers to a situation in which a quantity is partitioned off in some way or other and subtraction is required to calculate how many or how much remains. For example, there are 17 marbles in the box, 5 are removed, how many are left? (See Figure 4.3) The calculation to be entered on a calculator to correspond to this situation is 17 – 5. Partitioning is the structure that teachers (and consequently their pupils) most frequently connect with the subtraction symbol. It is strongly associated with the language 'take away' and 'how many (or how much) left'.

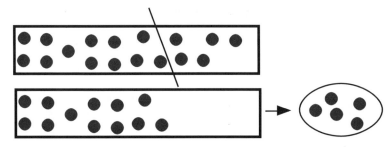

Figure 4.3   Subtraction as partitioning

The *reduction* structure is simply the reverse process of the augmentation structure of addition. It refers to a situation in which a quantity is reduced by some amount and the operation of subtraction is required to find the reduced value. For example, the price of a bicycle costing £149 is reduced by £25, what is the new price? The calculation that must be entered on a calculator to solve this problem is 149 – 25. The important language in this structure includes phrases such as 'reduced by' and 'goes down by'. This is the subtraction structure that lies behind the idea of counting back along a number line, as shown in Figure 4.4.

The *comparison* structure refers to a completely different set of situations, namely, those where subtraction is required to make a comparison between two quantities, as for example in Figure 4.5. How many

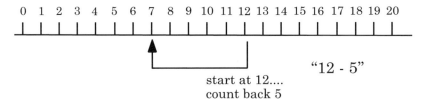

Figure 4.4   Subtraction as reduction

more blue cubes are there than red cubes? The calculation to be entered on a calculator to correspond to this situation is 12 – 7. Subtraction of the smaller number from the greater enables us to determine the *difference,* or to find out *how much greater* or *how much smaller* one quantity is than the other. Because making comparisons is such a fundamental process, with so many practical and social applications, the ability to recognize this subtraction structure and the confidence to handle the associated language patterns are particularly important.

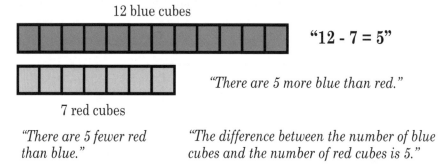

Figure 4.5   Subtraction as comparison

The *inverse-of-addition* structure refers to situations where we have to determine what must be added to a given quantity in order to reach some target. The phrase 'inverse-of-addition' underlines the idea that subtraction and addition are *inverse* processes. This means, for example, that since 28 + 52 comes to 80, then 80 – 52 must be 28. The subtraction of 52 'undoes' the effect of adding 52. Hence to solve a problem of the form 'what must be added to X to give Y?' we subtract X from Y. For example: the entrance fee is 80p, but I have only 52p, how much more do I need? The calculation that must be entered on a calculator to solve this problem is the subtraction, 80 – 52. Figure 4.6 shows how this subtraction structure might be interpreted as an action on the number line: starting at 52 we have to determine what must be added to get to 80.

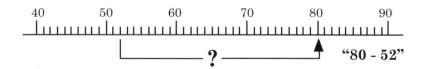

Figure 4.6   Subtraction as inverse-of-addition

What are some of the contexts in which pupils will meet the partitioning subtraction structure?

First this structure is encountered whenever we start with a given number of things in a set and a subset is taken away (removed, destroyed, eaten, killed, blown up, lost or whatever). In each case the question being asked is 'how many are left?' It also includes situations where a subset is identified as possessing some particular attribute and the question asked is, 'how many are not?' or 'how many do not?' For instance, there might be 58 children from a year group of 92 going on a field trip. The question, 'how many are not going?' has to be associated with the subtraction 92 – 58.

Then the structure has a number of significant occurrences in the context of money and shopping. For example, we might spend £72 from our savings of £240 and need to work out how much is left (that is, carry out the subtraction 240 – 72). Or we might need to calculate the amount of change from a £10 note if our bill in the shop comes to £6.75 (that is, carry out the subtraction 10 – 6.75).

Finally, there are various practical situations in the context of measurement where we encounter the partitioning subtraction structure. For example, when we have a given length of some material, plan to cut off a length of it and wish to calculate how much will be left; or where we have some cooking ingredients measured by mass or volume, plan to use a certain amount in a recipe and wish to calculate how much will be left.

What are some of the contexts in which pupils will meet subtraction in the reduction structure?

Realistic examples of the reduction structure mainly occur in the context of money. The key idea which signals the operation of subtraction is that of 'reducing', for example, reducing prices and costs, cutting wages and salaries. For example, if a person's council tax of £625 is cut by £59, the reduced tax is determined by the subtraction, 625 – 59. The structure may also be encountered occasionally in other measurement contexts, such as reduction in mass or temperatures falling.

What are some of the contexts in which pupils will meet subtraction in the comparison structure?

Almost any context! Wherever two numbers occur we will often find ourselves wanting to compare them, to determine the difference, or to find out how much greater or smaller one is than the other. First, we might wish to compare the numbers of items in two sets (for example, the numbers of marbles in two bags, the numbers of cards in two packs, the numbers of children in two classes, the numbers of counters in two piles, the numbers of pages in two books, and so on). To do this we have to connect the situation and the associated language of 'difference', 'how many more', 'how many less (or fewer)' with the operation of subtraction.

Then in the context of money we would encounter this subtraction structure whenever we are comparing the prices of articles or the costs of services. If holiday package A costs £716 and package B costs £589, then we would ask questions such as: 'how much more expensive is A?' 'How much cheaper is B?' 'How much dearer is A?' 'How much more does A cost than B?' 'How much less does B cost than A?' Note the range of language patterns used here – and that in each case the question is answered by the same subtraction, 716 – 589. Also, we might use subtraction to compare salaries and wages: for example, how much more does a police officer earn than a teacher?

Finally, the process of comparison is a central idea in all measurement contexts. If we had measured the heights of two pupils we would need a subtraction to compare them, to determine how much taller or shorter one pupil is than another. If we had measured the masses of two articles we could compare them by asking 'how much heavier' or 'how much lighter' – and again subtraction is involved.

The language of comparison in the contexts of measurement is extensive. For example, we might ask: how much longer, taller, higher, further, wider, shorter, nearer, narrower, in the context of length; how much heavier, lighter, in the context of weighing; holds how much more or how much less, in the context of capacity; how much longer or shorter in time taken, how much sooner, earlier, later, younger, older, in the context of time; how much hotter, colder, in the context of temperature; how much faster, slower, in the context of speed. The development of this range of language is crucial to an understanding of the measurement concepts, as well as being important in building up confidence in recognizing situations to be connected with subtraction.

What are some of the contexts in which pupils will meet subtraction in the inverse-of-addition structure?

This subtraction structure is often the most difficult to recognize for primary pupils because the language associated with it, such as 'how much more is needed?' and 'what must be added?', signals the idea of addition rather than subtraction.

There are many commonplace situations where we encounter this structure: for example, any situation where we have a number of objects or a number of individuals and we require some more in order to reach a target. The most convincing examples for many will be in the context of sport. For example, if I have scored 180 in darts how many more do I need to reach 401? This corresponds to the subtraction, 401 – 180. If we are chasing a score of 235 in cricket and we have scored 186 with eight overs remaining, how many more runs do we need? The calculation to be entered on a calculator to answer this is 235 – 186.

Other examples of the inverse-of-addition structure occur in the context of measurement, such as: how much further do you have to drive to complete a journey of 345 miles if you have so far driven 196 miles?

Perhaps the most relevant instances of the inverse-of-addition subtraction structure occur in the context of money. For example, if we have saved up £485 towards a holiday costing £716, we would need to do the subtraction, 716 – 485, in order to calculate how much more we need to save. Again, if the reader is uncertain about the assertion that this situation is an example of subtraction, it will help to ask: What is the calculation you would enter on a calculator to work this out?

Of course, when calculating a subtraction like 716 – 485 without a calculator, we might very well use a number-line image and the idea of adding-on from 485 to get to 716 (for example, 15 to get from 485 to 500, another 200 to get to 700, and another 16 to get to 716, as shown in Figure 4.7). This is a powerful mental strategy, as we shall see in the next chapter. It reinforces the importance of pupils associating subtraction with the full range of structures discussed above. This is not just so that they will know when a situation requires a subtraction calculation, but also that when a subtraction calculation is required they can interpret it in a number of different ways in order to deal with it.

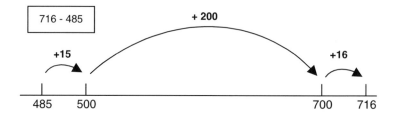

Figure 4.7   What must be added to 485 to get to 716?

Self-assessment questions

4.1: Make up a problem that corresponds to the addition 5.95 + 6.99 using the aggregation structure in the context of shopping.

4.2: Make up a problem that corresponds to the addition 9750 + 145 using the augmentation structure in the context of salaries.

4.3: Make up a problem that corresponds to the addition 250 + 125 using the aggregation structure and liquid volume in the context of cooking.

4.4: Make up a problem that corresponds to the addition 15 + 25 + 55 + 20 + 65 using the aggregation structure in the context of time.

4.5: An important event is planned for 1 January 2050. On 1 January 2002 how many years are there to wait? What is the calculation to be entered on a calculator to answer this? Of what subtraction structure is this an example?

4.6: There are 256 pages in my book. I have so far read 178 of them. How many more pages do I have to read? What is the calculation to be entered on a calculator to answer this? Of what subtraction structure is this an example?

4.7: I am 52 and my daughter is 25. How many years younger than me is she? What is the calculation to be entered on a calculator to answer this? Of what subtraction structure is this an example?

4.8: I have collected 565 points from my local service station, but I need 750 points to get the decanter from the free-gift catalogue: how many more points do I need? What is the calculation to be entered on a calcula-tor to answer this? Of what subtraction structure is this an example?

4.9: Make up a problem that corresponds to the subtraction 3.95 − 2.99 using the comparison structure in the context of shopping.

4.10: Make up a problem that corresponds to the subtraction 25 − (−6) using the comparison subtraction structure in the context of temperatures.

4.11: Make up a problem that corresponds to the subtraction 250 − 159 using the partitioning structure and the phrase 'how many do not . . . ?'.

4.12: Make up a problem in the context of shopping, that uses the inverse-of-addition structure, corresponding to 489 − 350.

Summary of teaching points

1. Pupils should learn to connect the operation of addition with a range of problems, including situations using the idea of aggregation and those using the idea of augmentation.

2. The key language to be developed in the aggregation structure of addition includes: *how many altogether, how much altogether, the total.*

3. The key language to be developed in the augmentation structure of addition includes: *count on, increased by, goes up by.*

4. Pupils should experience these addition structures in a range of relevant contexts, including, especially, money (shopping, bills, wages and salaries) and various aspects of measurement.

5. Make explicit to pupils the commutative law of addition and show them how to use it in addition calculations, particularly by starting with the bigger number when counting on.

6. Explain that subtraction is not commutative.

7. Pupils should learn to connect the operation of subtraction with a wide range of problems, including situations using the ideas of partitioning, reduction, comparison and inverse-of-addition.

8. Pupils should experience these subtraction structures in a range of practical and relevant contexts, including especially money (shopping, bills, wages and salaries) and various aspects of measurement.

9. The key language to be developed in the partitioning structure of subtraction includes: *Take away, how many left? How many are not? How many do not?*

10. Subtraction is not just 'take away'. Partitioning is only one subtraction structure. Teachers should not overemphasize the language of 'take away, how many left' at the expense of all the other important language that has to be associated with subtraction.

11. The key language to be developed in the reduction structure of subtraction includes: *reduced by, cut by, count back.*

12. The key language to be developed in the comparison structure of subtraction includes: *Difference, how many more? How many less (or fewer)? How much greater, smaller, longer, taller, higher, further, wider, shorter, nearer, narrower, heavier, lighter, longer or shorter in time taken, sooner, earlier, later, younger, older, hotter, colder, faster, slower? Holds how much more, how much less?*

13. The key language to be developed in the inverse-of-addition structure of subtraction includes: *What must be added? How many (much) more needed?*

14. The language of problems with the inverse-of-addition structure often signals addition rather than subtraction, so that many pupils will automatically add the two numbers in the question. They will need specific help to recognize the need for a subtraction.

15. Asking the question, 'what is the calculation to be entered on a calculator to solve this problem?', helps to focus the pupils' thinking on the underlying mathematical structure of the situation.

16. Familiarity with the range of subtraction structures will enable pupils to interpret a subtraction calculation in a number of ways and hence increase their ability to handle these calculations by a range of methods.

5

Mental Strategies for Addition and Subtraction

Pupils should be taught to: recall all addition and subtraction facts for each number up to 20; work out what they need to add to any two-digit number to make 100, then add or subtract any pair of two-digit whole numbers; understand how the commutative and associative laws can be used to do mental addition calculations more efficiently; handle (mentally) particular cases of three-digit and four-digit additions and subtractions by using compensation or other methods; choose and use an appropriate way to calculate and explain their reasoning; use correctly the symbol for 'equals'.

In this chapter there are explanations of

- the associative law for addition;
- counting forwards and backwards in ones, tens, hundreds;
- using multiples of 10 and 100 as stepping-stones;
- front-end addition and subtraction;
- compensation in addition and subtraction calculations;
- the correct use of the symbol for 'equals';
- using multiples of 5 in additions and subtractions;
- relating additions and subtractions to doubles; and
- using 'friendly' numbers.

What is the associative law of addition?

Like the commutative law $(a + b = b + a)$ discussed in the previous chapter, the associative law is a fundamental property of addition. Written formally, as a generalization, it is the assertion that for any numbers a, b and c:

$$a + (b + c) = (a + b) + c.$$

39

Using a particular example, this might be: 7 + (13 + 18) = (7 + 13) + 18. The brackets indicate which addition should be done first. In simple terms, the associative law says that if you have three numbers to add together you get the same answer whether you start by adding the second and third or start by adding the first and second. In the example above, it's probably easier to start by adding the 7 and 13, but you get the same answer if you start with 13 + 18. I like to remember the associative law by thinking of it as a picture of three political parties: sometimes the party in the centre associates with the right and sometimes it associates with the left, but it doesn't make any difference!

This law allows us to write down 7 + 13 + 18, without any brackets to indicate which two numbers should be added first. We can choose whichever we prefer. The commutative and associative laws combined give us the freedom to add a string of numbers together in any order we like. For example, 7 + (13 + 18) could be changed as follows:

$$
\begin{aligned}
7 + (13 + 18) &= 7 + (18 + 13) && \text{(using the commutative law)} \\
&= (7 + 18) + 13 && \text{(using the associative law)} \\
&= (18 + 7) + 13 && \text{(using the commutative law)} \\
&= 18 + (7 + 13) && \text{(using the associative law)} \\
&= 18 + (13 + 7) && \text{(using the commutative law)} \\
&= (18 + 13) + 7 && \text{(using the associative law)} \\
&= (13 + 18) + 7 && \text{(using the commutative law).}
\end{aligned}
$$

We shall see below that deciding on the most efficient way of adding up various bits of numbers is an important strategy for informal calculations, so the associative and commutative laws of addition are important – even though most people use them without realizing it.

An important point to make about associativity is that subtraction does not have this property. For example, 25 – (12 – 8) is not equal to (25 – 12) – 8. This means that we cannot write 25 – 12 – 8 to mean both of these! The convention is that 25 – 12 – 8 means (25 – 12) – 8, that is, that the subtractions are done in order from left to right, unless brackets are used to indicate otherwise.

How important is mental calculation?

The ability to calculate mentally using a range of strategies is recognized as the basis of being numerate. It is a reasonable expectation that most pupils in primary schools should be able to learn to add and subtract using informal, mental strategies with three-digit numbers. This does not mean, of course, that they do not write anything down. They may need to write the question down for a start, so they don't forget it – and it may be helpful to support their mental calculation with a few jottings along the way or with a picture such as a number-line.

It is now generally realized that most of the problems that pupils encounter in calculations in primary schools are associated with their being introduced too early to formal algorithms, written in a vertical format. Vertical layouts for additions and subtractions especially lead pupils to treat the digits in the numbers as though they are individual numbers and then to combine them in all kinds of bizarre and meaningless ways. Mental strategies by their very *ad hoc* nature lead you to build on what you understand and to use methods that make sense to you.

The decision as to which strategy to employ is guided by the actual numbers in the problem. For example, very few of us would use the same strategy for calculating 201 – 20 and 201 – 197. The first I would do essentially by counting back in tens from 201, and the second by counting on from 197. Both of these are very simple subtractions, of course, when written down horizontally and done by mental methods. But the potential for error when these are written down as vertical calculations and tackled by the conventional algorithm is considerable, as illustrated in Figure 5.1 (see self-assessment question 5.2 at the end of this chapter). A good suggestion is that pupils should be thoroughly confident in additions and subtractions written in horizontal format, using mental and informal strategies, before they are introduced to the vertical layout algorithms. There has been a great neglect of open discussion and specific teaching of mental strategies in many of our primary schools. Greater sharing of such methods will undoubtedly lead to greater confidence with number.

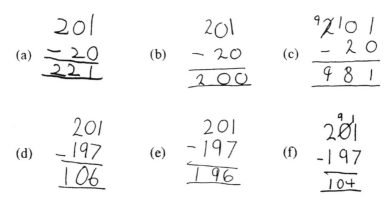

Figure 5.1   Examples of children's errors in vertical layout of subtractions

How does counting forwards and backwards help in mental calculations?

In Chapter 4 we saw how addition could be understood as counting-on and subtraction as counting-back, and that these ideas were strongly linked with movements along a number-line. These ideas are also central to much mental and informal calculation. Doing additions and subtractions on a hundred-square (see Figure 5.2) provides pupils with a strong image that supports the process of counting on and back in ones and tens. So 57 + 3 done by counting on in ones is associated with a movement to the right along a row: 57 . . . 58, 59, 60. And 57 – 3 done by counting back in ones is associated with a movement to the left along a row: 57 . . . 56, 55, 54. Then 57 + 30 done by counting on in tens is seen as a movement down a column: 57 . . . 67, 77, 87. And 57 – 30 done by counting back in tens is seen as a movement up a column: 57 . . . 47, 37, 27.

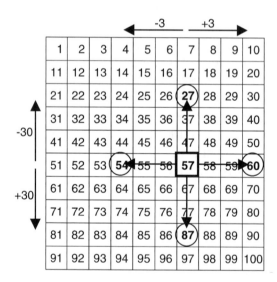

Figure 5.2   Using a hundred-square

These are important strategies that can be extended to counting in hundreds and which we combine with other strategies when we become more proficient calculators. A good target for primary school teachers is that their pupils should be able to count on or back in ones, tens and hundreds from any given number (up to three digits) by about the age of 9 years.

How do we use multiples of 10 and 100 as stepping-stones?

Notice what happens when we add 5 to 57 on the hundred-square. We have to break the 5 down into two bits, 3 and 2. The 3 gets us to the next multiple of 10 (60) and then we have 2 more to count on. This process of using a multiple of ten (60) as a stepping-stone is an important mental strategy for addition and subtraction. [*Note*: multiples of 10 are 10, 20, 30, 40, 50, 60, . . . and so on. Multiples are discussed more fully in Chapter 11.]

Here is how we might use this idea of a stepping-stone for calculating, say, 57 + 28. First we could count on in 10s, to deal with adding the 20: 57 . . . 67, 77. Then break the 8 up into 3 and 5, to enable us to use 80 as a stepping-stone: 77 + 8 = 77 + 3 + 5 = 80 + 5 = 85. A number line diagram is a useful image for supporting this kind of reasoning. Pupils can be taught to use an 'empty number-line', which is simply a line on which they can put whatever numbers they like, not worrying about the scale, just ensuring that numbers are in the right order relative to each other. Figure 5.3 shows an empty number-line representation of the calculation of 57 + 28, using 80 as a stepping-stone.

Figure 5.4 shows how we might use multiples of 100 as stepping-stones for calculating 542 – 275, using an empty number-line. Using the inverse-of-addition structure, the subtraction can be interpreted as

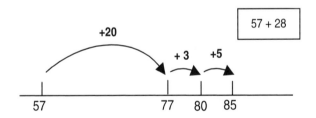

Figure 5.3   Using a multiple of 10 as a stepping-stone on an empty number-line

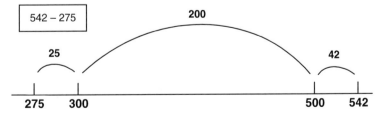

Figure 5.4   Using multiples of 100 as stepping-stones in a subtraction

'what do you add to 275 to get 542?'. This is done in three steps (25 + 200 + 42), with 300 and 500 as convenient stepping-stones lying between the 275 and the 542.

What is front-end addition and subtraction?

Most formal written algorithms for addition and subtraction work from right to left, starting with the units. In mental calculations it is much more common to work from left to right. This makes more sense, because you deal with the biggest and most significant bits of the numbers first. One strategy is mentally to break the numbers up into hundreds, tens and ones, and then to combine them bit by bit, starting with the hundreds. So, for example, given 459 + 347, we would think of the 459 as (400 + 50 + 9) and the 347 as (300 + 40 + 7). This process is sometimes called *partitioning into hundreds, tens and ones*. We would then use the freedom granted to us by the associative and commutative laws to add these bits in any order we like. The 'front-end approach' would deal with the hundreds first (400 + 300 = 700), then the tens (50 + 40 = 90, making 790 so far), then the ones (for example, 790 + 9 = 799; 799 + 7 = 799 + 1 + 6 = 806). Notice that I have used 800 as a stepping-stone for the last step here.

Writing this out in full, in a way which might explain my thinking to someone else:

$$459 + 347 = (400 + 50 + 9) + (300 + 40 + 7)$$
$$= (400 + 300) + (50 + 40) + (9 + 7)$$
$$= 700 + 90 + 9 + 7$$
$$= 799 + 7 = 799 + 1 + 6 = 800 + 6 = 806.$$

We will quite often use the front-end approach to get us started in a subtraction done mentally. For example, for 645 − 239, we would immediately deal with the hundreds (600 − 200 = 400) leaving us simply to think about 45 − 39. This gives us 6 (using 40 as a stepping-stone), so the answer is 400 + 6 = 406.

What is compensation in addition and subtraction?

You can often convert an addition or subtraction question into an easier question by temporarily adding or subtracting an appropriate small number. For example, many people would evaluate 673 + 99 by adding

1 temporarily to the 99, so the question becomes 673 + 100. This gives 773. Now take off the extra 1, to get the answer 772. This strategy is sometimes called *compensation*. Figure 5.5(a) shows how this way of finding 673 + 99 looks when carried out with a number-line diagram.

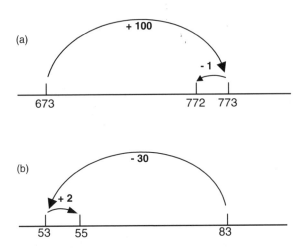

Figure 5.5   Using compensation to calculate (a) 673 + 99 and (b) 83 – 28

The trick in the strategy is always to be on the lookout for an easier calculation than the one that you have to do. This will often involve temporarily replacing a number ending in a 9 or an 8 with the next multiple of 10. For example, the subtraction 83 – 28 can temporarily be changed into the much easier calculation 83 – 30, which gives 53, with 2 to be added to this to compensate for the fact that we've actually taken away 2 more than required. This is illustrated with a number-line diagram in Figure 5.5(b).

The strategy can be used to change any subtraction into an easier one. For example, 453 – 178 looks a bit daunting. I would rather do 453 – 180. (But remember: I will have taken away 2 more than I should and this will have to be added on again later.) If I'm still struggling with 453 – 180, I could instead choose to do 453 – 200, which is 253. (Now I have to remember there's an extra 20 to add on.) So the answer is 253 + 20 + 2, which is a relatively easy addition, giving 275.

This approach is particularly effective with precisely those subtractions that cause most problems using the decomposition algorithm (see Chapter 6): those with zeros in the first number. For example, Figure 5.6(a) shows a typical error made by a 9-year-old boy attempting to calculate 101 – 97 set out in vertical format. He was then given the question in horizontal format and encouraged to work it out mentally. This he did successfully by first dealing with 100 – 97 by counting back

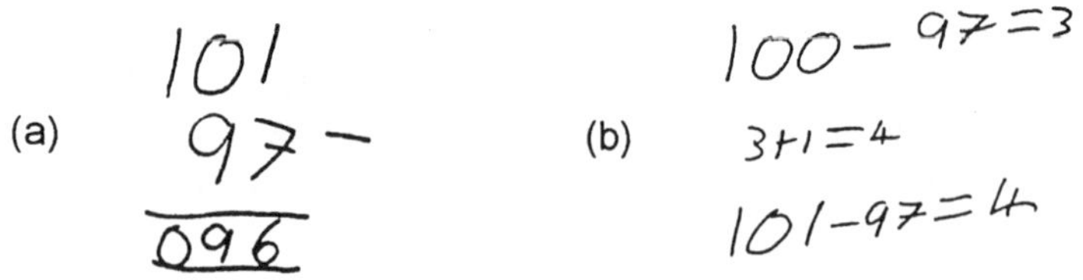

(a)
$$\begin{array}{r} 101 \\ 97\ - \\ \hline 096 \end{array}$$

(b)
$$100 - 97 = 3$$
$$3 + 1 = 4$$
$$101 - 97 = 4$$

Figure 5.6   (a) A 9-year-old's unsuccessful attempt to calculate 101 – 97; and (b) his successful use of compensation

and then compensating. Figure 5.6(b) is his response to the invitation to 'write down how you did it in a way that shows your thinking to someone else'.

Here's a more challenging example, written out in a way that might explain the thinking to someone else:

> To calculate 4003 – 3196.
> Add 4 to the second number: 4003 – 3200
> Add 800 to the second number: 4003 – 4000 = 3
> Now compensate: 3 + 4 + 800 = 807.

Obviously to use this strategy you have to be very good at recognizing what you need to make a number up to the next multiple of 10, the next multiple of 100, and so on. This skill should therefore be a very specific teaching focus with primary-school pupils.

There are other ways of using the strategy of compensation, all of which amount to changing one or more of the numbers in order to produce an easier calculation. We can use this approach to exploit our confidence in handling multiples of five, to relate additions and subtractions to doubles, or simply to replace one of the numbers by a more 'friendly' number. These are explained below.

How should the symbol for 'equals' be used in recording calculations?

As pupils begin to make more detailed written records of their calculations they can be encouraged to use the equals sign (=) to link only those things that are actually equal, as has been done in all the examples in this chapter. There is a tendency for pupils (and some teachers) to abuse the equals sign by employing it rather casually just to link the steps in a calculation, without it having any real meaning. For example, it is not uncommon to see this kind of thing written down: 103 – 87 = 103 – 90 =

13 + 3 = 16. Only the final equals sign here connects two expressions that are actually equal. Although this kind of recording might be acceptable behaviour in the privacy of your own scribbling-pad, you should be warned that it is likely seriously to upset pedantic mathematicians if done in public.

While I'm being pedantic, I might just mention the word 'sum'. Mathematically, a *sum* is the result of the *addition* of two or more numbers. Colloquially the word 'sum' is often used to refer to any *calculation*. Strictly it should apply only to additions. So, for example, 103 – 87 is not a sum.

How do multiples of 5 help in mental additions and subtractions?

Multiples of 5 (5, 10, 15, 20, 25, 30, . . .) are particularly easy to work with. Young children quickly learn to relate simple additions and subtractions to fives. For example, a 5-year-old might think of 6 + 7 as '5 and 1 and 5 and 2', and proceed by first combining the fives. This tendency to relate numbers to multiples of 5 is no doubt related to the way our early experience of counting on our fingers leads us to perceive 6, 7, 8 and 9 as '5 and some more'. It is then reinforced by our experience of handling money. We can exploit this confidence with multiples of 5 in many additions and subtractions done mentally. For example, 37 + 26 could be related to 35 + 25, which we would probably find much easier. This can be taught as a specific strategy. Here are some examples, written out in full to show what would, of course, be a mental process:

$$37 + 26 \quad = (35 + 25) + 2 + 1 \quad = 60 + 2 + 1 \quad = 63$$
$$77 + 24 \quad = (75 + 25) + 2 - 1 \quad = 100 + 2 - 1 \quad = 101$$
$$174 - 46 \quad = (175 - 45) - 1 - 1 \quad = 130 - 1 - 1 \quad = 128.$$

How do you relate additions and subtractions to doubles?

Sometimes in additions and subtractions we can exploit the fact that most people are fairly confident with the processes of doubling and halving. Even quite young primary school pupils will quickly show confidence with doubles and will often relate the calculation of 'near-doubles' to these. For example, many 5-year-olds would think of 6 + 7 as 'double 6 and 1 more'. This is another example of compensation, of course, turning the calculation into what most of us would find to be an easier one.

Using our facility for doubling with larger numbers could lead us to look at, for example, 36 + 37 and think 'double 36 and 1 more'. Here are some more examples of how we might use our confidence with doubling and halving to get us started on some additions and subtractions:

> 48 + 46 could be related to double 46
> $$46 + 46 = 92, \text{ so } 48 + 46 = 92 + 2 = 94$$
> 62 + 59 could be related to double 60
> $$60 + 60 = 120, \text{ so } 62 + 59 = 120 + 2 - 1 = 121$$
> 54 − 28 could be related to half 54 (27) or double 28 (56)
> $$54 - 27 = 27, \text{ so } 54 - 28 = 27 - 1 = 26$$
> $$56 - 28 = 28, \text{ so } 54 - 28 = 28 - 2 = 26.$$

How do you use 'friendly' numbers?

Most of us would much prefer to deal with 742 − 142 than 742 − 146, because the 142 and 742 are much more 'friendly' than the 146 and the 742. We always have as an option in addition and subtraction to use the compensation approach and temporarily replace one of the numbers in a calculation with one that is more friendly. This is especially useful in subtraction:

> Calculate 742 − 146:
> Change the 146 to 142: $742 - 142 = 600$
> Now compensate: $742 - 146 = 600 - 4 = 596.$
>
> Or,
> Change the 742 to 746: $746 - 146 = 600$
> Now compensate $742 - 146 = 600 - 4 = 596.$

Self-assessment questions

5.1: a) What sign should go in the box to make this true: $67 - (20 - 8) = (67 - 20) \square 8$? Try this with some other numbers and state a general rule. b) What sign should go in the box to make this true: $67 - (20 + 8) = (67 - 20) \square 8$? Try this with some other numbers and state a general rule.

5.2: Identify the errors made by the pupils in the examples in Figure 5.1.

5.3: Find the answer to 538 + 294 by the front-end approach, i.e. by partitioning the numbers into hundreds, tens and ones, then starting with the hundreds and working from left to right.

5.4: Calculate 423 + 98 mentally, using compensation.

5.5: Calculate 297 + 304 mentally, by relating it to a double.

5.6: Calculate 494 + 307 mentally, using 500 as a stepping-stone.

5.7: Calculate 26 + 77 mentally, by relating the numbers to multiples of 5.

5.8: Calculate 1000 − 458 mentally, using compensation.

5.9: Calculate 819 − 523 mentally, by making one of the numbers more friendly.

5.10: Calculate 732 − 389 mentally, by adding-on from 389, using 400 and 700 as stepping-stones.

5.11: Do these using any mental strategies that seem appropriate: a) 974 − 539; b) 400 − 237; c) 597 + 209; d) 7000 − 6; e) 7000 − 6998.

Summary of teaching points

1. Make it clear to pupils (and parents) that there is no 'proper' way of doing a calculation and that a mental or informal method is as valid as a formal written method.

2. Encourage pupils to try to do additions and subtractions by mental and informal methods first, before resorting to formal written algorithms.

3. Confidence in counting backwards and forwards in ones, tens and hundreds is an essential prerequisite for effective mental calculation, so these skills need to be taught specifically and reinforced frequently.

4. Other important prerequisite skills to be emphasized are: doubling single-digit and two-digit numbers; adding and subtracting multiples of 5; making a number up to the next ten or next hundred by adding-on.

5. Aim for all primary pupils to be able to handle addition and subtractions with three-digit numbers using mental methods, supported by jottings and empty number-line diagrams if necessary.

6. Teach pupils specifically the strategies outlined in this chapter and give them opportunities to discuss different ways of tackling additions and subtractions.

7. Explain mental strategies with reference to hundred-squares and number-lines, in order to provide pupils with mental images that will underpin their manipulation of numbers.

6

Written Methods for Addition and Subtraction

Pupils should be taught to: use written methods to add and subtract whole numbers less than 1000, then up to 10000.

In this chapter there are explanations of

- a variety of ways of introducing column addition and subtraction;
- the idea of 'carrying' in the formal addition algorithm;
- the decomposition method for doing subtraction calculations;
- the equal additions method for subtraction;
- how the two methods differ and why decomposition is preferred;
- the problem with zeros in the top number in a subtraction calculation; and
- the constant difference method for subtraction.

How can you introduce pupils to column addition?

When pupils begin to work with three-digit numbers they can be introduced to various ways of laying out their calculations that line up the hundreds, tens and ones in columns. These should build on some of the mental strategies outlined in the previous chapter, particularly the idea of partitioning the numbers into hundreds, tens and ones. Figure 6.1(a) shows how a 9-year-old might record the calculation 372 + 247, using this strategy and lining up the hundreds, tens and ones in columns. Figure 6.1(b) shows an alternative layout for recording the same thinking, which can then be abbreviated to the version in Figure 6.1(c). These ways of recording are a useful introduction to what we might call 'the formal addition algorithm', which is shown in Figure 6.1(d). The major source of pupil error in using this format is that it encourages pupils to think of the digits as separate numbers, losing any sense that they represent hundreds, tens or ones. The layouts in Figures 6.1(a), (b) and (c) have the advantage that they do not obscure the meaning of the digits and pupils should still be consciously aware that they are handling hundreds, tens and ones. Note that these layouts allow you to use the more natural procedure of working from left to right, dealing with the largest bits of the numbers first, as in the 'front-end' approach discussed in Chapter 5. Discussion of various ways of setting out calculations such as these also reinforces the important message that there is no 'proper' way of doing a calculation.

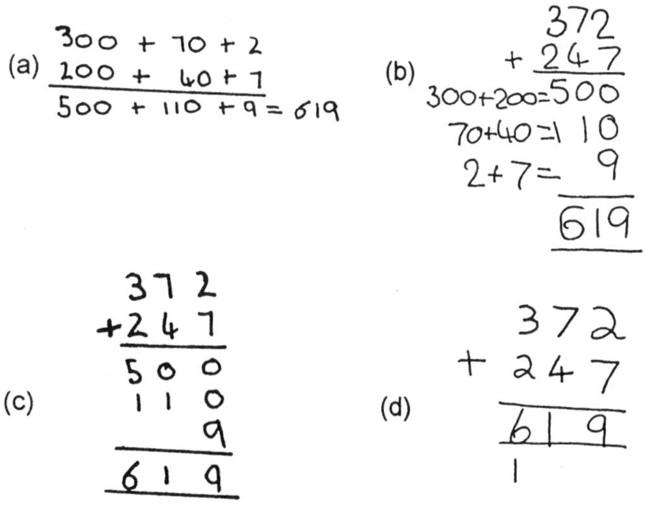

$$
\text{(a)} \quad
\begin{array}{r}
300 + 70 + 2 \\
100 + 40 + 7 \\
\hline
500 + 110 + 9 = 619
\end{array}
$$

$$
\text{(b)} \quad
\begin{array}{r}
372 \\
+ \ 247 \\
\hline
300+200 = 500 \\
70+40 = 110 \\
2+7 = \ \ 9 \\
\hline
619
\end{array}
$$

$$
\text{(c)} \quad
\begin{array}{r}
372 \\
+247 \\
\hline
500 \\
110 \\
9 \\
\hline
619
\end{array}
$$

$$
\text{(d)} \quad
\begin{array}{r}
372 \\
+ \ 247 \\
\hline
619 \\
1
\end{array}
$$

Figure 6.1   Four ways of recording 372 + 247 as a column addition

How do you explain what's going on when you 'carry one' in addition?

The conventional, formal written algorithm (shown in Figure 6.1(d)) is a very condensed and abstract record of a calculation. Teachers might therefore help pupils to understand what is going on here by making clear links between the written record and the manipulation of some form of base-ten materials that incorporate place-value principles (see Chapter 2). These could be, for example, base-ten blocks (units, longs and flats) or coins (pennies, ten-pences and pounds), representing the ones, tens and hundreds. This experience will, however, only be effective in promoting understanding if teachers help their pupils to make strong links between the manipulation of the materials and the written record of the addition. In particular, the 'carrying' procedure should be linked strongly with the physical act of 'carrying' a ten or a hundred from the bank when exchanging 'ten of these for one of those'.

To explain addition, then, I will use £1, 10p and 1p coins, which will be referred to as 'hundreds', 'tens' and 'ones'. (Some teachers prefer to refer to the 'ones' as 'units'. I have no strong views about this and tend to switch freely between the two words.) Clearly the principle that 'ten of these can be exchanged for one of those' applies to the ones and the tens, and to the tens and the hundreds. The process could (and with children, should) equally well be experienced with base-ten blocks.

So to take an example: 356 + 267. This calculation is set out with coins as shown in Figure 6.2, with 356 interpreted as 3 hundreds, 5 tens and 6 ones, and 267 interpreted as 2 hundreds, 6 tens and 7 ones. The two numbers now have to be combined to find the total. So where do you start? The standard algorithm usually involves working from right to left, that is, starting with the ones. This procedure of working from right to left conflicts to some extent with the natural mental strategies of starting with the biggest-value digits and working from left to right. When it comes to using the standard addition algorithm, all I can say is that with experience you find that it's easier to be systematic and to avoid getting in a muddle if you work from right to left. But in fact it really does not matter as long as you remember and apply correctly the principle that 'ten of these can be exchanged for one of those'.

So, in Figure 6.2, we first put together all the ones, making thirteen in all. Ten of these can then be exchanged at the bank for a ten. Since this

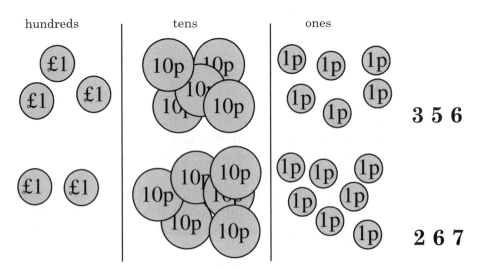

Figure 6.2   356 + 267 set out with coins

ten is literally 'carried' from the bank and placed in the tens column, the language of 'carrying one' is very appropriate – provided it is clear that we are carrying 'one of these' and not carrying 'a one'. The coins at this stage are arranged as shown in Figure 6.3. This also shows the recording so far, in which there is a direct relationship between what is done with the symbols and what has been done with coins. The 3 written in the ones column corresponds to the three remaining one-penny coins. The 1 written below the line in the tens column corresponds to the one ten which has been carried from the bank in exchange for ten ones.

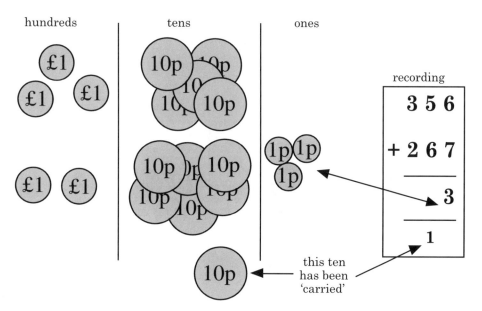

Figure 6.3   Carrying a ten

Next all the tens are combined: that's the 5 tens in the top row, plus the 6 tens in the next row, plus the 1 ten that has been carried. This gives a total of 12 tens. Ten of these are then exchanged for a hundred. So once again we are 'carrying one', but this time, of course, it is 'one hundred'. Figure 6.4 shows the situation at this stage and, once again, the direct correspondence between the recording in symbols and the manipulation of the coins.

The final stage in this calculation is to combine the hundreds: that's the 3 hundreds in the top row, plus the 2 hundreds in the next row, plus the 1 hundred that has been carried, giving a total of 6 hundreds. Figure 6.5 shows the final arrangement of the coins, with the 6 hundreds, 2 tens and 3 ones corresponding to the answer to the sum, namely 623.

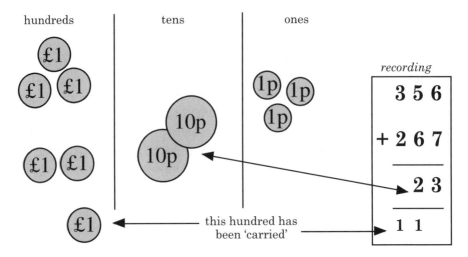

Figure 6.4   Carrying a hundred

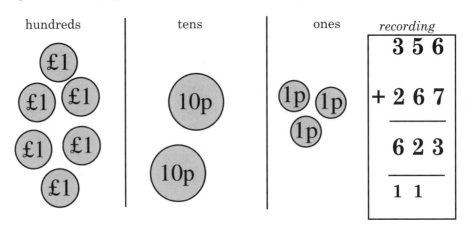

Figure 6.5   The result of adding 356 and 267

What about introducing column subtraction?

Subtractions are straightforward when each digit in the first number is greater than the corresponding digit in the second. For example, in calculating 576 – 324 we just take the 3 hundreds away from the 5 hundreds, the 2 tens away from the 7 tens, and the 4 units away from the 6 units, to get the answer 252. The problem comes when one or more of the digits in the first number is smaller than the corresponding digit in the second number, for example, 448 – 267. Of course, this is not a difficult calculation when tackled by some of the mental strategies outlined in the previous chapter. But, as the numbers get bigger, pupils will probably need to develop some kind of standard written procedure, lining up the hundreds, tens and ones in columns, in order to deal with subtraction. Historically, in Britain, there have been essentially two formal written algorithms for subtraction. Nowadays, nearly all primary schools, if they teach pupils a subtraction algorithm, use the method known as *subtraction by decomposition*. This has more or less completely ousted the method that most people of my age were taught at school, namely the method of *equal additions*. But even in the year 2000 I still find a significant proportion of student-teachers who have grown up using this method. These methods are explained later in this chapter. The bad news for any readers who were brought up on equal additions is that they will definitely have to become fluent in using the method of decomposition. On the other hand, those who use decomposition already have no need to try to master the method of equal additions. However, they will find it informative to try to understand it and, and as we shall see later, it can be the basis for a novel approach to subtraction calculations.

The reason for the shift towards decomposition is that it is much easier to *understand*, in the sense of making connections between the manipulation of concrete materials, the manipulations of the symbols and the corresponding language. Subtraction by equal additions can only really be taught to children by rote, as a procedure to be followed blindly with little real understanding of what is going on. The shift towards decomposition therefore coincided with a greater emphasis in teaching on learning mathematics with understanding.

Pupils can be introduced to the idea of lining up the hundreds, tens and ones in columns for subtraction using the same format as is suggested in Figure 6.1(a) for introducing addition. Figure 6.6 shows some ways in which pupils might record the calculation of 448 – 267, all of which start by partitioning the numbers into hundreds, tens and ones.

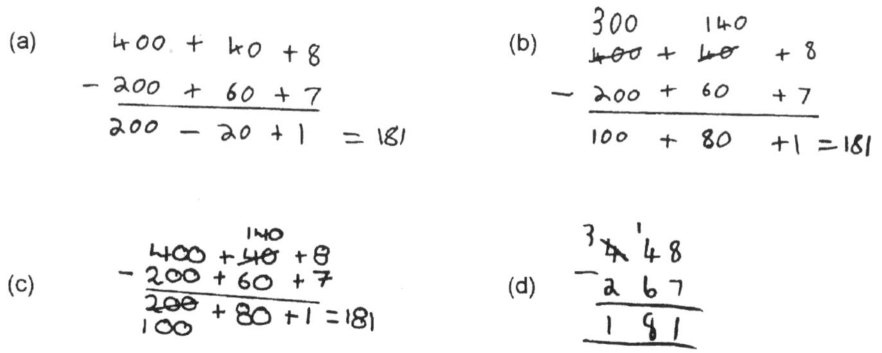

Figure 6.6   Four ways of calculating 448 – 267 using column subtraction

In the approach shown in Figure 6.6(a) the pupil has worked from left to right, subtracting the hundreds, then the tens, then the ones. The recording of –20 in the tens column does not require a sophisticated understanding of negative numbers. It can be understood simply as meaning that we have taken away 40 of the 60 in the second number, so we still have 20 to be taken away. The final step of calculating 200 – 20 + 1 is done mentally.

In Figure 6.6(b), the pupil is introduced to the idea of decomposition and encouraged to work from right to left. The thought process is as follows: starting with the ones, 8 – 7 = 1; then onto the tens; 40 take away 60 is a problem; so take 100 from the next column and add this to the 40, making 140; then 140 – 60 = 80; then deal with the hundreds; 300 – 200 = 100. The final calculation 100 + 80 + 1 is again done mentally.

Figure 6.6(c) shows a novel application of the idea of decomposition. The pupil is using a front-end approach, working from left to right. Having dealt with 400 – 200 = 200, the pupil then encounters the problem of 40 – 60. To deal with this, 100 is taken from the 200 in the answer in the hundreds column and added on to the 40. This gives 140 – 60 = 80.

The layout of Figure 6.6(b) especially is a helpful introductory procedure prior to the development of the formal decomposition algorithm shown in Figure 6.6(d). As with addition, the formal algorithm for subtraction is a highly condensed and abstract form of recording and can become a meaningless routine in which digits are manipulated without any thought as to what they represent. Again, to promote understanding of what is going on here, teachers might discuss with pupils the corresponding manipulation of some base-ten materials to represent hundreds, tens and ones. This would involve putting out a pile of hundreds, tens and ones to represent the first number, then taking away the second number, exchanging a hundred for ten tens, or a ten for ten ones when necessary. As with addition, pupils should be helped to connect the manipulation of the materials with the written record, step by step.

So how does subtraction by decomposition work?

As with addition calculations, the key to explaining the method is a sound grasp of *place value* and the use of some appropriate concrete embodiments of number, such as coins or base-ten blocks.

I will explain the method of decomposition with base-ten blocks, using the example of 443 – 267. First the 443 is set out with base-ten blocks, as shown in Figure 6.7: 4 hundreds, 4 tens and 3 units. The task is to take 267 away from this collection of blocks, that is, to remove 2 hundreds, 6 tens and 7 units. As with addition, the natural place to start might be to take away the biggest blocks first, that is, working from left to right, and this is how most of us would deal with a calculation of this kind if doing it mentally or by informal written methods. But again the standard written algorithm actually works from right to left. This is certainly not essential, but it is usually tidier to do it this way. So we start by trying to remove 7 units from the collection of blocks in Figure 6.7. Since there are only 3 units there we cannot do this – yet. So we take one of the tens (take it to the box of blocks) and exchange it for ten units.

Figure 6.8 shows the situation at this stage and the corresponding recording. Notice how the recording in symbols corresponds precisely to

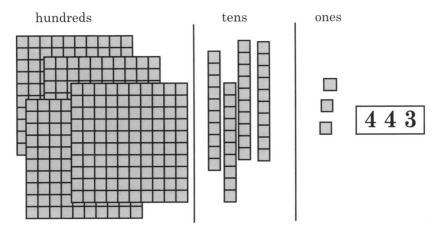

Figure 6.7   The number 443 set out with base-ten blocks

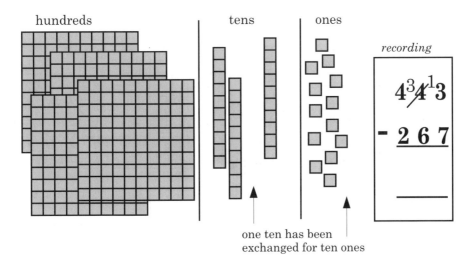

one ten has been
exchanged for ten ones

Figure 6.8   Exchanging one ten for ten ones

the manipulation of the materials. We have crossed out the 4 tens in the top number and replaced it by 3, because one of these tens has been exchanged for units and we do indeed now have 3 tens in our collection. The little 1 placed beside the 3 units in the top number is to indicate that we now have 13 units. We are now in a position to take away the 7 units as required, leaving 6 units. This is recorded as in Figure 6.9.

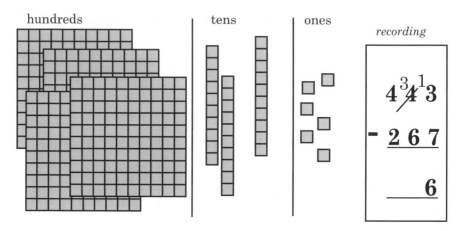

Figure 6.9   After 7 units have been taken away

The next step is to deal with the problem of removing 6 tens when we have only 3 of them. So we take one of the hundreds and exchange it for 10 tens, producing the situation shown in Figure 6.10. The recording indicates that after the exchanging process we now have 3 hundreds and

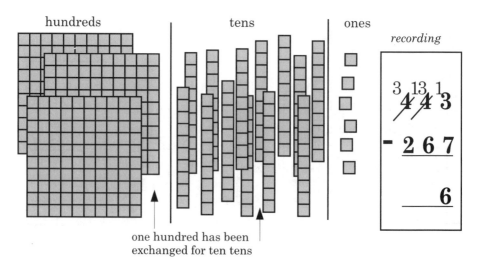

one hundred has been
exchanged for ten tens

Figure 6.10   Exchanging one hundred for 10 tens

13 tens. We can now complete the subtraction, taking away first the 6 tens and then the 2 hundreds.

Figure 6.11 shows the final arrangement of the blocks, with the remaining 1 hundred, 7 tens and 6 units corresponding to the result of the subtraction, namely 176.

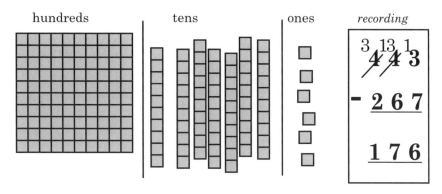

Figure 6.11   The result of subtracting 267 from 443

There are three important points to note about this method. First there is the quite natural idea of exchanging a block in one column for ten in the next column to the right when necessary. Second, there is the strong connection between the manipulation of the materials and the recording in symbols, supported by appropriate language. Third, notice that all the action in the recording takes place in the top line, that is, in the number you are working on, not the number you are subtracting.

How does the method of equal additions differ from this?

The method of equal additions differs in all three of these respects. It does not use the principle of exchange, it is not naturally rooted in the manipulation of materials and the method involves working on both numbers simultaneously. Although the method is not normally taught these days it will actually prove to be quite useful to explain it. My explanation will be merely in terms of numbers, without the support of coins or blocks, simply because the method is not easily understood in these terms.

The method is based on the comparison structure of subtraction (see Chapter 4) and uses the principle that the difference between two numbers remains the same if you add the same number to each one. For example, the difference between your height and my height is still the same if we stand together on a table rather than on the floor! Faced with the subtraction 443 – 267, the person using equal additions would manipulate the symbols as shown in Figure 6.12.

Unable to deal with '3 take away 7', we add 10 to both numbers, as shown in Figure 6.12(b). In the top number this 10 is added to the units digit, increasing the 3 to 13. This is shown by writing a little 1 in front of the 3. In the bottom number the 10 is added to the tens column, increasing the 6 to 7. I show this by striking through the 6 and writing 7, whereas some people indicate this by writing a little 1 somewhere in the tens column: various systems of recording are used for this step, but the principle of adding ten to both numbers is the same.

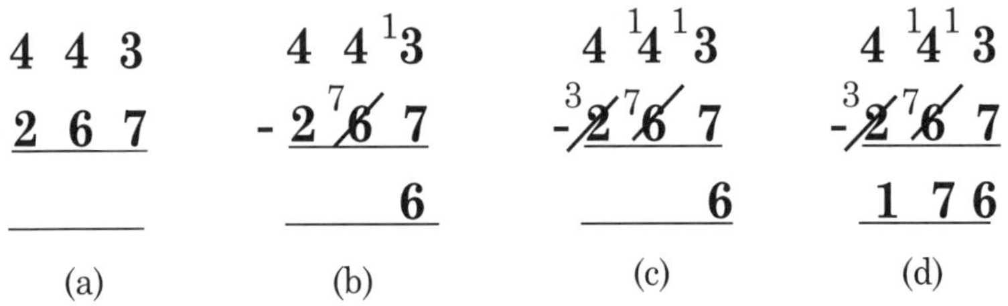

Figure 6.12   The method of equal additions

In Figure 6.12(b) we can now deal with the units, writing in 6 in the answer, but are faced with the problem of '4 subtract 7' in the tens column. We apply the same principle of adding the same thing to both numbers, but this time we actually add 100, as shown in Figure 6.12(c). This appears as 10 tens in the top number, increasing the number of tens from 4 to 14. Simultaneously, in the bottom number we add 1 to the hundreds digit, increasing it from 2 to 3. We are then able to complete the subtraction as shown in Figure 6.12(d). The reader may be encouraged to note that both methods produce the same answer.

What is 'borrowing' in subtraction?

I really don't know. When we did equal additions we were taught to say, 'Borrow one and pay it back'. I have never understood this phrase, since it is not at all clear from whom we were borrowing or even whether we were paying it back to the same source. I have therefore come to the conclusion that it was merely something to say to yourself, with no meaning, simply as a reminder that there were two things to do. We could equally well have said, 'Pick one up and put one down'. The intriguing thing is, though, that this language of 'borrowing' has actually survived the demise of the method for which it was invented! It is still commonplace to hear teachers talking about 'borrowing one' when

explaining the method of decomposition to children. I find this unhelpful. We are not 'borrowing one' in decomposition, we are *'exchanging
one of these for ten of those'*.

Of course, in practice no one ever thought consciously that what they
were doing, for example, was adding ten or a hundred to both numbers:
they were simply 'borrowing one and paying it back'! Thus subtraction by
equal additions was always taught by rote, with no real attempt to understand what was going on. This is the real advantage of decomposition: that
there is the potential in the method for pupils to understand it in terms of
concrete experiences of coins or blocks, supported by meaningful language.

The reader may wonder therefore why everyone did not always teach
the method of decomposition. The reason is that unfortunately there is
sometimes a slight problem in using the decomposition method when
there is a zero in the top number. A modification in the process of
decomposition is required, whereas with equal additions zeros in the
top number make no difference to the routine. However, the modification is a natural process, still easily understood if related strongly to
concrete materials and the appropriate language of exchange.

What is the problem in decomposition with a zero in
the top number?

Figure 6.13 shows the steps involved in tackling 802 – 247 by decomposition. In Figure 6.13(a) the person doing the calculation is faced with
the problem of '2 subtract 7'. The decomposition method requires a ten
to be exchanged for ten units, but in the 802 the zero indicates that
there are no tens. This is the problem! However, it is not difficult to see
that the thing to do is to go across to the hundreds column and exchange this for 10 tens, as shown in Figure 6.13(b), then to take one of
these and exchange it for ten units, as shown in Figure 6.13(c). The
subtraction can then be completed, as in Figure 6.13(d). Of course, all
this can be carried out and understood easily in terms of base-ten blocks
or coins, representing hundreds, tens and ones (units).

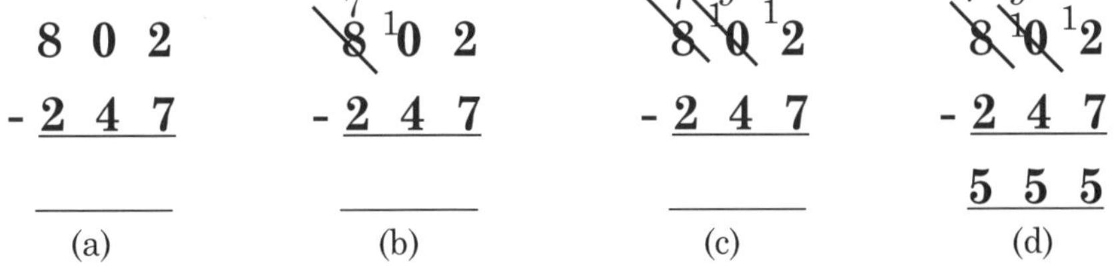

Figure 6.13   The problem of a zero in the top number

However, let me remind you that these subtractions with zeros in the first number, that are most problematic when done by the formal de-composition algorithm, are often very straightforward when tackled using mental strategies such as compensation, as explained in Chapter 5. (For example, 802 – 247 is a cinch if you start with 802 – 250 and then compensate for the additional 3 taken away.) The method of constant differences explained below is an alternative approach that is also par-ticularly effective when there are zeros in the first number.

What is the constant difference method?

Surprisingly, in view of what I have said above, the principle of equal additions is not redundant, but is actually an important tool in the collection of strategies that we might use for mental or informal methods of doing subtraction calculations. But it does not have to be just 10 or 100 that you add. For instance, to work out 87 – 48 we could simply add 2 to both numbers and change it to 89 – 50, thus converting it into a much easier calculation. This adhocorithm can almost be de-veloped into an algorithm that some pupils might find more to their liking than the formal method of decomposition. I call it the *constant difference method*, because as we change the subtraction into easier sub-tractions, we keep the difference between the numbers constant.

So, for example, returning to 802 – 247, we could proceed like this:

The problem is 802 – 247
Add 3 to both numbers: 805 – 250   (that makes it easier)
Add 50 to both numbers: 855 – 300   (that makes it really easy!)
So the answer is 555.

This approach can be combined where appropriate with subtracting the same thing from both numbers. For example, to calculate 918 – 436:

The problem is 918 – 436   (no problem with the units)
Subtract 6 from both: 912 – 430   (getting easier)
Add 70 to both numbers: 982 – 500   (really easy!)
So the answer is 482.

With a bit of practice, this method of converting the second number into a multiple of 10 or a multiple of 100 by adding the same thing to both numbers, or subtracting the same thing from both numbers, can become extremely efficient and just as quick as any other.

Self-assessment questions

6.1: Using the same kind of explanation with coins as that given above, work through the addition of 208, 156 and 97.

6.2: Using the column addition layout in Figure 6.1(a), what would be the last line in the calculation of 357 + 587?

6.3: Practise the explanation of the process of subtraction by decomposition using coins (1p, 10p and £1 to represents ones, tens and hundreds) and appropriate examples, such as 623 – 471.

6.4: Using the column subtraction layout in Figure 6.6(b), what would be the last line in the calculation of 652 – 464?

6.5: Practise the explanation of the process of decomposition using base-ten blocks to represent units, tens, hundreds and thousands, with examples with zero in the first number, such as 2006 – 438.

6.6: Find the answer to 2006 – 438 using the constant difference method.

Summary of teaching points

1. Introduce pupils to column addition and subtraction using some of the methods shown in Figures 6.1 and 6.6 that build upon the idea of partitioning the numbers into hundreds, tens and ones, and which do not obscure the meaning of the digits.

2. Important language used in the addition algorithm includes: *hundreds, tens, ones (units), 'ten of these can be exchanged for one of those', carrying.*

3. The two most effective concrete embodiments of the place-value principle with which the addition algorithm can be explained to pupils and experienced by them are coins (hundreds, tens and ones) and base-ten blocks.

4. To develop their understanding of the addition algorithm, pupils should have opportunities to connect the manipulation of the materials (both coins and blocks) with the manipulation of the symbols and the corresponding language.

5. When pupils need a formal algorithm for subtraction, teach the method of decomposition.

6. Explain the method in a way that encourages understanding of the process, not just as a recipe without meaning.

7. Provide pupils with plenty of opportunity to connect the manipulation of coins (1p, 10p and £1) and base-ten blocks with the manipulation of the symbols in the process of subtraction by decomposition, supported by the appropriate language.

8. Don't use the language of 'borrowing' when explaining subtraction by decomposition. It has no place there. Emphasize the idea of 'exchanging'.
9. Encourage pupils to set out written subtraction calculations generously, to give themselves plenty of room for their working.
10. Be alert to the possibility of parents and grandparents confusing children by trying to teach them the formal method of equal additions.
11. Discuss with pupils how the principle of adding the same thing to both numbers (or subtracting the same thing from both) can convert a subtraction question into an easier calculation (the constant difference method).

7

Multiplication and Division Structures

Pupils should be taught to: understand multiplication as repeated addition; understand division as grouping (repeated subtraction); use vocabulary associated with multiplication and division; develop further their understanding of multiplication and division and the inverse relationship between them; understand why the commutative law applies to multiplication; choose and use multiplication or division to solve problems in 'real life', money or measures of lengths, mass, capacity or time.

In this chapter there are explanations of

- two different structures of real-life problems modelled by multiplication;
- the contexts in which pupils will meet these multiplication structures;
- the commutative law of multiplication;
- the idea of a rectangular array associated with multiplication;
- three different structures of real-life problems modelled by division; and
- the contexts in which pupils will meet these division structures.

What are the different kinds of situation to which the operation of multiplication applies?

There are essentially two categories of situation that have a structure that corresponds to the mathematical operation represented by the symbol for multiplication. These two structures, which are essentially extensions of the two structures of addition, discussed in Chapter 4, are

- the repeated aggregation structure; and
- the scaling structure.

Repeated aggregation is the elementary idea that multiplication means 'so many sets of' or 'so many lots of'. If I have '10 sets of 3 counters' then the question, 'how many counters altogether?', is associated with the multiplication, 3 × 10 (see Figure 7.1). This structure is simply an extension of the aggregation structure of addition, with, for example, the repeated addition, 3 + 3 + 3 + 3 + 3 + 3 + 3 + 3 + 3 + 3, becoming the multiplication, 3 × 10.

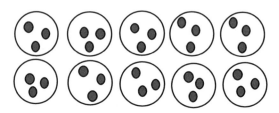

Figure 7.1   Multiplication as repeated aggregation, 3 × 10

The *scaling* structure is a rather more difficult idea. It is an extension of the augmentation structure of addition. That structure referred to addition as meaning that we increase a quantity by a certain amount. With multiplication we also increase a quantity, but we increase it by a *scale factor*. So multiplication by 10 would be interpreted in this structure as scaling a quantity by a factor of 10, as illustrated in Figure 7.2.

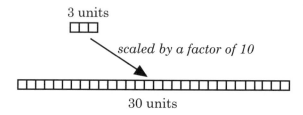

Figure 7.2   Multiplication as scaling, 3 × 10

It should perhaps be mentioned here that multiplication by a number less than 1 would correspond to a scaling that *reduces* the size of the quantity, not increases it. For example, scaling 3 by a factor of 0.5 would reduce it to 1.5, corresponding to the multiplication, 3 × 0.5 = 1.5.

I'm not sure whether 3 × 5 means '3 lots of 5' or '5 lots of 3'

Which of the pictures in Figure 7.3 would we connect with 3 × 5? If I were to be really pedantic, I suppose I would have to say that, strictly speaking, 3 × 5 means '5 lots of 3'. You start with 3, and multiply it by 5. That is, you reproduce the three, five times in all, as illustrated in Figure 7.3(a). But I would prefer to let the meaning of the symbol be determined by how it is used. It seems to me that, in practice, people use the symbols 3 × 5 to mean both '3 lots of 5' and '5 lots of 3', in other words, both the examples shown in Figures 7.3(a) and 7.3(b). I am happy therefore to let 3 × 5 refer to either (a) or (b). And the same goes for 5 × 3. One symbol having more than one meaning is something we have to learn to live with in mathematics – as well as being a feature which makes mathematical symbols so powerful in their application.

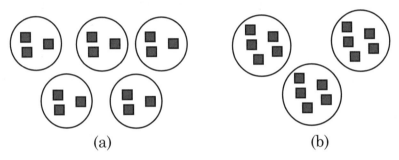

(a)   (b)

Figure 7.3   (a) 5 sets of 3; (b) 3 sets of 5

The underlying mathematical principle here is what is called the *commutative law of multiplication*. This refers to the fact that when you are multiplying two numbers together the order in which you write them down does not make any difference. We have already seen in Chapter 4 that addition also has this property. We recognize this commutative property formally by the following generalization, which is true whatever the numbers *a* and *b*:

$$b \times a = a \times b.$$

There are two important points to note about the commutative property in relation to multiplication. First it is important to realize that division does *not* have this property. For example, 10 ÷ 5 is not equal to 5 ÷ 10. Second, use of the commutative property enables us to simplify some calculations. For example, many of us would evaluate '5 lots of 14' by changing the question to the equivalent, '14 lots of 5' – because fives are much easier to handle than fourteens! Grasping the principle of commutativity also cuts down significantly the number of different results we have to memorize from the multiplication tables: if I know seven fives, for example, then I know five sevens.

Is there a picture that can usefully be associated with the multiplication symbol?

It is interesting to note first that the commutative property of multiplication is by no means obvious. Other than by counting the numbers in each picture, we would not immediately recognize that (a) and (b) in Figure 7.3 have the same number of counters. So this picture is not especially helpful. But there is one very significant picture of multiplication which does make this commutative property obvious. This is the association of multiplication with the image of a *rectangular array*. Figure 7.4 shows some examples of rectangular arrays that correspond to 3 × 5 (or 5 × 3). This is the image of multiplication that we should carry round in our heads, particularly when we want to talk to children about multiplication and to illustrate our discussions with diagrams. This picture really does make the commutative property transparently obvious. We can actually see that 3 sets of 5 and 5 sets of 3 come to the same thing, because the array can be thought of as 3 rows of 5, using vertical rows, or 5 rows of 3, using horizontal rows.

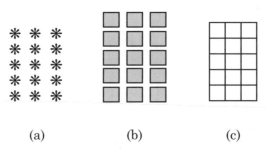

(a)   (b)   (c)

Figure 7.4   Examples of rectangular arrays for 3 × 5

There are other good reasons for strongly associating this image of a rectangular array with multiplication. For example, this idea leads on naturally to the use of multiplication for determining the area of a rectangle. In example (c) in Figure 7.4, 3 × 5 gives the number of square units in the rectangle and therefore determines its area. We can also extend this idea to develop an effective method for multiplying together larger numbers (see Chapter 9).

Apart from 'so many sets of so many,' are there other contexts in which pupils will meet multiplication in the repeated aggregation structure?

Any situation in which we aggregate a certain number of portions of a given quantity, such as mass, liquid volume, length and time, provides an application of this multiplication structure. For example: finding the total mileage for 42 journeys of 38 miles each (42 × 38); finding the total volume of drink required to fill 32 glasses if each holds 225 ml (32 × 225); finding the total time required for 12 events each lasting 25 minutes (12 × 25).

But, not surprisingly, the most important context will be shopping, particularly where we have to find the cost of a number of items given the *unit cost*. Two important words here are *each* and *per*. For example, we might need to find the cost of 25 cans of drink at 39p *each* (25 × 39). Or we might purchase 25 tickets at £3.50 *per* ticket (25 × 3.50). In both cases we have to associate the language and the structure of the example with the operation of multiplication.

Then there are important situations where we encounter repeated aggregation in the context of *cost per unit of measurement*. For example, if we purchase 28 litres of petrol at £0.84 per litre, we should recognize that a multiplication (25 × 0.84) is required to determine the total cost, although, of course, in practice the petrol pump will do it for us. Likewise, we should connect multiplication with situations such as finding the cost of so many metres of material given the cost per metre, or someone's earnings for so many hours of work given the rate of pay per hour, and so on.

What are some of the contexts in which pupils will meet multiplication in the scaling structure?

Most obviously, this structure is associated with scale models and scale drawings. For example, if a scale model is built using a scale factor of 1 to 10, then each linear measurement in the actual object is 10 times the corresponding measurement in the model. Similarly, if we have a plan of the classroom made using a scale factor 1 to 100 and the width of the chalkboard in the drawing is 2 cm, then the width of the actual chalkboard will be 200 cm (2 × 100).

This is also the multiplication structure that lies behind the idea of a *pro rata* increase. For example, if we all get a 13% increase in our salary, then all our salaries get multiplied by the same scale factor, namely 1.13 (see Chapter 16 for an explanation of percentage increases). The simplest experience of this structure is when we talk about *doubling* or *trebling* a given quantity: this is simply increasing the given quantity by applying the scale factors 2 or 3 respectively.

Then we also sometimes use this multiplication structure in order to express a comparison between two numbers or amounts, where we make statements using phrases such as 'so many times as much (or as many)' or 'so many times bigger (longer, heavier, etc.)'. For example, 125 × 3 would be the calculation corresponding to this situation: John earns £125 a week, but his brother earns three times as much; how much does his brother earn? The phrase *three times as much* is what should prompt the association with multiplication by 3.

What are the different kinds of situation to which the operation of division applies?

There is a wide range of situations in which we have to learn to recognize that the appropriate operation is division. These can be categorized into at least the following three structures:

- the equal-sharing structure;
- the inverse-of-multiplication structure; and
- the ratio structure.

As with the other operations of addition, subtraction and multiplication, it helps us to connect these mathematical structures with the operation of division if we ask ourselves the question: 'What is the calculation I would enter on a calculator in order to solve this problem?' In each case the answer will involve using the division key on the calculator. As we saw earlier, particularly with subtraction in Chapter 4, one of the difficulties in understanding the meanings of the symbols we use in mathematics is that one symbol can have a number of strikingly different meanings. This is certainly the case with the division symbol.

The *equal-sharing* structure refers to a situation in which a quantity is shared out equally into a given number of portions and we are asked to determine how many or how much there is in each portion. For example, 20 marbles might be shared equally between 4 pupils in a game, as shown in Figure 7.5. The calculation to be entered on a calculator to

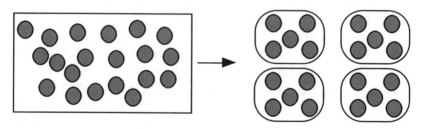

Figure 7.5   Division as equal sharing, 20 ÷ 4

correspond to this situation is 20 ÷ 4. This is the structure that teachers most naturally connect with division and is strongly associated with the language 'sharing' and 'how many (or how much) each?'

The *inverse-of-multiplication* structure, however, interprets 20 ÷ 4 in a completely different way, as shown in Figure 7.6. Now the question being asked is: 'How many groups of 4 marbles are there in the set of 20 marbles?'

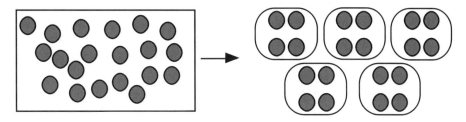

Figure 7.6   Division as inverse-of-multiplication, 20 ÷ 4

Both Figures 7.5 and 7.6 are equally valid interpretations of the division, 20 ÷ 4, even though they are answering two different questions:

1. Share 20 equally into 4 groups: how many in each group? (Figure 7.5.)
2. Share 20 into groups of 4: how many groups? (Figure 7.6.)

The phrase 'inverse-of-multiplication' underlines the idea that division and multiplication are *inverse* processes. This means, for example, that since 6 × 9 comes to 54, then 54 ÷ 9 must be 6. The division by 9 'undoes' the effect of multiplying by 9. Hence to solve a problem of the form 'what must *A* be multiplied by to give *B*?' we divide *B* by *A*. For example: How many tickets costing £1.50 each do I need to sell to raise £90? The calculation that must be entered on a calculator to solve this problem is the division, 90 ÷ 1.50.

The actual problems that occur in practice which have this inverse-of-multiplication structure can be further subdivided. There are problems that incorporate the notion of *repeated subtraction from a given quantity*, such as 'how many sets of 4 can I get from a set of 20?' And there are those that incorporate the idea of *repeated addition to reach a target*, such as 'how many sets of 4 do you need to get a set of 20?' First, the process of sharing out the 20 marbles in the above example can be thought of as *repeatedly subtracting* 4 marbles from the set of 20 until there are none left, counting the number of groups as you do this. But the problem might also be based on the idea of repeated addition to reach a target. The question, 'how many groups of 4 marbles are there in a set of 20 marbles?' could mean, in practical terms, *repeatedly adding* sets of 4 marbles until the target of 20 is achieved, counting the number of sets required as you do this. In Chapter 10 we shall see that this distinction between the repeated subtraction idea and the repeated addition idea in the inverse-of-multiplication structure is particularly significant when the answer to the division is not a whole number.

The *ratio* division structure refers to situations where we use division to compare two quantities. As has already been discussed in Chapter 4, in a situation where a comparison has to be made between two numbers, sums of money or measurements of some kind, we can make the comparison by subtraction, focusing on the difference between the quantities. For example, if A earns £300 a week and B earns £900 a week, one way of comparing them is to state that B earns £600 more than A, or A earns £600 less than B. The 600 is arrived at by the subtraction, 900 − 300. But we could also compare A's and B's earnings by looking at their ratio, stating, for example, that B earns three times more than A. The three is obtained by the division, 900 ÷ 300. This process is simply the inverse of the scaling structure of multiplication described above, since what we are doing here is finding the scale factor by which one quantity must be increased in order to match the other; in the above example, the question would be, by what factor must 300 be multiplied to give 900?

The reader may have noticed that all the examples of division used in this chapter so far have had whole-number answers and no remainders. The problems of remainders and rounding are dealt with in Chapter 10.

What are some of the contexts in which pupils will meet division in the equal-sharing structure?

At first sight we might think that sharing is a very familiar experience for pupils: sharing sweets, sharing pencils, sharing books, sharing toys, and so on. But this idea of sharing a set into subsets corresponds to division only under certain conditions. First, the set must be shared into *equal* subsets, which is certainly not always the case in children's experience of sharing. Second, it is important to note that the language is *sharing between* rather than *sharing with*. Children's normal experience is to share sets of things *with* a number of friends. Division requires sharing them *between* a number of people. The division 12 ÷ 3 does not correspond to 'I have 12 marbles and I share them *with* my 3 friends'. The situation required is: 'Share 12 marbles equally *between* 3 people'. This is a somewhat artificial process and may not be encountered as often in the pupils' experience as we might imagine at first sight. So, sharing does not always correspond to division: it must be not just 'sharing', nor just 'sharing equally', but 'sharing equally between'.

In the context of measurement it is not difficult to come up with imaginary situations where we might share a given quantity into a number of equal portions. Cutting up a 750-cm length of wood into 6 equal lengths, or pouring out 750 ml of wine equally into 6 glasses, or sharing out 750 g of chocolate equally between 6 children, for example, all correspond to the division 750 ÷ 6. But these problems tend to feel like situations contrived for mathematics lessons rather than genuine problems.

The context of money does, however, provide some of the more natural examples in real life for this structure of the division operation. For example, a group of people might share a prize in a lottery, or share a bill in a restaurant: in both cases it is likely that we would *share equally between* the people in the group. An important class of everyday situations is where items are sold in multiple packs: a familiar requirement is to want to know the price per item. So, for example, if a shop is selling a pack of 9 audio-cassettes for £7.92, the cost per cassette, in pence, is found by the division 792 ÷ 9. We can think to ourselves that the 792 pence are being shared equally between the 9 cassettes.

This then extends naturally to the idea of price per unit of measurement. For example, to find the cost per litre of a 6-litre flagon of milk costing 210p, we should recognize that the calculation to be entered on a calculator is the division, 210 ÷ 6. It is as though the 210 pence are being shared out equally between the 6 litres, giving 35p for each litre. Once again the word 'per', meaning 'for each', plays an important part in our understanding of this kind of situation.

This idea of 'per' turns up in numerous other situations in everyday life. For example, when calculating for a purchase how many or how much we get per penny or per pound, when finding miles per litre, determining how much someone earns per hour, an average speed in miles per hour, the number of words typed per minute, and so on: all these situations would correspond to the operation of division using the equal-sharing structure.

What are some of the contexts in which pupils will meet division in the inverse-of-multiplication structure?

There are many practical situations in which a set is to be sorted out into subsets of a given size and the question to be answered is, 'how many subsets are there?' For example, the head of a school with 240 pupils may wish to organize them into classes of 30 children. How many classes do we need? This is modelled by 240 ÷ 30, in other words, how many 30s make 240? Then the teacher with a class of 30 children may wish to organize them into groups of 5 children and ask: How many groups? This is modelled by 30 ÷ 5, in other words, how many 5s in 30?

The structure extends quite naturally into the context of money. A familiar question is: How many of these can I afford? This kind of question incorporates the idea of *repeated subtraction from a given quantity*. For example, how many items costing £6 each can I buy with £150? The question is basically 'how many 6s can I get out of 150?' We could imagine repeatedly spending (subtracting) £6 until all the £150 is used up. Similar situations occur in the context of measurement. For instance, the question, 'how many 150-ml servings of wine from a 750-ml bottle?' is an example of the inverse-of-multiplication division structure, in the context of liquid volume and capacity, corresponding to the calculation, 750 ÷ 150, in other words, how many 150s make 750? Again the notion of repeated subtraction from a given quantity is evident here. We can imagine repeatedly pouring out (subtracting) 150 ml servings, until the 750 ml is used up.

Then there are problems in the context of money and measurement that ask the question: How many do we need? This kind of question incorporates the idea of *repeated addition to reach a target*. For example, how many items priced at £6 each must I sell to raise £150? We could imagine repeatedly adding £6 to our takings until we reach the target of £150. In spite of the language used, the problem is modelled by the division, 150 ÷ 6.

The word 'per' turns up again in this division structure. For example, if we know the price per kg of potatoes is 50p, then we might find ourselves asking a question like, 'how many kilograms can I get for £10 (1000p)?' Similarly, if I save 50p per week, I might ask the question, 'how long will it take to save £10?' Or, if the price of petrol is 50p per litre, the question might be, 'how many litres can I get for £10?' Each of these is, of course, another instance of 'how many 50s make 1000?', so they are again examples of the inverse-of-multiplication structure, corresponding in these cases to the division, 1000 ÷ 50.

Exactly the same mathematical structure occurs in finding the time for a journey given the average speed. For example, the question, 'how long will it take me to drive 1000 miles, if I average 50 miles per hour?', is equivalent again to the question, 'how many 50s make 1000?', and hence, using the inverse-of-multiplication structure, to the division, 1000 ÷ 50.

What about situations using the ratio division structure?

Many primary-school pupils can learn to recognize the need to use division to compare two quantities by ratio. Situations where comparisons could be made between numbers in sets, between amounts of money or between measurements of various kinds are readily available. The problem is, however, that in practice, unless the questions are contrived carefully, the answers tend to be quite difficult to interpret. It's easy enough to deal with, say, comparing two children's journeys to school of 10 minutes and 30 minutes, and, using division (30 ÷ 10), making the statement that one pupil's journey is three times longer than the other. But it's a huge step from interpreting a statement like that with whole numbers to making sense of, say, comparing the heights of two pupils, 125 cm and 145 cm, using a calculator to do the division (145 ÷ 125 = 1.16), and concluding that one pupil is 1.16 times taller than the other.

Self-assessment questions

7.1: Give two problems associated with the multiplication 29 × 12, one using the idea of '29 lots of 12' and the other using '12 lots of 29'.

7.2: Make up a problem using the repeated aggregation structure and the word *per*, in the context of shopping, corresponding to the multiplication, 12 × 25.

7.3: A box of yoghurts consists of 4 rows of 6 cartons arranged in a rectangular array. How would you use this as an example to illustrate the commutative property of multiplication?

7.4: A model of an aeroplane is built on a scale of 1 to 25. Make up a question about the model and the actual aeroplane, using the scaling structure.

7.5: A headteacher earning £2827 a month gets a 12% pay rise. Model this situation with a multiplication by a scale factor and use a calculator to find her new monthly salary.

7.6: The real car is 300 cm long and the model car is 15 cm long: how many times longer is the real car? (i.e. what is the scale factor?) What is the calculation to be entered on a calculator to answer this? Of what division structure is this an example?

7.7: A sack of apples weighing 28 pounds costs £7: what is the price per pound-weight of apples? What is the calculation to be entered on a calculator to answer this? Of what structure of division is this an example?

7.8: How many CDs costing £12.50 each can I afford to buy with £100? What is the calculation to be entered on a calculator to answer this? Of what division structure is this an example?

7.9: How many months do I need to save up £300 if I save £12 a month? What is the calculation to be entered on a calculator to answer this? Of what division structure is this an example?

7.10: Make up a problem that corresponds to the division, 60 ÷ 4, using the equal-sharing structure in the context of shopping.

7.11: Make up a problem that corresponds to the division, 60 ÷ 4, using the inverse-of-multiplication structure, incorporating the idea of repeated subtraction from a given quantity, in the context of shopping.

7.12: Make up a problem using the ratio structure in the context of salaries. Use a calculator to answer your own problem.

Summary of teaching points

1. Primary-school pupils' main experience of multiplication will be through the structure of repeated aggregation, although they may also meet some examples of multiplication used for scaling.

2. There is no need to make a fuss about whether $a \times b$ means 'a lots of b' or 'b lots of a'.

3. The key language to be developed in the repeated aggregation of multiplication structure includes: *so many lots (sets) of so many, how many (how much) altogether, per, each*.

4. Give special attention to helping pupils to use the word *per* with confidence and to associate the practical problems about unit cost and cost per unit of measurement with the corresponding multiplications.

5. The key language to be developed in the scaling structure of multiplication includes: *scaling, scale factor, so many times bigger (longer, heavier, etc. . . .), so many times as much (or as many)*.

6. Work hard with your pupils to establish the commutative principle in multiplication and encourage them to use it in recalling results from the multiplication tables.

7. Use rectangular arrays frequently to illustrate and to support your explanations about multiplication, particularly for reinforcing the commutative principle.

8. Pupils should learn to connect the operation of division with a wide range of problems, including situations with the structures of equal-sharing, inverse-of-multiplication (including both repeated subtraction from a given quantity and repeated addition to reach a target) and, possibly, ratio.

9. Pupils should experience these division structures in a range of practical and relevant contexts, including especially shopping, rates of pay and the many kinds of problems associated with the word *per*, such as 'price per unit'.

10. The key idea in the equal-sharing structure of divison is *sharing equally between*.

11. Division is not just 'sharing'. Equal sharing is only one division structure. Teachers should not overemphasize the language and imagery of sharing at the expense of the other important language and imagery which has to be associated with division, particularly inverse-of-multiplication.

12. Two key ideas in the inverse-of-multiplication structure of division are *how many Bs make A?* (repeated addition to reach a target) and *how many times can B be taken away from A until there's nothing left?* (repeated subtraction from a given quantity). Both these have to be connected with the division, $A \div B$.

13. Particularly important are division problems with questions such as 'how many can I afford?', which incorporate the idea of repeated subtraction from a given quantity, and 'how many do I need?', which incorporate the idea of repeated addition to reach a target.

14. Primary pupils can be introduced to the idea of using division to find the ratio between two quantities in order to compare them, but the results are difficult to interpret if they are not whole numbers.

15. Asking the question, 'what is the calculation to be entered on a calculator to solve this problem?', helps to focus the pupils' thinking on the underlying mathematical structure of the situation and hence to make the connection with division.

16. Familiarity with the range of multiplication and division structures discussed in this chapter will enable pupils to interpret multiplication and division calculations in a variety of ways and hence increase their ability to handle these calculations by a range of methods.

8

Mental Strategies for Multiplication and Division

Pupils should be taught to: recall multiplication facts to 10 × 10 and use them to derive quickly the corresponding division facts; double and halve any two-digit number; understand how the commutative, associative and distributive laws can be used to do mental multiplication calculations more efficiently; multiply and divide (mentally), at first in the range 1 to 100, then for particular cases of larger numbers by using factors, distribution or other methods; choose and use an appropriate way to calculate and explain their reasoning.

In this chapter there are explanations of

- product, quotient, dividend and divisor;
- the commutative, associative, distributive laws of multiplication;
- the distributive laws of division;
- how these laws are used in multiplication and division calculation strategies;
- some prerequisite skills for being efficient in mental multiplication and division calculations;
- how factors can be used to simplify multiplications;
- how doubling can be used as an *ad hoc* approach to multiplication;
- the use of *ad hoc* additions and subtractions in multiplication and division; and
- the constant ratio method for a division calculation.

What are products, quotients, dividends and divisors?

These are four technical words that are used in the context of multiplication and division calculations. The result of multiplying together some numbers is called their *product*. For example, the product of 7 and 8 is 56.

The terms used to identify the numbers in a division calculation are perhaps less familiar, but it is nevertheless useful to have them available when explaining division strategies. The result of dividing one number by another is called the *quotient*. For example, if 56 is divided by 8 (56 ÷ 8 = 7) the quotient is 7. The first number in the division, that which is to be divided (in this example, 56), is called the *dividend*. The number by which it is divided (in this example, 8) is called the *divisor*.

How are the commutative, associative and distributive laws useful in multiplication calculations?

These fundamental laws of arithmetic, written formally as algebraic generalizations, look like this:

Commutative law of multiplication: $a \times b = b \times a$

Associative law of multiplication: $(a \times b) \times c = a \times (b \times c)$

Distributive laws of multiplication: $a \times (b + c) = (a \times b) + (a \times c)$
$a \times (b - c) = (a \times b) - (a \times c).$

These statements are true whatever numbers are chosen for *a*, *b* and *c*. (The reader should compare the commutative and associative laws for addition discussed in Chapters 4 and 5, and see also the discussion of the commutative law of multiplication in Chapter 7.)

Written down baldly, as they are above, the three fundamental laws of multiplication look a bit daunting and obscure. But, rather like Monsieur Jourdain in *Le Bourgeois Gentilhomme*, who discovered to his delight that he had been speaking prose for more than 40 years without knowing it, readers can be assured that they probably use one or another of these laws unconsciously every time they undertake a multiplication calculation!

For example, take the calculation of 5 × 28. First, I would prefer to think of this as 28 fives, rather than five 28s, simply because I am better at my 5-times table than I am at my 28-times table. It is the commutative law that allows me to switch the order of two numbers in a multiplication freely like this:

$$5 \times 28 = 28 \times 5.$$

Now to work out 28 × 5, I could think of the 28 as 14 × 2, choose to do 2 × 5 first (to get 10) and then multiply this by 14 (14 × 10 = 140).

What I am using here is the associative law. I am 'associating' the 2 with the 5, rather than with the 14, in order to make the calculation easier:

$$(14 \times 2) \times 5 = 14 \times (2 \times 5).$$

An alternative approach to calculating 28×5 would be to split the 28 into 20 + 8 and then to multiply the 20 and 8 separately by the 5, to get 100 and 40, which add up to 140. This is using the distributive law! The multiplication by 5 is being 'distributed' across the addition of 20 and 8. Written down formally the first step of this strategy might look like this:

$$5 \times (20 + 8) = (5 \times 20) + (5 \times 8).$$

Finally, we could choose to think of the 28 as 30 – 2 and then 'distribute' the multiplication by 5 across this subtraction: 5×30 is 150, 5×2 is 10, so the answer is 150 – 10, which is 140. This is using the second of the distributive laws of multiplication:

$$5 \times (30 - 2) = (5 \times 30) - (5 \times 2).$$

The commutative and associative laws together give us the freedom to rearrange two or more numbers in a product. For example,

$$
\begin{aligned}
(5 \times 3) \times 8 \quad &= \quad 5 \times (3 \times 8) \quad \text{(using the associative law)} \\
&= \quad 5 \times (8 \times 3) \quad \text{(using the commutative law)} \\
&= \quad (5 \times 8) \times 3 \quad \text{(using the associative law)} \\
&= \quad 40 \times 3 = 120.
\end{aligned}
$$

This means that we can just write down $5 \times 3 \times 8$ without any brackets, recognizing that we can multiply the numbers together in any order we like.

The distributive laws give us the option to deal with a complicated multiplication in easy stages, breaking up the numbers into easier components. We shall see below that these three laws are really all we need to become very efficient at multiplication with informal mental strategies.

What about laws of division?

We have already noted in Chapter 7 that division (like subtraction) is not commutative. We should note here that division is also not associative (again like subtraction). For example, $(24 \div 6) \div 2$ is not equal to 24

$\div (6 \div 2)$. Dealing with the divisions in the brackets first, in the first of these we get the answer 2, whereas in the second we get the answer 8.

But, division can be distributed across addition and subtraction. There are the following two distributive laws for division that are true whatever numbers are chosen for a, b and c (provided you do not choose $c = 0$, since division by zero is not possible).

Distributive laws of division: $(a + b) \div c = (a \div c) + (b \div c)$
$$(a - b) \div c = (a \div c) - (b \div c).$$

Informally the first of these means that if the dividend can be thought of as the sum of two numbers $(a + b)$, then you can divide each of a and b separately by the divisor (c) and add up the results. And the second means that if the dividend can be thought of as the difference between two numbers $(a - b)$ then you can divide each of a and b separately by the divisor (c) and find the difference between the results.

Again, the reader should recognize these as the basis of some very familiar procedures in the way we handle division calculations. We often employ this principle to simplify division questions. For example, since $45 = 30 + 15$, you can think of $45 \div 3$ as $(30 + 15) \div 3$, which, using the distributive law, can be split up into $30 \div 3$ and $15 \div 3$. The trick is to transform the 45 into $30 + 15$, being guided by your awareness that with a divisor of 3, numbers like 30 and 15 are highly desirable.

In using the distributive law in an *ad hoc* approach we should always look for numbers that are easy to handle with the particular divisor. So, tackling $143 \div 11$, I might make use of the fact that 99 is a good number to have around when dividing by 11, and think of 143 as $99 + 44$ as follows:

Think of $143 \div 11$ as $(99 + 44) \div 11$
$(99 + 44) \div 11 = (99 \div 11) + (44 \div 11)$ (note the distributive law
$\qquad\qquad\quad = 9 + 4 = 13.$ being used here)

Of course, there's no need to set out the working as formally as I have done here. It will probably be done mentally with a few numbers written down to keep track of where you are.

Here's an example where we might use the same trick but with subtraction, for calculating $162 \div 9$. The trick here is to spot that 162 is not too far from 180, which is an easy number to divide by 9:

Think of $162 \div 9$ as $(180 - 18) \div 9$
$(180 - 18) \div 9 = (180 \div 9) - (18 \div 9)$ (note the distributive law
$\qquad\qquad\quad = 20 - 2 = 18.$ being used here)

Again, there is no need to set out the working in full like this, unless, like me, you are trying to explain your strategy to someone else.

What are the prerequisite skills for being efficient at mental strategies for multiplication and division?

The first prerequisite is that you know thoroughly and can recall instantly all the results in the multiplication tables up to 10 × 10. If you are still struggling with this basic knowledge then develop some strategies for working out what you do not know from what you do know. For example, if you are not sure of the product of 6 and 8, start with 6 × 2 = 12, double it to get 6 × 4 = 24 and double it again to get 6 × 8 = 48. Then if you cannot remember the product of 7 and 8, but you now know 6 × 8 = 48, then you can get 7 × 8 = 56 by adding on another 8. Or you could use 5 × 8 = 40 and 2 × 8 = 16 to deduce that 7 × 8 = 40 + 16.

Second, you should be able to derive from any one of these results a whole series of results for multiplications involving multiples of 10 and 100. For example, knowing 7 × 8 = 56, we should be able to deduce the following:

70	×	8	=	560
7	×	80	=	560
70	×	80	=	5600
7	×	800	=	5600
700	×	8	=	5600
70	×	800	=	56 000
700	×	80	=	56 000.

It helps enormously just to notice that the total number of zeros written in the numbers on the left-hand side of each of these results is the same as the extra number of zeros written after the 56 on the right-hand side. To help understand this, using the example 700 × 80, we can think of the 700 as 7 × 100 and the 80 as 8 × 10. Then the whole calculation becomes: 7 × 100 × 8 × 10. Using the freedom granted to us by the commutative and associative laws of multiplication to rearrange this how we like, we can think of it as (7 × 8) × (100 × 10), which leads to 56 × 1000 = 56 000.

Third, you should be able to recognize all the division results that are simply the inverses of any of the above results. For example,

$$56 \div \quad 8 = 7$$
$$56 \div \quad 7 = 8$$
$$560 \div \quad 8 = 70$$
$$5600 \div \quad 70 = 80$$
$$56\,000 \div 800 = 70.$$

Once you have these skills in place you will be able to use a wide range of strategies, such as: the use of factors and doubling as *ad hoc* approaches to multiplications; *ad hoc* additions and subtractions in multiplication and division; and the constant ratio method for division.

How can factors be used as an *ad hoc* approach to multiplication?

When we think of a number such as 6 as 3×2 we are splitting it up into what are called *factors*. (Factors are discussed in more detail in Chapter 11.) As we have already seen above, we can use the associative law to enable us to multiply by each factor in turn, in order to simplify a product.

For example, one way to tackle 37×6 would be to think of the 6 as 3×2:

$$
\begin{aligned}
37 \times 6 \quad &= 37 \times (3 \times 2) \\
&= (37 \times 3) \times 2 \quad \text{(using the associative law)} \\
&= 111 \times 2 = 222.
\end{aligned}
$$

This strategy is particularly effective when there are numbers ending in 5 around, since they are especially easy to multiply by 2 or 4. For example, to calculate 26×15 and 25×32, we should jump at the opportunities to make use of the facts that $2 \times 15 = 30$ and $25 \times 4 = 100$. To achieve this, we split the 26 into factors as 13×2 and the 32 into factors as 4×8:

$$
\begin{aligned}
26 \times 15 \quad &= (13 \times 2) \times 15 \\
&= 13 \times (2 \times 15) \quad \text{(using the associative law)} \\
&= 13 \times 30 = 390
\end{aligned}
$$

$$
\begin{aligned}
25 \times 32 \quad &= 25 \times (4 \times 8) \\
&= (25 \times 4) \times 8 \quad \text{(using the associative law)} \\
&= 100 \times 8 = 800.
\end{aligned}
$$

Again, it should be stressed that I am writing these out in detail only to explain the mathematical basis of what will be essentially a mental process. Figure 8.1 shows some examples of an 11-year-old using factors to assist with some multiplications, writing down her method in a way that shows her thinking to someone else.

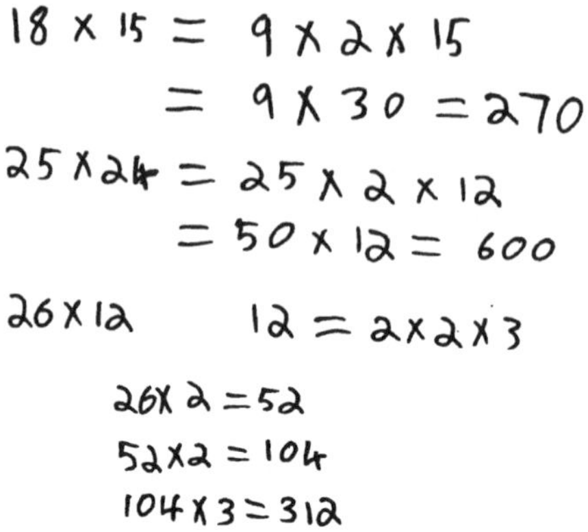

$$18 \times 15 = 9 \times 2 \times 15$$
$$= 9 \times 30 = 270$$
$$25 \times 24 = 25 \times 2 \times 12$$
$$= 50 \times 12 = 600$$
$$26 \times 12 \qquad 12 = 2 \times 2 \times 3$$
$$26 \times 2 = 52$$
$$52 \times 2 = 104$$
$$104 \times 3 = 312$$

Figure 8.1   An 11-year-old using factors in multiplication

How can doubling be used as an *ad hoc* approach to multiplication?

We have previously noted (in Chapter 5) that we can make use of our confidence in doubling numbers in informal approaches to additions and subtractions. We can also deal with *any* multiplication with whole numbers simply by a process of doubling! Approaches to multiplication based on doubling have in fact been around much longer than what people regard as the 'traditional' method for long multiplication. The trick here is to note that any number can be obtained by adding together some of the following numbers (called the powers of 2): 1, 2, 4, 8, 16, 32, 64 . . . and so on. For example, 23 = 16 + 4 + 2 + 1. This means that we can multiply a number by 23 (using the distributive law) in bits, multiplying by 16, 4, 2 and 1, and adding up the results. For example, to calculate 26 × 23 the working might look like this:

First, by repeatedly doubling the 26:
26 ×   1 =   26
26 ×   2 =   52
26 ×   4 = 104
26 ×   8 = 208
26 × 16 = 416.

So, 26 × 23 = (26 × 16) + (26 × 4) + (26 × 2) + (26 × 1)
        = 416 + 104 + 52 + 26 = 598.

Again, I have provided more detail than would be necessary for an informal calculation, as illustrated in Figure 8.2 in which an 11-year-old uses this method in a shopping context.

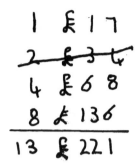

Figure 8.2   Using doubling to find the cost of 13 items at £17 each

How do you use *ad hoc* additions and subtractions in multiplications and divisions?

As with all calculations we can always make use of those number facts and relationships with which we are confident to find our own individual approaches that make sense to us. Again there is great value in encouraging pupils, even in primary schools, to build on their growing confidence with number in order to develop their own approaches and to share different approaches to the same calculation. The distributive law gives us the freedom to break up a number in a multiplication or the divisor in a division calculation in any way we like, using an *ad hoc* combination of additions and subtractions of whatever numbers are easiest to handle.

For instance, here are two *ad hoc* ways of evaluating 26×34. First, by breaking up the 26 into $10 + 10 + 2 + 2 + 2$, on the basis that I am confident in multiplying by 10 and by 2, we can transform 26×34 into $(10 \times 34) + (10 \times 34) + (2 \times 34) + (2 \times 34) + (2 \times 34)$, as follows:

$$
\begin{aligned}
10 \times 34 &= 340 \\
10 \times 34 &= 340 \\
2 \times 34 &= 68 \\
2 \times 34 &= 68 \\
2 \times 34 &= 68 \\
\hline
26 \times 34 &= 884.
\end{aligned}
$$

then adding up the numbers on the right

Visually, this method is represented by the diagram in Figure 8.3. The trick in this kind of approach is to make sure you only ever multiply by easy numbers, like 1, 2, 5 and 10.

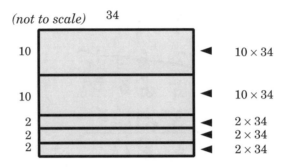

Figure 8.3   An ad hoc *approach to 26 × 34*

A second *ad hoc* approach to this calculation would be to think of the 34 as 10 + 10 + 10 + 5 −1, so that 26 × 34 becomes (26 × 10) + (26 × 10) + (26 × 10) + (26 × 5) − (26 × 1), as follows:

$$26 \times 10 = 260$$
$$26 \times 10 = 260$$
$$26 \times 10 = 260$$
$$\underline{26 \times 5 = 130}$$

adding the numbers on the right 26 × 35 = 910
and finally subtracting one 26 $\underline{26 \times 1 = 26}$
26 × 34 = 884.

In the same way, you can sometimes make a division much simpler by writing it as the sum or difference of numbers that are easier to divide by the given divisor. For example, if you have your wits about you, given 608 ÷ 32 you might spot that it would have been much nicer if the question had been 640 ÷ 32 (answer 20). So, we could deal with this division as follows:

$$608 \div 32 \quad = (640 - 32) \div 32$$
$$= (640 \div 32) - (32 \div 32)$$
$$= 20 - 1 = 19$$

In practice, the context of the problem that gave rise to the calculation will often suggest an appropriate *ad hoc* approach. For example, in Figure 8.4 a pupil is calculating how many classes of 32 pupils would be needed for a school of 608. The pupil's approach is to build up to the given total of 608, by an *ad hoc* process of addition, using first 10 classes, then another 5, then a further 2 and another 2. Formally, the pupil is breaking the 608 up into 320 + 160 + 64 + 64 and distributing the division by 32 across this addition as follows:

$$608 \div 32 \quad = (320 + 160 + 64 + 64) \div 32$$
$$= (320 \div 32) + (160 \div 32) + (64 \div 32) + (64 \div 32)$$
$$= 10 + 5 + 2 + 2 = 19.$$

The pupil's own way of writing down the thinking involved is clear and is, of course, perfectly acceptable. Many pupils are very successful in dealing with division calculations by this kind of *ad hoc* addition, building up to the given target. In the next chapter I will explain how an approach based on *ad hoc* repeated subtraction can be used to develop an efficient written method for division calculations.

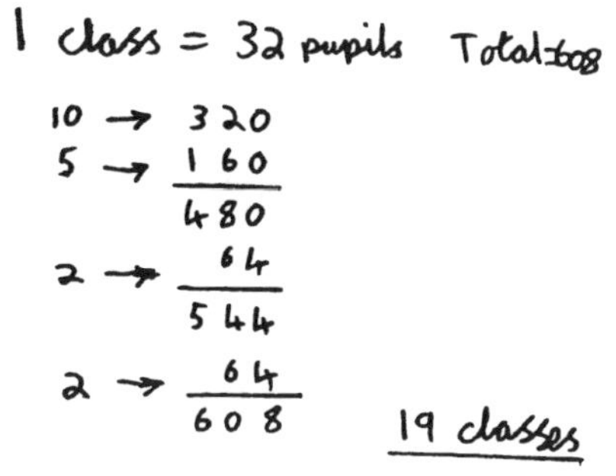

Figure 8.4 Ad hoc *repeated addition used to solve a division problem*

What is the constant ratio method for division?

We have here a parallel with the constant difference method for subtraction explained in Chapter 6. We make use of this important principle: that we do not change the answer to a division calculation if we multiply both the numbers by the same thing. To understand this it might help to think of the division in terms of the ratio structure: if both quantities are scaled by the same factor, then their ratio does not change – just as when you add the same thing to two numbers their difference does not change. For instance, all these divisions give the same result as 6 ÷ 2, because in each case the two numbers 6 and 2 have been multiplied by the same scale factor:

$60 \div 20$ (multiply both numbers by 10)
$12 \div 4$ (multiply both numbers by 2)
$30 \div 10$ (multiply both numbers by 5)
$6000 \div 2000$ (multiply both numbers by 1000).

The division $75 \div 5$ can be used to illustrate the application of this principle. Multiply both numbers by 2 and the question becomes: $150 \div 10$. So the answer is clearly 15. This approach is particularly useful when it comes to divisions involving decimals, as we shall see in Chapter 15. For example, to handle $6 \div 1.5$, which looks tricky, we could multiply both numbers by 2, to give $12 \div 3$, which is easy!

You can also use the reverse principle: that we do not change the answer to a division calculation if we *divide* both the numbers by the same thing. I might use this principle if I was dealing with, for example, $648 \div 24$, as follows:

$648 \div 24$ is the same as $324 \div 12$ (dividing both numbers by 2)
$324 \div 12$ is the same as $108 \div 4$ (dividing both numbers by 3)
$108 \div 4$ is the same as $54 \div 2$ (dividing both numbers by 2), which is 27.

These two principles can be combined, as in the following example, where I might spot that multiplying both numbers by 2 would turn $225 \div 15$ into an easier question:

$225 \div 15 = 450 \div 30$ (multiplying both numbers by 2)
$450 \div 30 = 45 \div 3$ (dividing both numbers by 10)
$45 \div 3 = 15$.

Although this constant ratio method is mathematically sound the reader should be warned that it could lead you astray if you are dealing with a division that does not work out exactly and you wish to give the answer with a remainder. For example, if the question was $48 \div 5$ and you doubled both numbers you would produce the equivalent ratio $96 \div 10$. The exact value of this quotient (9.6) is indeed the correct answer to $48 \div 5$. However, $96 \div 10$ expressed as '9 remainder 6' is not the correct result for $48 \div 5$, because the remainder has been doubled as well.

Self-assessment questions

8.1: What is the product of 1, 2, 3, 4 and 5?
8.2: A carton holds 6 bottles of squash. I have 288 bottles to put in cartons: How many cartons will I need? In the division calculation arising from this

problem, which number is the dividend, which the divisor and which the quotient?

8.3: How would the commutative law help in calculating the number of pupils in 25 groups of 16?

8.4: Jo calculated 25 × 24 by writing it as 25 × (4 × 6) and then using the associative law. Complete Jo's calculation.

8.5: Sam calculated 25 × 24 by writing it as 25 × (20 + 4) and then using the distributive law. Complete Sam's calculation.

8.6: Bev calculated 22 × 38 by writing it as 22 × (40 − 2) and then using the distributive law. Complete Bev's calculation.

8.7: Deduce eight other multiplication results, involving 4, 40, 400, 9, 90 and 900, from the result 4 × 9 = 36.

8.8: Use an *ad hoc* method, based on factors, to find 48 × 25.

8.9: Use the fact that 26 = 2 + 8 + 16 and the doubling strategy to find 103 × 26.

8.10: Use the fact that 26 = 10 + 10 + 2 + 2 + 2 to find 103 × 26.

8.11: Use the distributive law and the fact that 154 = 88 + 66 to find the answer to 154 ÷ 22; now do this again using the fact that 154 = 220 − 66.

8.12: Find 483 ÷ 21 by *ad hoc* addition of groups of 21, building up to the total of 483.

8.13: Find 385 ÷ 55 by using the constant ratio method.

Summary of teaching points

1. Make sure pupils are thoroughly confident with their multiplication tables up to 10 × 10 before they embark on multiplying bigger numbers.

2. Teach pupils some strategies for working out multiplication results they do not know from those they do know.

3. Teach pupils how to multiply simple multiples of 10, such as 20 × 3, 2 × 30 and 20 × 30, before going on to multiplication with two-digit numbers.

4. Teach pupils how to multiply simple multiples of 10 and 100, such as 2 × 300 and 20 × 300, before going on to multiplication with three-digit numbers.

5. Give pupils plenty of practice in changing the multiplication results above into division statements.

6. Value and encourage informal, *ad hoc* methods of tackling multiplications and divisions that build on the pupils' personal confidence with number and number relationships.

7. Explore with pupils the way in which factors can sometimes be used to simplify a multiplication.

8. Encourage pupils to build on their confidence with doubling to develop an informal strategy for multiplication.

9. Show pupils how, by breaking down one of the numbers in the multiplication into smaller numbers, you can always get away with multiplying only by easy numbers such as 1, 2, 5 and 10.

10. Discuss with pupils how division can be done by *ad hoc* addition of multiples of the divisor building up to the total dividend.

11. Provide pupils with plenty of practice in mental multiplication by 1, 2, 5, 10, 20 and 50: this is all that is required by way of multiplication to be efficient in doing multiplications and divisions using *ad hoc* repeated addition and subtraction.

12. Make explicit the principle that you do not change the ratio if you multiply or divide two numbers by the same thing, and use this principle in various examples.

9

Written Methods for Multiplication and Division

Pupils should be taught to: use written methods for short multiplication and division by a single-digit number of a two-digit number, then three-digit and four-digit numbers; understand how the commutative, associative and distributive laws can be used to do written calculations more efficiently; use long multiplication at first for two-digit by two-digit calculations, then for three-digit by two-digit; extend division to informal methods of dividing by a two-digit divisor.

In this chapter there are explanations of

- the long multiplication algorithm;
- a simpler method for multiplication using areas of rectangles;
- the *ad hoc* repeated subtraction method of doing division calculations; and
- the algorithm known as short division.

I can't remember how to do long multiplication. I don't think I ever understood it anyway

The standard algorithm for multiplying together two numbers with two or more digits is usually called *long multiplication*. Figure 9.1 shows how the method might be set out for calculating 26 × 34.

The method is based on the distributive law for division distributed over addition, explained in the previous chapter. Effectively what happens is that one of the numbers is broken up into the sum of its tens and units, and the multiplication by the other number is distributed across these. Applying this principle to 26 × 34, we can think of it as 26 × (30 + 4) and get the answer by multiplying the 26 first by the 30 and then by the 4, and then adding up the results. This is precisely what goes on in long multiplication, as shown in Figure 9.1. But the problem with the

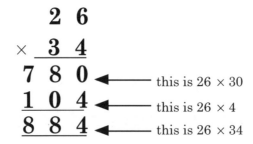

Figure 9.1   *Long multiplication, 26 × 34*

method is that multiplications like 26 × 30 and 26 × 4 are themselves quite difficult calculations and there is consequently some potential for errors and confusion.

So is there a simpler method for multiplication of two-digit numbers which is easier to understand?

Yes, there is a simpler method. It is based on the idea of splitting up *both* the numbers being multiplied into their tens and units. So the 26 becomes 20 + 6 and the 34 becomes 30 + 4. Then we have to multiply the 20 by the 30, the 20 by the 4, the 6 by the 30 and the 6 by the 4. To make sense of this we can visualize the multiplication as a question of finding the number of counters in a rectangular array of 26 by 34 (see Chapter 7), as shown in Figure 9.2. Thinking of the 26 and the 34 as 20 + 6 and 30 + 4 respectively suggests that we can split the array up into four separate arrays, representing 20 × 30, 20 × 4, 6 × 30 and 6 × 4.

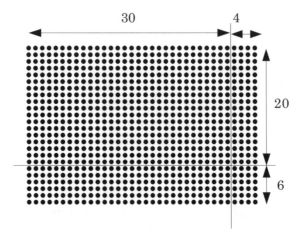

Figure 9.2   *A simpler approach for 26 × 34*

Drawing pictures with hundreds of counters in them, like Figure 9.2, helps to explain the method, but it's very tedious. A more efficient picture, therefore, uses the idea, suggested in Chapter 7, that we can extend the notion of a rectangular array into that of the area of a rectangle. We can then explain 26 × 34 very simply using the diagram shown in Figure 9.3. The answer to the multiplication is then obtained by working out the areas of the four separate rectangles and adding them up. The actual calculation can be written out as follows:

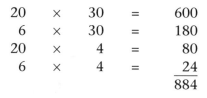

$$
\begin{array}{rcrcr}
20 & \times & 30 & = & 600 \\
6 & \times & 30 & = & 180 \\
20 & \times & 4 & = & 80 \\
6 & \times & 4 & = & \underline{24} \\
& & & & 884
\end{array}
$$

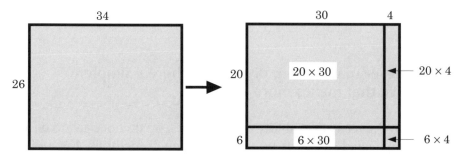

Figure 9.3   Using area to interpret 26 × 34

Can this method be used with three-digit numbers?

The method extends quite easily to multiplications involving three-digit numbers. Figure 9.4 shows a rough sketch that might be used to visualize 348 × 25. (The rectangles in the diagram are not intended to be drawn to scale.) Clearly, in this example, there are now six bits to deal with separately, and then to be added. This leads to the calculation being set out, for example, as follows:

$$
\begin{array}{rcrcr}
300 & \times & 20 & = & 6000 \\
40 & \times & 20 & = & 800 \\
8 & \times & 20 & = & 160 \\
300 & \times & 5 & = & 1500 \\
40 & \times & 5 & = & 200 \\
8 & \times & 5 & = & \underline{40} \\
& & & & 8700
\end{array}
$$

So we conclude that 348 × 25 = 8700. Multiplications of this level of difficulty are about as far as most primary-school children would need to go. It should be noted again, as explained in the previous chapter, that essential prerequisite skills for multiplication with two- and three-digit numbers include confidence in multiplication of multiples of 10 and 100.

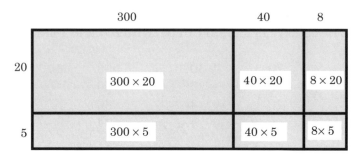

Figure 9.4   The area approach applied to 348 × 25

I could never master long division. Is there a simpler alternative that makes more sense?

Since, with the ready availability of calculators, we do not need to be able to do complicated divisions by paper-and-pencil methods, I would en-courage the use of a more *ad hoc* method described below, which builds on the mental and informal approaches to division discussed in Chapter 8. It works very well with problems up to the level of difficulty with which most people should be able to cope, dividing a three-digit number by a two-digit number. The approach builds on the individual's personal con-fidence with multiplication and the process is easily understood. This contrasts with the conventional algorithm, known as long division, which can involve some tricky multiplications and is, to say the least, not easy to make sense of. I do not intend therefore to explain 'long division'. In my view, it is a method that could well be laid to rest in the twenty-first century. To be honest, this is mainly because I have been singularly un-successful whenever I have attempted to teach the method!

So, take as an example the division, 648 ÷ 24. The method uses the inverse-of-multiplication structure and the idea of repeated subtraction, explained in Chapter 7. Hence the question is interpreted as: How many 24s make 648? (Not: Share 648 between 24.) We approach this step by step, using whatever multiplications we are confident with, repeatedly subtracting from the dividend various multiples of the divisor, in an *ad hoc* manner.

For example, we should know easily that ten 24s make 240. We subtract this 240 from the 648. That leaves us with 408 to find. At this stage our working might be as shown in Figure 9.5(a). Try another ten 24s. That's a further 240, leaving us with 168, as shown in Figure 9.5(b). We do not have enough for a further ten 24s, so we might try two 24s (or one 24, if we prefer it, or whatever we are confident to do mentally). This gives us the situation shown in Figure 9.5(c). And so we proceed, until we've used up all the 648, as shown in Figure 9.5(d). Totting up the numbers of 24s we've used down the left-hand side gives us the answer to the calculation: $10 + 10 + 2 + 2 + 2 + 1 = 27$. Someone with greater confidence with multiplication might get to the result more quickly, as shown in Figure 9.6. Here I have gone straight in with twenty 24s ($20 \times 24 = 480$), followed this up with five 24s ($5 \times 24 = 120$) and finished off with two 24s ($2 \times 24 = 48$).

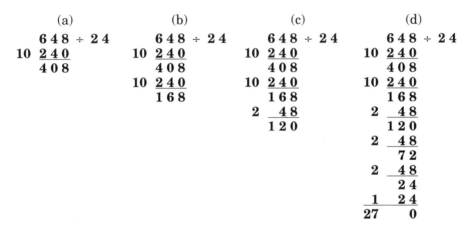

Figure 9.5   Ad hoc *repeated subtraction approach to 648 ÷ 24*

$$
\begin{array}{r r}
 & 6\,4\,8 \div 2\,4 \\
20 & \underline{4\,8\,0} \\
 & 1\,6\,8 \\
5 & \underline{1\,2\,0} \\
 & 4\,8 \\
2 & \underline{4\,8} \\
\hline
27 & 0 \\
\end{array}
$$

Figure 9.6   *648 ÷ 24 with fewer steps*

We should note that you would not get far with this method for division by a two-digit number if you were not fluent in subtraction. And it also helps to be really at ease with multiplying by at least 1, 2, 5, 10, 20 and 50. The reader should compare this method with the reverse process of *ad hoc* addition of multiples of the divisor building up to the given dividend, explained in the previous chapter.

Does this method work when there's a remainder?

Yes. Take as an example 437 ÷ 18 (Figure 9.7). This time I have started with twenty 18s, because I can do that in my head easily (20 × 18 = 360), then followed it up with two 18s and a further two 18s. At this stage I'm left with 5. Since this is less than the divisor, 18, I can go no further. The answer to the question is therefore '24 remainder 5'. The meaning of this answer will, of course, depend on the actual practical situation that gave rise to the calculation. Remainders in various division situations are discussed in Chapter 10.

$$
\begin{array}{r}
437 \div 18 \\
20 \quad 360 \\
77 \\
2 \quad 36 \\
41 \\
2 \quad 36 \\
24 \text{ rem } 5
\end{array}
$$

Figure 9.7   An example with a remainder, 437 ÷ 18

Since this approach to division is likely to be unfamiliar to many readers I have provided some further examples of the method in use in Figure 9.8.

$$
\begin{array}{r}
475 \div 25 \\
10 \quad 250 \\
225 \\
1 \quad 25 \\
200 \\
4 \quad 100 \\
100 \\
4 \quad 100 \\
19 \quad 0
\end{array}
\qquad
\begin{array}{r}
669 \div 12 \\
50 \quad 600 \\
69 \\
5 \quad 60 \\
55 \text{ rem } 9
\end{array}
\qquad
\begin{array}{r}
806 \div 31 \\
20 \quad 620 \\
186 \\
2 \quad 62 \\
124 \\
2 \quad 62 \\
62 \\
2 \quad 62 \\
26 \quad 0
\end{array}
$$

Figure 9.8   Further examples of the ad hoc *repeated subtraction method of division*

What about short division? How does that work?

Short division is the standard algorithm often used for dividing by a single-digit number. It can be demonstrated clearly using the equal-sharing structure for division and either coins (1p, 10p and £1) or base-ten blocks to represent the numbers. For example, Figure 9.9 shows the division, 75 ÷ 5, interpreted with 10p and 1p coins. The 7 tens and 5 ones in the dividend are to be shared equally between five recipients.

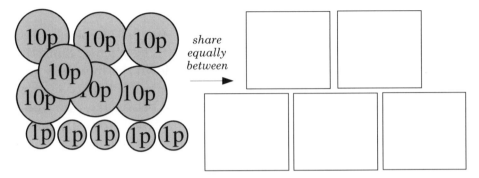

Figure 9.9   Interpreting 75 ÷ 5

In Figure 9.10, 1 ten has been given to each of the five recipients and the remaining 2 tens have been exchanged for 20 ones. There is therefore a total of 25 ones still to be shared out. When this is done each recipient gets 1 ten and 5 ones. Hence the answer is clearly 15.

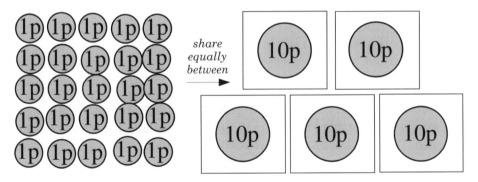

Figure 9.10   Dealing with the tens for 75 ÷ 5

One of the standard ways of recording this process is shown in Figure 9.11. The little 2 represents the 2 tens that have been exchanged for 20 ones; written in front of the 5, it indicates that at that stage there are 25 ones to be shared out. The 15 written above the line represents the 1 ten and 5 ones that each of the recipients gets when 75 is shared between five.

The problem with this explanation is that, in practice, when using the short division algorithm, particularly with bigger numbers, you probably do not use the equal-sharing structure consistently, but switch between this and the inverse-of-multiplication structure. So, for

$$\begin{array}{r} 1\ 5\ \\ \hline 5\,\big|\,7\,{}^{2}5 \end{array}$$

Figure 9.11   Short division, 75 ÷ 5

example, in Figure 9.12(a), tackling 438 ÷ 6, the first question I find myself asking might be: Can I share 4 (hundreds) between 6? Since the answer is 'no' (at least, not without breaking down the hundreds into tens), I exchange these 4 hundreds for 40 tens, giving a total of 43 tens, and so I am now looking at '43 tens to be shared between 6'. I now find myself saying: How many 6s in 43? I have switched from sharing to inverse-of-multiplication. The answer is 7 with 1 (ten) remaining, which is exchanged for 10 ones, giving a total of 18 ones still to be shared out between the 6. Again, I will probably switch to inverse-of-multiplication and think: How many 6s in 18? The calculation is completed as shown in Figure 9.12(b). But the explanation gets unwieldy and very wordy.

$$\begin{array}{r} \\ \hline 6\,\big|\,4\ 3\ 8 \end{array} \qquad \begin{array}{r} 7\ 3\ \\ \hline 6\,\big|\,4\ 3\,{}^{1}8 \end{array}$$

(a)   (b)

Figure 9.12   Short division, 438 ÷ 6

On balance, I prefer therefore when teaching division by single-digit numbers to introduce the *ad hoc* repeated subtraction approach I have outlined above, rather than plump for the standard short division algorithm. Figure 9.13 shows this repeated subtraction method applied to the two examples just considered, namely, 75 ÷ 5 and 438 ÷ 6. Clearly, the method gets easier the more fluent we are with mental multiplication. It therefore encourages us to handle calculations like 50 × 6 and 20 × 6 mentally.

Figure 9.13   The ad hoc *repeated subtraction alternative to short division*

Self-assessment questions

9.1: Use the method of Figure 9.3 to find 42 × 37.

9.2: Use the method of Figure 9.4 to find 345 × 17.

9.3: Write down the values of: 7 × 3, 7 × 5, 7 × 10. Now find 126 ÷ 7, using the method of *ad hoc* repeated subtraction.

9.4: Write down the values of: 23 × 2, 23 × 5, 23 × 10, 23 × 20. Now find 851 ÷ 23, using the method of *ad hoc* repeated subtraction.

9.5: Write down the values of: 8 × 5, 8 × 10, 8 × 50. Now find 529 ÷ 8, using the method of *ad hoc* repeated subtraction.

Summary of teaching points

1. When primary-school pupils are to be taught a method for multiplying together two two-digit numbers, encourage the method based on the areas of four rectangles, splitting each of the two numbers into tens and units (as shown in Figure 9.3).

2. Some pupils in primary schools may be able to go on to extend this approach to multiply together a three-digit number and a two-digit number (as shown in Figure 9.4), using six areas.

3. Note again the importance of pupils being thoroughly confident in multiplication with multiples of 10 and 100 as a prerequisite for going on to multiply two- and three-digit numbers.

4. Teach pupils the *ad hoc* repeated subtraction method for dividing first by single-digit numbers and then by two-digit numbers.

5. You might wish to teach short division as a method for dividing by a single-digit number, explaining it with coins or base-ten blocks.

6. The conventional long division algorithm, as a method for dividing by a two-digit number, is not recommended by this author.

7. Provide pupils with plenty of practice in mental multiplication by 1, 2, 5, 10, 20 and 50: this is all that is required by way of multiplication to be efficient in doing divisions by the *ad hoc* repeated subtraction method.

8. Another prerequisite for success with this approach is fluency in subtraction.

10

Remainders and Rounding

Pupils should be taught to: find remainders after division; round a whole number to the nearest 10 or 100 and then 1000; round a number with one or two decimal places to the nearest whole number or tenth; round up or down after division, depending on the context.

In this chapter there are explanations of

- the different interpretations required for the results of division calculations done on a calculator and those done by methods which produce a remainder;
- the relationship between the answer with a remainder and the calculator answer;
- the way in which the context determines whether to round a result up or down;
- the idea of rounding to the nearest something; and
- how to give answers to so many decimal places or significant figures.

I get confused between the figures after the decimal point in a calculator answer to a division calculation and the remainder

Consider the problem of seating 250 pupils in coaches that hold 60 pupils each. Using the process of mathematical modelling (see Chapter 3), we would model this problem with the division, $250 \div 60$. It is interesting to contrast the kind of reasoning involved in interpreting the answer to this division calculation when we do it with or without a calculator. If we divide 250 by 60, using whatever mental or written procedure we are confident with, we might get to the result '4 remainder 10'. To interpret this result we should note that the 'remainder 10' does not stand for 10 coaches; it represents the 10 pupils who would be left out if you ordered only 4 coaches. When we do the calculation on a calculator, however, and get the result '4.1666666', the '.1666666' represents a bit of a coach, not a bit of a pupil. So, in this example, the figures after the decimal point represent a bit of a coach, whereas the remainder represents a number of pupils. They are certainly not the same thing. This is a very significant observation, requiring careful explanation to pupils, through discussion of a variety of examples. The way we interpret back in the real world the mathematical solution to a calculation involving a division actually depends on: a) whether the manipulation of the symbols has led to an answer with a remainder or an answer with figures after the decimal point; and b) whether the problem giving rise to the division is an *equal-sharing* structure or an *inverse-of-multiplication* structure (see Chapter 7).

How does the interpretation of the results differ for the different division structures?

Consider the division, 150 ÷ 18. If I do this by mental or written methods I may get to the result '8 remainder 6'. But if I do it on a calculator I get '8.3333333'.

First, we will analyse how these results are interpreted if the problem giving rise to the calculation is an *equal-sharing* structure, of the form '150 things shared between 18'. For example, if I share 150 pencils equally between 18 people, how many do they each get? In interpreting the answer '8 remainder 6', the remainder represents the 6 pencils left over after you have done the sharing, giving 8 pencils to each person. But the figures after the decimal point in the calculator answer (the .3333333 part of 8.3333333) represent the portion of a pencil that each person would get if you were able to share out the remainder equally. This would, of course, involve cutting up the pencils into bits. So both the remainder and the figures after the decimal point in this example refer to pencils, although the first refers to pencils left over and the second to portions of pencils received if the left-overs are shared out.

Whether or not you can actually share out the remainder in practice will, of course, depend on what you are dealing with. For example, people and pencils are not usually cut up into smaller bits, so the answer with the remainder is actually more useful. But lengths, areas, weights and volumes can be further subdivided into smaller units, so the calculator answer might make more sense in examples in measurement contexts.

Now consider the interpretation of the two results if the problem giving rise to 150 ÷ 18 is an *inverse-of-multiplication* structure, which would be a question of the form: 'How many sets of 18 can you get from 150 things?' For example, how many boxes that hold 18 pencils each do you need to store 150 pencils? Now we notice that the remainder 6 represents the surplus of pencils after you have filled up 8 boxes of 18. The figures after the decimal point in the calculator answer (the .3333333 part of 8.3333333) then represent what fraction this surplus is of a full set of 18. In our example, the .3333333 means the fraction of a box that would be taken up by the 6 remaining pencils. So the *remainder* in this division problem represents surplus pencils, but the *figures after the decimal point* represent 'a bit of a box'. In simple language, we might say either 'we need eight boxes and there will be six pencils left over', referring to the answer with the remainder, or 'we need eight boxes and a bit of a box', referring to the answer with figures after the decimal point.

How can you get from the calculator answer to the remainder, and vice versa?

We will compare the calculator answer for a division question with the answer with a remainder obtained by some written or mental method:

- Calculator: 100 ÷ 7 = 14.285714.
- Written or mental method: 100 ÷ 7 = 14 remainder 2.

Note that the calculator answer is truncated (see Chapter 3) and would actually continue as a recurring decimal, 14.2857142857142857 . . ., if the calculator were able to display more than eight digits.

Now, the 14 is common to both answers. The question is: how does the .285714 in the first answer relate to the remainder 2 in the second? The easiest way to see this is to imagine that the division is modelling a problem with an equal-sharing structure in a measuring context; for example, sharing 100 cl (that is a litre) of wine equally between 7 glasses (for reference, a centilitre is one-hundredth of a litre). The 14 represents 14 whole centilitres of wine in each portion, and the remainder 2 represents 2 centilitres of wine left over. If this 2 cl is also shared out between the 7 glasses, then each glass will get a further portion of wine corresponding to the answer to the division, 2 ÷ 7. Doing this on the calculator gives the result 0.2857142, which is clearly the same as the bit after the decimal point in the calculator answer to the original question, allowing for the calculator's truncation of the result. So the figures after the decimal point are the result of dividing the remainder by the divisor.

This means, of course, that, since multiplication and division are inverse processes, the remainder should be the result of multiplying the bit after the decimal point by the divisor. Checking this with the above example, we would multiply 0.2857142 by 7 and expect to get the remainder, 2. What I actually get on my calculator is 1.9999994, which is *nearly* equal to 2, but not quite. The discrepancy is due to the tiny bit of the answer to 2 ÷ 7 that the calculator discarded when it truncated the result.

Another way of getting from the calculator answer (14.285714) to the remainder (2) is simply to multiply the whole number part of the calculator answer (14) by the divisor (7) and subtract the result (98) from the dividend (100). The reasoning here is that the 14 represents the 14 whole centilitres in each glass. Since there are 7 glasses, this amounts to 98 cl (since 14 × 7 = 98). Taking this 98 cl away from the original 100 cl leaves the remainder of 2 cl.

So, in summary, allowing for small errors resulting from truncation:

1. The figures after the decimal point are the result of dividing the remainder by the divisor.
2. The remainder is the result of multiplying the figures after the decimal point by the divisor.
3. The remainder is also obtained by multiplying the whole number part of the calculator answer by the divisor and subtracting the result from the dividend.

What about rounding?

Numbers obtained from measurements or as the results of calculations in practical situations often have to be rounded in some way in order to make sense and to be of any use to us. Sometimes we round up and sometimes we round down. The first consideration must always be the *context* that gives rise to the numbers. For example, when buying wallpaper most people find it helpful to round *up* in their calculation of how many rolls to purchase, to be on the safe side. On the other hand if we were planning to catch the 8.48 train we might well decide to round this *down* to 'about a quarter to nine', since rounding this time *up* to 'about ten to nine' would result in our missing the train. So sometimes the context requires us to round *down* in our calculations and sometimes to round *up*. This consideration of the context is much more important than any rule we might remember from school about digits being greater or smaller than five.

Are there particular kinds of division problems that can be given to pupils where the context requires that you have to round up or round down?

Consider these two examples, both of which are problems modelled by 44 ÷ 6, with the inverse-of-multiplication structure. Both are of the form 'how many sixes make 44?'

1. You can fit six children on a bench. How many benches do we need if we have 44 children to be seated?
2. A pencil costs 6p. How many pencils can I buy with 44p?

For each problem I might enter '44 ÷ 6 =' on my calculator and get the result 7.3333333 displayed. The answer is a recurring decimal (7.̇3) that has been truncated by the calculator to show just eight figures and is interpreted as 'about 7.3333333 benches'.

Clearly, in problem (1), we cannot bring in 7.3333333 benches, so, since seven benches would not be enough for everyone to get a seat, we conclude that eight benches are needed. In this case the context determines that we round the 7.3333333 *up* to 8.

Then, in example (2), obviously we can only purchase whole pencils, so the answer 'about 7.3333333 pencils' must again be rounded. In this case, however, the context determines that we round the answer *down*. We can clearly afford only 7 pencils.

In explaining what is going on to pupils, we could talk about the '.3333333' in example (1) as representing 'a bit of a bench'. We need 7 benches and a bit of a bench: so we must get 8 benches, otherwise some people will be left standing. Similarly, the '.3333333' in example (2) represents 'a bit of a pencil': we can afford 7 pencils and a bit of a pencil, but we will only be able to buy 7 pencils.

These two examples illustrate the point noted in Chapter 7 that a division problem with the inverse-of-multiplication structure often takes one of two forms. First, there are those that incorporate the idea of *repeated addition to reach a target*, such as problems that use the question, 'how many do we need?' Problems of this kind, such as problem (1) above, require a calculator answer with superfluous figures to be rounded *up*. Then there are those that incorporate the idea of *repeated subtraction from a given quantity*, such as problems that use the question, 'how many can we afford?'. Problems of this kind, such as problem (2) above, require a calculator answer with superfluous figures to be rounded *down*.

This analysis will be useful for teachers in generating division problems for pupils, to ensure that the pupils are given examples of both kinds and therefore experience a range of situations where the contexts require both rounding up and rounding down.

What about the rule of rounding up when the next digit is 5 or more?

In practice it is the context that most often determines that we should round up or that we should round down. In some situations, however, there is a convention that we should round an answer to the nearest something. In fact, such situations are fairly rare in practice, since there is more often than not a contextual reason for rounding up or down, particularly when dealing with money. One situation where 'rounding to the nearest something' is sometimes employed is in recording measurements.

Think of examples from everyday life where measurements are recorded in some form. It is nearly always the case that the measurement is actually recorded to the nearest something. For example, when the petrol pump says that I have put 15.8 litres in my tank this presumably means that the amount of petrol I have taken is really 15.8 litres to the nearest tenth of a litre. So it could actually be slightly more than that or slightly less. When I stand on the bathroom scales and record my weight as 12 stone 3 pounds, I am actually recording my weight to the nearest pound: I sometimes have to decide whether the pointer on the scales is nearer to, say, 3 pounds or 4 pounds. When I read that someone has run 100 metres in 9.84 seconds, the time is presumably rounded to the nearest one-hundredth of a second. In all these examples the measurement is recorded to the nearest something. The reasons for this are sometimes the limitations of the measuring device and sometimes simply that no practical purpose would be served by having a more accurate measurement.

It is in the handling of statistical data that the convention of rounding to the nearest something is employed most frequently. For example, you may well need to round your answer in this way when calculating averages (means). If my scores one cricket season are 50, 34, 0, 12, 0 and 43, I would calculate my average score by adding these up and dividing by 6 (see Chapter 18 for a discussion of averages). Doing this on a calculator I get the result 23.166666. Normally I would not wish to record all these figures, so I might round my average score to the nearest whole number, which would be 23, or possibly to the nearest tenth, which would be 23.2.

So how does the process of rounding to the nearest something work?

It is helpful to note that the concept of 'nearest' is essentially a spatial one, so it helps in this process to imagine the position of the number concerned on a number line, as shown in Figure 10.1. Clearly the decision to round down or up is determined by whether the number is less or more than halfway along the line between two marks on the scale. The crucial questions in this process are always: 1) what number would be halfway? 2) is my number less or more than this? So, to express 23.166666 to the nearest whole number, we have to decide between 23 and 24. The number halfway between 23 and 24 is 23.5, so we round *down* to 23, because our number is *less* than 23.5. But to express 23.166666 to the nearest tenth we have to decide between 23.1 and 23.2. The number halfway between 23.1 and 23.2 is 23.15, so we round *up* to 23.2, because our number is more than 23.15.

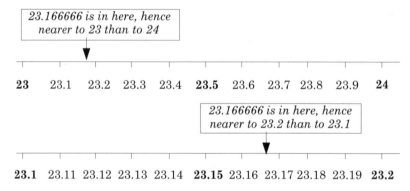

Figure 10.1   Rounding to the nearest something

This is just the same principle as when you are rounding to the nearest ten, the nearest hundred, the nearest thousand, and so on. For example, imagine I had worked out the estimated cost for renovating a classroom to be £8357. In discussions with the governors I might find it appropriate to round this figure to the nearest hundred, or even the nearest thousand. To the nearest hundred I have to choose between £8300 and £8400. Halfway between these two figures is £8350. My figure of £8357 is more than this, so I would round *up* and say that we estimate the cost to be about £8400. But if it is sufficient to discuss the cost to the nearest thousand, then I now have to choose between £8000 and £9000. Once again I ask what is halfway between these two figures. The answer is clearly £8500 and, since my estimated cost of £8357 is less than this, we would round *down* and say that the cost is going to be about £8000, to the nearest thousand.

But what do you do if the number you are dealing with is exactly halfway between your two marks on the scale?

Someone always asks this question. My answer is normally not to do anything. There really isn't much point, for example, in pretending to round a figure like £8500 to the nearest thousand. Just give it as £8500 and leave it at that. If I normally work my batting average out to the nearest whole number and one year it happens to come out exactly as 23.5, well, I think I will just leave it like that: at least I will be able to deduce from my records that I did a bit better than last year when my average to the nearest whole number was 23.

What about rounding to so many decimal places and significant figures?

When we are rounding a number like 23.166666, it is unnecessarily complex to talk about rounding it to the nearest tenth, hundredth, thousandth, ten thousandth, and so on. Apart from anything else, most of us find it difficult to articulate a word like 'thousandth' in a way that distinguishes it from 'thousand'. It is much easier therefore to talk about rounding *to so many decimal places*.

For example, 23.166666 is:

> 23, when rounded to the nearest whole number
> 23.2, when rounded to one decimal place
> 23.17, when rounded to two decimal places
> 23.167, when rounded to three decimal places
> 23.1667, when rounded to four decimal places.

A bit trickier, but often more appropriate, is the idea of rounding *to so many significant figures*. A full consideration of this is properly beyond the scope of this book, but for the sake of completeness I will try to clarify the main idea. The point is that in many practical situations we are really only interested in the approximate size of an answer to a calculation, and just the first two or three figures are normally enough.

If you are applying for a new job, you are not going to get terribly concerned about whether the salary offered is £17,437 or £17,431. In either case, the salary is about £17,400. When you are talking about thousands of pounds the choice between an additional £37 or £31 is not likely to be particularly significant. If, however, I am buying a pair of trousers then the difference between £37 and £31 becomes quite significant. It is this kind of reasoning that is the basis of the practice of rounding to a certain number of significant figures.

Giving the salaries above as 'about £17,400' in either case is the result of rounding them to three significant figures. The first significant figure, indeed the most significant figure, is the 1, since this represents the largest part of the salary, namely, ten thousand pounds. Then the 7 and the 4 are the second and third significant figures respectively. This might be all we want to know, since we would reckon that the figures in the tens and units columns are relatively insignificant. Below are some simple examples of rounding to significant figures.

On my monthly trip to the supermarket I spend £270.96. When I get home my wife asks me how big the bill was.

Exact statement: *The bill came to £270.96.*
Using just one significant figure: *The bill came to about £300.*
(This is to the nearest hundred pounds.)
Using two significant figures: *The bill came to about £270.*
(This is to the nearest ten pounds.)
Using three significant figures: *The bill came to about £271.*
(This is to the nearest pound.)

A rich man left £270,550 to be shared equally between four children. Mathematical model: 270550 ÷ 4 = 67637.5.

Exact solution: *They each inherit £67,637.50.*
To two significant figures we say: *They each inherit about £68,000.*
(This is giving the figure to the nearest thousand pounds.)
To three significant figures we say: *They each inherit about £67,600.*
(This is giving the figure to the nearest hundred pounds.)
To four significant figures we say: *They each inherit about £67,640.*
(This is giving the figure to the nearest ten pounds.)

In most practical situations, when approximate answers are required it is rarely useful to use more than three significant figures.

Self-assessment questions

10.1: A teacher wants to order 124 copies of a mathematics book costing £5.95. She must report the total cost of the order to the year-group meeting. What is the mathematical model of this problem? Obtain the mathematical solution, using a calculator. Interpret the mathematical solution as an exact statement back in the real world. What would the teacher say if she reports the total cost to the nearest ten pounds? What would the teacher say if she reports the total cost to three significant figures?

10.2: Jackie knows there are 365 days in a year and 7 days in a week. She wants to work out how many weeks in a year. What is the mathematical model of Jackie's problem? Use a non-calculator method to solve the mathematical problem, giving the answer with a remainder. What is the answer to Jackie's question? What is the meaning of the remainder? Now obtain the mathematical solution using a calculator. Is this calculator answer: a) an exact, appropriate answer; b) an exact but inappropriate answer; or c) an answer that has been truncated? (See Chapter 3.) What do the figures after the decimal point in the calculator answer represent?

10.3: Would you round your calculator answers up or down in the following situations? a) There are 327 children on a school trip and a coach can hold 40. How many coaches are needed? ($327 \div 40 = \ldots$); b) how many cakes costing 65p each can I buy with £5? ($500 \div 65 = \ldots$).

10.4: What is the average (mean) height, *to the nearest centimetre*, of 9 pupils with heights, 114 cm, 121 cm, 122 cm, 130 cm, 131 cm, 136 cm, 139 cm, 146 cm, 148 cm? (See Chapter 18: use a calculator, add up the heights, divide by 9.)

10.5: There was a total of 1459 goals in 462 matches in a football league one season. How many goals is this per match, on average? ($1459 \div 462 = \ldots$) Do this on a calculator and give the answer: a) rounded to the nearest whole number; b) rounded to one decimal place; and c) rounded to two decimal places.

10.6: A batch of 3500 books is to be shared equally between 17 shops. Using a calculator, I get $3500 \div 17 = 205.88235$. How many books are there for each shop? What is the remainder?

Summary of teaching points

1. Explicitly discuss with pupils the difference in meaning between the remainder in a division problem and the figures after the decimal point in the calculator answer.
2. Use the phrase 'a bit of a . . .' to explain informally the figures after the decimal point.
3. Provide pupils with a range of examples of real-life division problems, including those with the equal-sharing structure and those with the inverse-of-multiplication structure, to be done both by a method produc-

ing a remainder and on a calculator. Each time discuss what the remainder means and what the figures after the decimal point mean.

4. Explain, with examples of equal-sharing in measurement contexts, the
   relationship between the calculator answer to a division problem and the
   answer with the remainder.

5. When considering practical division problems with the inverse-of-
   multiplication structure that do not work out exactly when done on a
   calculator, discuss from the context whether to round up or to round
   down.

6. Use problems that incorporate both the ideas of repeated addition, such
   as those that ask 'how many do we need?', and repeated subtraction,
   such as those that ask 'how many can we afford?'

7. Emphasize the idea of recording measurements 'to the nearest something' when doing practical measuring tasks.

8. Use a number-line explanation of rounding to the nearest something,
   making use of the crucial questions in this process: a) what number
   would be halfway? and b) is my number less or more than this? Emphasize that we do not always use this process, and that it is most important
   that we first consider the context of the calculation to decide whether we
   should round up, round down or round to the nearest something.

11

Multiples, Factors and Primes

Pupils should be taught to: recognize and describe number patterns, including two- and three-digit multiples of 2, 5 or 10; recognize prime numbers to 20; find factor pairs and all the prime factors of any two-digit whole number.

In this chapter there are explanations of

- natural numbers;
- multiples, including lowest common multiple;
- some ways of spotting multiples of various numbers;
- digital sums and digital roots;
- factors, including highest common factor;
- the transitive property of multiples and factors; and
- prime numbers and composite (rectangular) numbers.

What are multiples?

First it should be made clear that in this chapter we will deal only with what are called the *natural numbers*. These are the numbers we use for counting: 1, 2, 3, 4, 5, 6, and so on, *ad infinitum*. So when you read the word 'number' in this chapter it refers to one of these. We are therefore excluding zero, negative numbers and anything other than positive whole numbers.

The *multiples* of any given number are obtained by multiplying the number in turn by each of the natural numbers, 1, 2, 3, 4, 5, 6, and so on. For example

- multiples of 3 are: 3, 6, 9, 12, 15, 18, 21, 24, 27, 30, 33, 36, 39, 42, 45, etc.;

- multiples of 7 are: 7, 14, 21, 28, 35, 42, 49, 56, 63, 70, 77, 84, 91, etc.; and
- multiples of 37 are: 37, 74, 111, 148, 185, 222, 259, 296, 333, 370, etc.

You can easily generate the multiples of a given number using a simple calculator with a constant facility (most have this). Enter the number, for example, 37, on to the calculator, press +, then repeatedly press the equals button. The calculator responds by repeatedly adding 37 to itself and thus produces the multiples of 37.

The mathematical relationship 'is a multiple of' applied to numbers possesses what is called the *transitive property*. Formally, this means that if A is a multiple of B and B is a multiple of C then it follows that A is a multiple of C. This is illustrated in general terms in Figure 11.1(a). Figure 11.1b gives an example: any number that is a multiple of 6, such as 24, must also be a multiple of 3, because 6 itself is a multiple of 3. Applying this principle, we can deduce that all multiples of 6 are multiples of 3 (but not vice versa). Similarly, all multiples of 28 must be multiples of 7, because 28 is itself a multiple of 7.

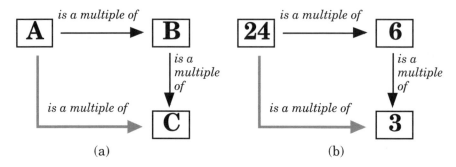

Figure 11.1   The transitive property of multiples

Is there anything else to know about multiples?

Being able to recognize multiples and having an awareness of some of the patterns and relationships within them help to develop a high level of confidence and pleasure in working with numbers. For example, this pattern in the multiples of 37 may appeal to some readers:

$$3 \times 37 = 111$$
$$6 \times 37 = 222$$
$$9 \times 37 = 333$$
$$12 \times 37 = 444 \text{ and so on.}$$

The pattern in the multiples of 9, with the tens digit increasing by one and the units digit decreasing by one each time, is a useful aid for learning the nine-times table:

$$1 \times 9 = 09$$
$$2 \times 9 = 18$$
$$3 \times 9 = 27$$
$$4 \times 9 = 36$$
$$5 \times 9 = 45 \text{ and so on.}$$

There are a number of ways of spotting certain multiples. For example, you will surely be able to tell at a glance that all these numbers are multiples of ten: 20, 450, 980, 7620. That's using a very obvious pattern, namely, that all multiples of ten end with the digit zero. Similarly, you probably know that all multiples of two (even numbers) end in 0, 2, 4, 6 or 8; and that all multiples of five end in 0 or 5.

There's a simple way to spot whether a number greater than 100 is a multiple of 4. Since 100 is a multiple of 4, then any multiple of 100 is a multiple of 4. So, given, for example, 4528, we can think of it as 4500 + 28. We know that the 4500 is a multiple of 4, because it's a multiple of 100. So all we need to decide is whether the 28 is a multiple of 4, which it is. So if you have a number with three or more digits you need only look at the last two digits to determine whether or not you are dealing with a multiple of 4.

Would you spot immediately that all these are multiples of nine: 18, 72, 315, 567, 4986? If so, you may be making use of the *digital sum* for each number. This is the number you get if you add up the digits in the given number. If you then add up the digits in the digital sum, and keep going with this process of adding the digits until a single-digit answer is obtained, the number you get is called the *digital root*. For example, 4986 has a digital sum of 27. This is itself a multiple of nine! This is true for any multiple of 9: the digital sum is itself a multiple of 9. If you then add up the digits of this digital sum (2 + 7) you get the single-digit number, 9, which is therefore the digital root. Fascinatingly, the digital root of a multiple of 9 is always 9.

Here is a summary of some useful tricks for spotting various multiples:

- Every natural number is a multiple of 1.
- Multiples of 2 are even numbers and end in 0, 2, 4, 6 or 8.
- The digital sum of a multiple of 3 is always a multiple of 3; and the digital root is always 3, 6 or 9.

- The number given by the last two digits of a multiple of 4 must be a multiple of 4.
- Multiples of 5 always end in 0 or 5.
- Multiples of 6 are multiples of 2 *and* multiples of 3; so they must end in 0, 2, 4, 6 or 8 *and* have a digital root of 3, 6 or 9.
- The number given by the last three digits of a multiple of 8 must be a multiple of 8.
- The digital sum of a multiple of 9 is always a multiple of 9; and the digital root is always 9.
- Multiples of 10 always end in zero.

What is a 'lowest common multiple'?

If we list all the multiples of each of two numbers, then inevitably there will be some multiples common to the two sets. For example, with 6 and 10, we obtain the following sets of multiples:

- Multiples of 6: 6, 12, 18, 24, 30, 36, 42, 48, 54, 60, 66, . . .
- Multiples of 10: 10, 20, 30, 40, 50, 60, 70, . . .

The numbers common to the two sets are: 30, 60, 90, 120, and so on. The smallest of these (30) is known sometimes as *the lowest common multiple*. The lowest common multiple of 6 and 10 is therefore the small-est number that can be split up into groups of 6 and into groups of 10. This concept occurs in a number of practical situations. For example, a class of 30 children is the smallest class-size that can be organized into groups of 6 children for mathematics and teams of 10 for games. Or, if I have to feed one plant every six days and another plant every ten days, then the lowest common multiple indicates the first day on which both plants have to be fed, namely the thirtieth day. Or, if I can only buy a certain kind of biscuit in packets of 10 and I want to share the biscuits equally between 6 people, the number of biscuits I buy must be a multi-ple of both 6 and 10; so the smallest number I can purchase is the lowest common multiple, which is 30 biscuits.

What is a factor?

The concept of *factor* is simply the reverse of multiple. If A is a multiple of B then B is a factor of A. For example, 24 is a multiple of 6, so 6 is a factor of 24. Colloquially, we say '6 goes into 24'. So the factors of 24 are all those natural numbers by which 24 can be divided exactly: 1, 2, 3, 4, 6, 8, 12 and 24. Notice that 1 and 24 are included as factors of 24. Of course, 1 is a factor of all numbers and every number is a factor of itself. Recognizing quickly all the factors of a given number is, of course, very useful. For example, with a set of 24 people we can know instantly that they can be put into groups of 2, 3, 4, 6, 8 or 12. This makes a number like 24, with lots of factors, much more useful for many practical purposes than a number like 23, which has no factors other than 1 and itself.

The idea of a *rectangular array*, introduced in Chapter 7, provides a good illustration of the concept of a factor. Figure 11.2 shows all the different rectangular arrays possible with a set of 24 crosses. The dimensions of these arrays are all the possible pairs of factors of 24: 1 and 24, 2 and 12, 3 and 8, 4 and 6.

```
× × × × × × × × × × × × × × × × × × × × × × × ×        × × × ×
                                                        × × × ×
                   1 by 24                              × × × ×
                                                        × × × ×
                                × × × × × × × ×          × × × ×
× × × × × × × × × × × ×          × × × × × × × ×          × × × ×
× × × × × × × × × × × ×          × × × × × × × ×
        2 by 12                      3 by 8              4 by 6
```

Figure 11.2   Factors of 24 shown in rectangular arrays

A calculator can be used to determine whether or not a number is a factor of a given number. Divide the given number by the possible factor: if the answer is a whole number it is a factor, otherwise it is not. For example, is 23 a factor of 1955? Using a calculator, I get 1955 ÷ 23 = 85, so 23 *is* a factor of 1955. Is 15 a factor of 1955? Using a calculator, I get 1955 ÷ 15 = 130.33333, so 15 is *not* a factor of 1955.

The mathematical relationship, 'is a factor of', also possesses the transitive property as illustrated in Figure 11.3. So, for example, any factor of 12 must be a factor of 24, because 12 is a factor of 24.

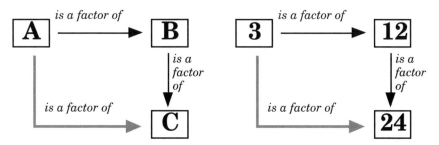

Figure 11.3   The transitive property of factors

What about the 'highest common factor'?

This is a similar idea to the lowest common multiple. If we list all the factors of two numbers, the two sets of factors may have some numbers in common. (Since 1 is a factor of all numbers they must at least have this number in common!) The largest of these common factors is sometimes called the *highest common factor*. For example, with 24 and 30 we have the following two sets of factors:

- Factors of 24: 1, 2, 3, 4, 6, 8, 12, 24.
- Factors of 30: 1, 2, 3, 5, 6, 10, 15, 30.

The factors in common are 1, 2, 3 and 6. So the highest common factor is 6. This concept occurs in many practical situations. For example, imagine that two classes in a year group have 24 and 30 children respectively, and that we wish to divide them up into a number of groups, with each class of children shared equally between the groups. The number of groups must clearly be a factor of both 24 and 30. The largest possible number of groups is therefore 6, since this is the highest common factor.

The idea of the highest common factor can be illustrated with a rectangular array. The geometric problem would be to arrange, say, 24 crosses and 30 noughts in a rectangular array, with the same combination of noughts and crosses in each row. It is possible to achieve this with 1 row, 2 rows, 3 rows or 6 rows. So the highest common factor, 6, is the greatest number of rows possible. This is shown in Figure 11.4, where the 24 crosses and 30 noughts have been arranged in 6 rows: with 4 crosses and 5 noughts in each row.

$$\times \times \times \times \; O \; O \; O \; O \; O$$
$$\times \times \times \times \; O \; O \; O \; O \; O$$
$$\times \times \times \times \; O \; O \; O \; O \; O$$
$$\times \times \times \times \; O \; O \; O \; O \; O$$
$$\times \times \times \times \; O \; O \; O \; O \; O$$
$$\times \times \times \times \; O \; O \; O \; O \; O$$

Figure 11.4   The highest common factor of 24 and 30 shown in a rectangular array

What is a prime number?

Any number that has precisely two factors, and no more than two, is called a *prime number*. This is the strict mathematical definition. In practice we think of a prime number as a number that cannot be divided exactly by any number apart from 1 and itself. So, for example, 7 is a prime number because it has precisely two factors, namely 1 and 7. But 10 is not a prime number because it has four factors, namely 1, 2, 5 and 10. A number, such as 10, with more than two factors is sometimes called a *composite number*, or, because it can be arranged as a rectangular array with more than one row (see Figure 11.5), a *rectangular number*. Prime numbers cannot be arranged as rectangular arrays, other than with a single row. The first twenty prime numbers are: 2, 3, 5, 7, 11, 13, 17, 19, 23, 29, 31, 37, 41, 43, 47, 53, 59, 61, 67 and 71.

(a) 10   (b) 7

Figure 11.5   (a) 10 is a composite number; (b) 7 is a prime number

Notice that according to the strict mathematical definition, the number 1 is *not* a prime number since, uniquely, it has only one factor (itself). So 1 is the only number that is neither prime nor composite. The exclusion of 1 from the set of prime numbers often puzzles students of mathematics. The reason is related to the most important property of prime numbers: given any composite number whatsoever, there is only one combination of prime numbers that multiplied together give the number. I will illustrate this with the number 24. This number can be obtained by multiplying together various combinations of numbers, such as: 2×12, $2 \times 2 \times 6$, $1 \times 2 \times 3 \times 4$, and so on. If, however, we stipulate that only *prime* numbers can be used, there's only one combination that will produce 24: namely, $2 \times 2 \times 2 \times 3$. This is called the *prime factorization* of 24. This is such a powerful property of prime numbers that it would be a pity to mess it up by allowing 1 to be a prime number! If we did, then the prime factorization of 24, for example, would not be unique, because we could also get to 24 with $1 \times 2 \times 2 \times 2 \times 3$, or $1 \times 1 \times 2 \times 2 \times 2 \times 3$, and so on.

The study of primes is a fascinating branch of number theory. Computers have been employed to search for very large numbers that are prime. At the time of writing, to my knowledge, the largest known prime number is '$2^{697259} - 1$'. (This means 6 972 593 twos multiplied together, minus 1: this produces a number with over 2 million digits!) This was discovered, after his computer had worked on the problem for 111 days, by Nayan Hajratwala in Michigan, USA, on 1 June 1999. However, this is definitely not the largest prime number because, as the Greek mathematician, Euclid, proved, as long ago as 300 BC, there is no largest prime number. The really annoying facet of prime numbers is that there is no pattern or formula that will generate the complete set of prime numbers.

What is the point of learning about multiples, factors and primes?

I recall once, in response to this question, asking a student whether she felt differently about the numbers 47 and 48. I was surprised to be told that she did not! To me, 48 seems such a friendly number, flexible and amenable. If I have 48 in a group there are so many ways I can reorganize them: 6 sets of 8, 3 sets of 16, 4 sets of 12, and so on. By contrast, 47 is such an awkward number! The difference, of course, is that 47 is prime, but 48 has lots of factors. This is all part of what is sometimes called 'having a feel for number'. Our confidence in responding to numbers in the everyday situations where they occur will be improved enormously by having this kind of feel for numbers; by being aware of the significant relationships between them; and by recognizing at a glance which properties they possess and which they do not. And the more we are aware of properties like multiples, factors and primes, the more we learn to delight in the pattern and fascination of number. Being able to spot at a glance which car registration numbers are multiples of eleven, or how many of the hymn numbers in church on Sunday morning are prime, might be diverting but is of no immediate practical use. But it all leads to yet greater confidence when we have to respond to numerical situations that do matter. Whether the reader is convinced or not by this argument will, no doubt, be evident in the level of enthusiasm with which they tackle the self-assessment questions which follow.

Self-assessment questions

11.1: Continue the pattern shown earlier in this chapter for certain multiples of 37, until the pattern breaks down.

11.2: Multiply each of these numbers by 9 (use a calculator if necessary) and check that the digital root in each case is 9: a) 47; b) 172; and c) 9876543.

11.3: Use some of the methods for spotting multiples to decide whether the following numbers are multiples of 2, 3, 4, 5, 6, 8, or 9: a) 2652; b) 6570; and c) 2401.

11.4: These car registration numbers are all multiples of 11: a) 561; b) 594; c) 418; d) 979; and e) 330. Add up the two outside digits and subtract the middle one. Do this with a few more three-digit multiples of 11. Can you state a rule?

11.5: What is the smallest number of people that can be split up equally into groups of 8 and groups of 12? What mathematical concept is used in solving this problem?

11.6: Find all the factors of a) 95; b) 96; and c) 97. Which of these two numbers would be most flexible as a year-group size for breaking up into smaller-sized groups for various activities?

11.7: List all the factors of 48 and 80. What are the common factors? If there are 48 blue chairs and 80 red chairs to be arranged in rows, with the same combination of reds and blues in each row, how can this be done?

11.8: List all the prime numbers between 70 and 100.

11.9: By trying each prime number in turn, using a calculator to help you, find the prime numbers that multiply together to give 4403.

11.10: Starting with 1, add 4, add 2, add 4, add 2, and continue this sequence until you pass 60. How many of the answers are prime?

11.11: A famous unproven theorem, called Goldbach's conjecture (Christian Goldbach, 1690–1764), states that every even number greater than 2 is the sum of two primes. For example, $52 = 5 + 47$. Test this conjecture with all the even numbers from 4 to 30. (At the time of writing the conjecture has been tested and shown to work for all even numbers up to 4×10^{14}, which is 4 followed by 14 zeros!)

11.12: Find a number that is a multiple of all the numbers from 1 to 10 inclusive.

Summary of teaching points

1. Encourage pupils to be fascinated by number and patterns in number.
2. Build up pupils' confidence in responding to numerical situations by exploring the concepts and properties of multiples, factors and prime numbers.
3. Share with pupils some of the ways of testing for various multiples.
4. Use calculators to explore factors, multiples and primes.
5. Use rectangular arrays to illustrate the concepts of factor, prime number and composite (rectangular) number.

12

Squares, Cubes and Number Shapes

Pupils should be taught to: recognize and describe number patterns, using these to make predictions; recognize square numbers up to 10×10.

In this chapter there are explanations of

- square numbers;
- cube numbers;
- square roots and cube roots;
- the trial and improvement method for finding square roots and cube roots using a calculator;
- use of the inequality signs (>, <) for recording 'greater than', 'less than' and 'lies between';
- the relationship between sequences of geometric patterns and sets of numbers;
- triangle numbers; and
- the theorem of Pythagoras.

Why are some numbers called squares? A square is a shape, isn't it?

Connecting pictures with number concepts helps to build up our understanding and confidence, as was seen in the previous chapter with concepts like 'factor' and 'multiple'. In particular we saw that a prime number, like 7, could be represented as a rectangle of dots only with one row, whereas a composite (rectangular) number, like 10, could be shown as a rectangular array with more than one row (see Figure 11.5). Now, some rectangles have equal sides: these are the rectangles that are called squares. So numbers, such as 1, 4, 9, 16, 25, and so on, which can be represented by square arrays, as shown in Figure 12.1, are called *square numbers*. If we use an array of small squares, called square units, as in Figure 12.1(b), rather than just dots, as in Figure 12.1(a), then the number of squares in the array also corresponds to the total area. For example, the area of the 5 by 5 square grid is 25 square units. Of course, square numbers are also composite (rectangular) numbers, just as squares are rectangles. (Strictly speaking, there is one exception: the number 1 is considered a square number but, as we saw in the previous chapter, it is neither prime nor composite.)

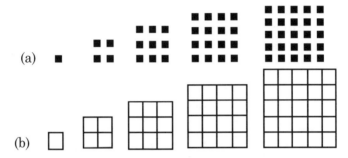

Figure 12.1   Pictures of square numbers: (a) using dots; (b) using a square grid

This explains the geometric idea of square numbers. The arithmetic idea that corresponds to this is that a square number is any number that is obtained by multiplying a (whole) number by itself. The number 16 is represented in Figure 12.1 by 4 rows of 4 dots, or 4 rows of 4 squares, which, of course, corresponds to the multiplication 4×4. Likewise, the representation of 25 as a square corresponds to 5×5. There is a special mathematical notation that can be used as a shorthand for writing 5×5. This is 5^2, which means simply that there are two fives to be multiplied together. This is read as 'five squared' or 'five to the power two' (see the discussion about powers of 10 in Chapter 2). The square numbers can be obtained easily using a calculator. For example, to find 6 squared, just enter: 6, $\times$, =. This is the numerical pattern for the set of square numbers:

$$1 \times 1 = 1^2 = \ 1$$
$$2 \times 2 = 2^2 = \ 4$$
$$3 \times 3 = 3^2 = \ 9$$
$$4 \times 4 = 4^2 = 16$$
$$5 \times 5 = 5^2 = 25$$
$$6 \times 6 = 6^2 = 36 \text{ and so on.}$$

What about cube numbers?

Just as some numbers can be represented by square arrays, there are those, such as 1, 8 and 27, that can be represented by arrangements in the shape of a cube. Figure 12.2 shows how the first three cube numbers are constructed from small cubes, called cubic units. The first three cube numbers are made from 1 cubic unit, from 8 cubic units and from 27 cubic units, respectively. The 27, for example, is produced by 3 layers of cubes, with 3 rows of 3 cubes in each layer, and is therefore equal to $3 \times 3 \times 3$. The number of cubic units in the whole construction corresponds to the total volume of the cube. For example, the volume of the 3 by 3 by 3 cube is 27 cubic units. It is difficult, of course, to represent these cubic constructions in a two-dimensional picture, so readers are encouraged to build various-sized cubes from cubic units and to generate these cube numbers for themselves.

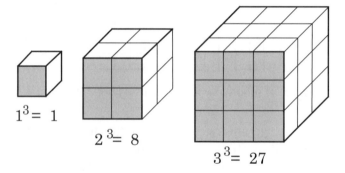

$1^3 = 1$

$2^3 = 8$

$3^3 = 27$

Figure 12.2   Examples of cube numbers

The same kind of notation is used for cube numbers as for square numbers: $3 \times 3 \times 3$ is abbreviated to 3^3 and read as 'three cubed' or 'three to the power three'. Again, it is easy to generate cube numbers using a simple calculator; for example, to obtain 6 cubed, simply enter: 6, ×, =, =. By analogy with the square numbers above, we can construct the following pattern for the cube numbers:

$$1 \times 1 \times 1 = 1^3 = 1$$
$$2 \times 2 \times 2 = 2^3 = 8$$
$$3 \times 3 \times 3 = 3^3 = 27$$
$$4 \times 4 \times 4 = 4^3 = 64$$
$$5 \times 5 \times 5 = 5^3 = 125$$
$$6 \times 6 \times 6 = 6^3 = 216 \text{ and so on.}$$

What are square roots and cube roots?

What is the length of the side of a square that has an area of 729 square units? Another way of asking the same question is: Which number when multiplied by itself gives 729? Or, which number has a square equal to 729? The answer (27) is called the *square root* of 729. (Strictly speaking, 27 is the *positive* square root of 729; you can also get 729 by multiplying the negative number, –27, by itself, but we are not concerned with negative numbers in this chapter.) The mathematical abbreviation for 'the (positive) square root of' is: $\sqrt{}$. So we could write, for example, $\sqrt{729} = 27$. Finding a square root is the *inverse* process of finding a square. This means that one process undoes the effect of the other, for example:

$$2^2 = 4 \quad \text{so} \quad \sqrt{4} = 2$$
$$3^2 = 9 \quad \text{so} \quad \sqrt{9} = 3$$
$$4^2 = 16 \quad \text{so} \quad \sqrt{16} = 4$$
$$27^2 = 729 \quad \text{so} \quad \sqrt{729} = 27$$

The idea of a *cube root* follows the same logic. In geometric terms the question would be: What is the length of the side of a cube with a total volume of 729 cubic units? Or, in arithmetic terms, what number has a cube equal to 729? The answer (9) is called the cube root of 729. As with square roots we can think in terms of an *inverse* process: finding the cube root is the inverse process of finding the cube. For example, the cube of 14 is 2744, so the cube root of 2744 is 14. The symbol for a cube root is: $\sqrt[3]{}$. So, for example, we could write: $\sqrt[3]{2744} = 14$.

How can you find square roots and cube roots?

Using a basic calculator, finding a square root is very simple, since it will usually have a square root key, with the symbol for square root ($\sqrt{}$) written on it. So, for example, to find the square root of 361, you simply enter: 361, $\sqrt{}$. The calculator displays the answer, 19. It is also instructive to try to find some square roots without using the square root key, since this introduces a mathematical process, sometimes called *trial and improvement*, which can then be applied to other problems. For example, the problem might be to find the side of a square with a total area of 3844 square units. Using a calculator, we simply try various numbers, square them and decide whether the results are too high or too low, gradually refining our guesses so that we home in on the solution. Like this:

Try 50 . . . square it (enter 50, ×, =) . . . answer: 2500 . . . too low.
Try 60 . . . square it (enter 60, ×, =) . . . answer: 3600 . . . too low.
Try 70 . . . square it (enter 70, ×, =) . . . answer: 4900 . . . too high.
So, the answer lies between 60 and 70 . . .
Try 65 . . . square it (enter 65, ×, =) . . . answer: 4225 . . . too high.
Try 63 . . . square it (enter 63, ×, =) . . . answer: 3969 . . . too high.
Getting close!
Try 62 . . . square it (enter 62, ×, =) . . . answer: 3844 . . . got it.

So the square root of 3844 is 62. This is really the only way to find a cube root using a simple calculator. For example, to find the cube root of 85 184:

Try 50 . . . cube it (enter 50, ×, =, =) . . . answer: 125 000 . . . too high.
Try 30 . . . cube it (enter 30, ×, =, =) . . . answer: 27 000 . . . too low.
Try 40 . . . cube it (enter 40, ×, =, =) . . . answer: 64 000 . . . too low.
Try 45 . . . cube it (enter 45, ×, =, =) . . . answer: 91 125 . . . too high.
Try 43 . . . cube it (enter 43, ×, =, =) . . . answer: 79 507 . . . too low
Try 44 . . . cube it (enter 44, ×, =, =) . . . answer: 85 184 . . . got it.

In the two examples above the numbers were chosen carefully so that there was an exact whole number which was the square root or the cube root. In real situations where a square root or cube root is required, this is unlikely to be the case. For example, if I want to build a square patio with an area of 200 square metres, the length of the side in metres must be the square root of 200. However, my calculator tells me that $14^2 = 196$ (too low) and $15^2 = 225$ (too high). So the answer lies between 14 and 15. There is, in fact, no number that I can enter on a calculator that is the exact square root of 200. (This is because $\sqrt{200}$ is an irrational number: see Chapter 14.) But using the trial and improvement method, we can get an answer as close as we wish, by going into decimals. For example, since I find that $14.1^2 = 198.81$ (too low) and $14.2^2 = 201.64$ (too high), the answer must lie between 14.1 and 14.2. Readers confident in handling decimals may wish to pursue this in questions 12.6 and 12.7 in the self-assessment questions at the end of the chapter.

We should note here that the mathematical signs for *inequality* (> and <) can be used in this context for recording results rather more concisely. Some examples are given below.

$\sqrt{200}$ is less than 15	can be recorded as:	$\sqrt{200} < 15$
15 is greater than $\sqrt{200}$	can be recorded as:	$15 > \sqrt{200}$
$\sqrt{200}$ is greater than 14	can be recorded as:	$\sqrt{200} > 14$

14 is less than $\sqrt{200}$ can be recorded as: $14 < \sqrt{200}$
$\sqrt{200}$ lies between 14 and 15   can be recorded as: $14 < \sqrt{200} < 15$

Note that this last statement is saying effectively: 14 is less than $\sqrt{200}$ which is less than 15. It could also be written the other way round using greater-than signs: $15 > \sqrt{200} > 14$.

People with little experience of mathematics are often uneasy about this kind of trial-and-improvement approach, feeling that it is not respectable mathematics. So let me assure you that it is! There are many problems in advanced mathematics which were at one time practically impossible, but which can now be solved by using numerical methods of this kind, employing a calculator or a computer to do the hard grind of the successive calculations involved.

How are squares and square roots used in applying the theorem of Pythagoras?

Pythagoras (569 to 500 BC) was a Greek mathematician and philosopher, most famous for the theorem about right-angled triangles that is attributed to him. The longest side of a right-angled triangle, the side opposite the right-angle, is called the *hypotenuse*. Pythagoras is said to have discovered that, for any right-angled triangle, the square of the length of the hypotenuse is equal to the sum of the squares of the lengths of the other two sides. He went on to prove this conjecture with a formal mathematical argument, which I do not intend to reproduce here. In relation to the right-angled triangle shown in Figure 12.3, the generalization that Pythagoras came up with can be written as $c^2 = a^2 + b^2$. So if we know the lengths of the two shorter sides in a right-angled triangle, we can calculate the length of the hypotenuse, using our facility with squares and square roots. For example, if a = 12 units and b = 16 units, then $c^2 = 12^2 + 16^2 = 144 + 256 = 400$. Now, if $c^2 = 400$, then $c = \sqrt{400} = 20$ units.

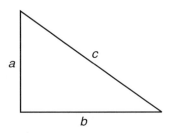

Figure 12.3   The theorem of Pythagoras: $c^2 = a^2 + b^2$

When the three sides of a right-angled triangle work out to be natural numbers, such as the numbers 12, 16 and 20 in the example above, they are called a *Pythagorean triple*. Other well-known examples of Pythagorean triples are 3, 4, 5 (because 9 + 16 = 25) and 5, 12, 13 (because 25 + 144 = 169). Often though, when the lengths a and b are natural numbers the hypotenuse will not work out exactly. For example, if a = 1 unit and b = 2 units, then $c^2 = 1^2 + 2^2 = 1 + 4 = 5$, so c = $\sqrt{5}$. Using either a calculator key or a trial-and-improvement method to find the square root of 5, we get that c is approximately 2.236 units. (The length of c in this case, $\sqrt{5}$, is an irrational number: see Chapter 14.)

Are there any other geometric shapes, in addition to squares and cubes, that describe sets of numbers?

Almost any sequence of geometric shapes or patterns, such as those shown in Figure 12.4, can be used to generate a corresponding set of numbers. Exploring these kinds of sequences, trying to relate the geometric and numerical patterns, can produce some intriguing mathematics. For example, the reader might consider why the first sequence of patterns in Figure 12.4 generates the odd numbers: 1, 3, 5, 7, 9 and so on ; and why the second sequence generates the multiples of 3: 3, 6, 9, 12, and so on.

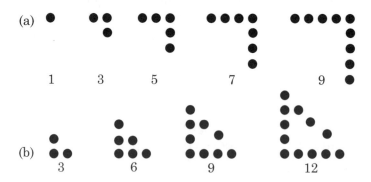

Figure 12.4   Geometric patterns generating sets of numbers

Some of these patterns turn out to be particularly interesting and are given special names. For example, you may come across the so-called *triangle numbers*. These are the numbers that correspond to the particular pattern of triangles of dots shown in Figure 12.5: 1, 3, 6, 10, 15, and so on. Notice that you get the second triangle by adding two dots to the first; the third by adding three dots to the second; the fourth by adding four dots to the third; and so on.

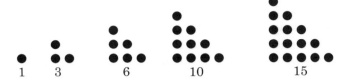

Figure 12.5   Triangle numbers

The geometric arrangements of dots show that these triangle numbers have the following numerical pattern:

$$1 = 1$$
$$3 = 1 + 2$$
$$6 = 1 + 2 + 3$$
$$10 = 1 + 2 + 3 + 4$$
$$15 = 1 + 2 + 3 + 4 + 5, \text{ and so on.}$$

A general formula for triangle numbers is given in Chapter 20. Self-assessment questions 12.3 and 12.8 below provide two examples of explaining patterns in number sequences by thinking about the geometric patterns to which they correspond.

Self-assessment questions

12.1: Drawing on the ideas of this and the previous chapter, find at least one interesting thing to say about each of the numbers from 20 to 29.

12.2: Find a triangle number that is also a square number.

12.3: Look at the sequence of square numbers: 1, 4, 9, 16, 25, 36, and so on. Find the differences between successive numbers in this sequence. What do you notice? Can you explain this in terms of patterns of dots?

12.4: Use a calculator. Choose a number. Square it, then cube the answer. Cube it, then square the answer. Are the results the same? Can you find a whole number less than 100 that is both a cube number and a square number?

12.5: Use the trial and improvement method to find: a) the square root of 3249; and b) the cube root of 4913.

12.6: For those confident with decimals: continue with the trial and improvement method for finding the square root of 200, until you can give the length of the side of the square patio with area of 200 square metres to the nearest centimetre.

12.7: To construct a cube with a volume of 500 cubic centimetres, what should be the length of the sides of the cube? Use a calculator and trial-and-improvement to answer this to a practical level of accuracy.

12.8: List all the triangle numbers less than 100. Find the sums of successive pairs of triangle numbers, for example, $1 + 3 = 4$, $3 + 6 = 9$, $6 + 10 = 16$, and so on. What do you notice about the answers? Can you explain this numerical pattern by reference to the geometric patterns for these numbers?

12.9: Use a calculator with a square-root key to help you to find a Pythagorean triple in which the smallest of the three natural numbers is 20.

12.10: What is the length of the diagonal of a square of side 10 cm?

12.11: Insert the correct inequality signs (> or <) in the gaps in the following: a) $10 \ldots \sqrt{50}$; b) $\sqrt[3]{100} \ldots 5$; c) $8 \ldots \sqrt{70} \ldots 9$.

12.12: Find two consecutive whole numbers that will go in the boxes: $\square < \sqrt{150} < \square$.

Summary of teaching points

1. Use geometric pictures such as square arrays of dots and square grids to explain square numbers, and cubes constructed from cubic units to explain cube numbers.

2. Connect the square of a number with the area of a square grid, given by counting the number of square units in the grid.

3. Connect the cube of a number with the volume of a cube, given by counting the number of cubic units used to construct it.

4. Emphasize the idea of inverse processes when discussing squares and square roots, i.e. that one process undoes the effect of the other.

5. Explicitly teach pupils the calculator key sequences for finding squares (number, ×, =) and cubes (number, ×, =, =).

6. Introduce primary pupils to the method of trial and improvement, using a calculator to find square roots (without using the square root key) and cube roots.

7. Encourage pupils to explore the relationships between sequences of geometric patterns of dots and the corresponding sequences of numbers.

13

Integers: Positive and Negative

Pupils should extend their understanding of the number system to include integers. They should be taught to: recognize and continue number sequences formed by counting on or back in steps of constant size from any integer, extending to negative integers when counting back; order a set of negative integers, explaining methods and reasoning.

In this chapter there are explanations of

- integers;
- the cardinal and ordinal aspects of number;
- contexts for understanding positive and negative numbers;
- situations in the contexts of temperatures and bank balances that are modelled by the addition and subtraction of positive and negative numbers; and
- how to enter negative numbers on a basic calculator.

What are integers?

The mathematical word *integer* is related to words such as 'integral' (forming a whole) and 'integrity' (wholeness). So integers are simply *whole numbers*. But this includes both positive and negative whole numbers, and zero. So the set of integers includes the set of *natural numbers* described in Chapter 11.

People have difficulty with the concept of a negative number, mainly because we overemphasize the idea that a number represents a set of things. So when a teacher wants to demonstrate to a young child, say, 3 + 4, the first thing they do is to put out a set of 3 things (counters, blocks, fingers, etc.) and a set of 4 things, and put the two sets together to form a new set. This is the so-called *cardinal aspect* of number. The problem is that we cannot conceive of a set of negative three things! But this does not mean that negative numbers are some kind of mysterious, abstract mathematical notion, because numbers are not just sets of things. For instance, the numeral 3 can also be thought of as representing a point on a number line, such as that shown in Figure 13.1, and the instruction, 'add 4', interpreted as moving 4 steps further along the number line. It is this *ordinal aspect* of number that extends our understanding of number quite naturally and simply to include negative numbers: the idea that numbers are also labels used for putting things in order. In Figure 13.1 the numbers are just that: they are labels for putting in order the particular points that have been marked on the line.

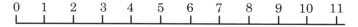

Figure 13.1   Numbers as points on a line

So, extending the number line in the other direction, as shown in Figure 13.2, some further symbols, those for negative numbers, are needed to label the points less than zero. We now have the set of numbers called the integers: {. . . , –5, –4, –3, –2, –1, 0, +1, +2, +3, +4, +5, . . .} going on for ever in both directions. Note that we would not normally write, for example, +4, for 'positive four', but would simply write 4, unless in the context it is particularly helpful to signal the distinction between the negative and the positive integers. Pupils can have fun generating the integers on a calculator. To produce the positive integers, just enter: +, 1, =, =, =, =, . . . and continue pressing the equals sign as many times as you wish. To produce the negative integers, just enter: –, 1, =, =, =, =, . . . The reader should be warned, however, that various calculators have different ways of displaying negative numbers.

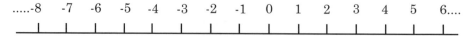

Figure 13.2   Extending the number line

The number line, either drawn left to right, as in Figures 13.1 and 13.2, or, preferably, drawn vertically with positive numbers going up and negative numbers going down, is the most straightforward image for us to associate with positive and negative integers. There are some other contexts that also help us to make sense of negative numbers especially.

The most familiar is probably the context of temperature. Quite young children can grasp the idea of the temperature falling below zero, associating this with feeling cold and icy roads, and are often familiar with the use of negative numbers to describe this. One small point about different uses of language should be made here. Mathematicians might prefer to refer to the integer, –5, as 'negative five' rather than 'minus five', using the word 'minus' as a synonym for the operation of subtraction. But weather forecasters tend to say that the temperature is falling to 'minus five degrees'. Similarly, they might refer to a positive temperature as 'plus five' rather than 'positive five'. However, these are not serious difficulties and temperature is still one of the best contexts for experiencing positive and negative numbers.

We can also associate positive and negative integers with levels in, say, a multistorey car park or department store, with, for example, 1 being the first floor, 0 being ground level, –1 being one floor below ground level, and –2 being two floors below ground level, and so on. We have a department store locally that has the buttons in the lift labelled in this way. Similarly, the specification of heights of locations above and below sea level provides another application for positive and negative numbers.

For some people the context of bank balances is one where negative numbers make real, if painful, sense. For example, being overdrawn by £5 at the bank can be represented by the negative number, –5.

Finally, in football league tables we find another application of positive and negative integers. If two teams have the same number of points, their order in the table is determined by their goal difference, which is 'the number of goals-for subtract the number of goals-against'. So, for example, a team with 28 goals-for and 23 goals-against has a goal difference of +5. But a team with 23 goals-for and 28 goals-against has a goal difference of –5. Many pupils find this a relevant and realistic context for experiencing the process of putting in order a set of positive and negative numbers.

How do you explain addition of positive and negative integers?

The difficulty in making sense of the ways in which we manipulate positive and negative integers is that we really need to use different images to support different operations. With addition, we need contexts and problems that help us to make sense of such calculations as:

1. $10 + (-2)$.
2. $2 + (-7)$.
3. $(-3) + 4$.
4. $(-5) + (-3)$.

Let's try bank balances. Interpret the addition as follows: the first number represents your starting balance, the second number represents either a credit (a positive number) or a debit (a negative number). So, with this interpretation, each of the examples (1) to (4) above can be seen as a mathematical model (see Chapter 3) for a real-life situation, as follows.

In example (1), we start with £10 and add a debit of £2: the result is a balance of £8. The corresponding mathematical model is: $10 + (-2) = 8$. In example (2), we start with a balance of £2 and add a debit of £7: the result is a balance of £5 overdrawn. The corresponding mathematical model is: $2 + (-7) = -5$. In example (3), we start with a balance of £3 overdrawn and add a credit of £4: the result is a balance of £1. The corresponding mathematical model is: $(-3) + 4 = 1$. Then, in example (4), we start with a balance of £5 overdrawn and add a debit of £3: the result is a balance of £8 overdrawn. The corresponding mathematical model is: $(-5) + (-3) = -8$.

We could also interpret these collections of symbols in the context of temperatures, with the first number being a starting temperature and the second being either a rise or a fall in temperature; or, on the number line, which, of course, is just like the scale on a thermometer, with the first number being the starting point and the second number a move in either the positive or the negative direction. The reader is invited to construct problems of this kind in self-assessment question 13.3 below.

What about subtraction? Why do 'two minuses make a plus'?

The key to making sense of subtraction with positive and negative integers is to get out of our heads the idea of subtraction meaning 'take away'. This structure only applies to positive numbers: you cannot 'take away' a negative number. The calculation $6 - (-3)$, for example, cannot model a problem about having a set of 6 things and 'taking away negative three things': the words here are just nonsense. We make sense of subtracting with negative numbers by drawing on situations that incorporate some of the other structures for subtraction, notably the comparison and the inverse-of-addition structures (see Chapter 4).

The kinds of calculations to which we need to give meaning through experience in context would include:

(a) $6 - (-3)$
(b) $(-3) - (-8)$
(c) $6 - 9$
(d) $(-3) - 4.$

Let's look at these in the context of temperatures. First we will think in terms of the comparison structure for subtraction. In this structure, the subtraction $a - b$ models a question of the form, 'How much greater is a than b?' Problems that incorporate the comparison structure for subtraction would require us therefore to find how much hotter is the first temperature than the second. So, in example (a), the problem might be to find how much higher is a temperature of 6 degrees indoors than a temperature of –3 degrees outdoors. Reference to the number line in Figure 13.3(a) makes it clear that the difference between the two temperatures is 9 degrees. The corresponding mathematical model is therefore: $6 - (-3) = 9$. Then in example (b) we might be comparing a temperature of –3 degrees in the morning with the overnight temperature of –8 degrees, deducing that the morning temperature is 5 degrees higher than the overnight. The corresponding mathematical model is therefore: $(-3) - (-8) = 5$.

This idea of comparison makes a lot of sense when we are using a subtraction to model a situation in which the first temperature is higher than the second. Personally, I would restrict primary-school pupils' experience of subtracting with negative numbers to problems of this kind,

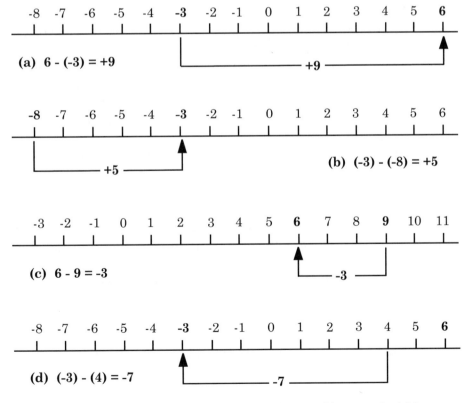

Figure 13.3   Subtractions interpreted as comparison and inverse-of-addition

namely comparing two temperatures, one or both of which might be negative, to find the difference. This will always correspond then to a subtraction in which the first number is the higher temperature.

In examples (c) and (d), as can be seen in Figure 13.3, the first temperature is *lower* than the second. Because of this the answers to the question, 'how much higher is the first temperature?', are negative numbers. This gets a bit confusing. So perhaps it is easier to relate these examples to problems with the inverse-of-addition structure. In this structure, the subtraction $a - b$ models a question of the form, 'What must be added to b to give a?' So, in the context of temperatures, we are asking what change in temperature takes us from the *second* temperature to the *first*. Note the order here. So, in example (a) in Figure 13.3, the +9 could represent a rise of 9 degrees which has to be added to a temperature of –3 degrees to produce a temperature of 6 degrees. In (b), the +5 could represent a rise of 5 degrees which has to be added to a temperature of –8 degrees to produce a temperature of –3 degrees. Example (c) then is related to the question: What change in temperature takes you from 9 degrees to 6 degrees? Clearly this is a fall of 3 degrees, represented by –3. The corresponding mathematical model is therefore: $6 - 9 = -3$. Finally, in example (d), the question is: What change in temperature takes you from 4 degrees to –3 degrees? Clearly this is a fall of 7 degrees, represented by –7. The corresponding mathematical model is therefore: $(-3) - (4) = -7$.

Alternatively, it would be possible to pose exactly corresponding problems, modelled by these same subtractions, with a starting and a finishing bank balance, and then asking what credit or debit has been added. The reader is invited to construct problems of this kind in self-assessment question 13.4 below.

I hope that these illustrations make it clear that we do not need a nonsense rule like, 'two minuses make a plus'. Apart from anything else, to be just a little pedantic, in a question such as $6 - (-3)$, the first '–' is a minus sign, indicating subtraction, and the second is a negative sign, indicating a negative number. If we simply interpret the subtraction as 'compare the first number with the second' or 'what must be added to the second to give the first?' and put these questions into contexts such as temperatures and bank balances, then there is some chance of actually understanding what is going on.

How do you put negative numbers on to a calculator?

Some calculators have a special key, usually labelled '+/–', which does this for you. To enter –78, for example, you press this key sequence: 78,

+/–. So to do a calculation such as, 184 – (–78), you could use this key sequence: 184, – , 78, +/–, =. Many basic calculators do not have this special key. But most of them do have a memory and a key labelled something like 'M–' that allows you to subtract a number from whatever is in the memory. This enables us very easily to put a number like –78 into the memory. First ensure the memory is clear (on my calculator I do this by pressing a key labelled MRC twice), then press: 78, M–. This subtracts 78 from the zero in the memory, to give –78. There is then a key on the calculator that enables you to recall what is in the memory. This is often the same key as the one that clears the memory, for example, the MRC key. So, to do a calculation such as, 184 – (–78), you might use this key sequence: MRC, MRC (to clear the memory), 78, M– (puts –78 in the memory), 184, –, MRC (recalls the –78 from the memory), =. The reader should try this on his or her own calculator: it is not nearly as complicated as it looks in print!

However, having explained all that, I should say that the context that gives rise to the problem will very often suggest that the actual calculation which you do makes no use of negative numbers whatsoever. For example, if the problem had been to find the difference in height between two points, one 184 metres above sea level and the other 78 metres below sea level, then the image formed in my mind by the context leads me simply to add 184 and 78.

My conclusion therefore is that we rarely need to use calculations with negative numbers to solve real-life problems; but we do need the real-life problems to help to explain the way we manipulate positive and negative numbers when we are doing abstract mathematical calculations!

Self-assessment questions

13.1: Which of these are integers: 6.8, 472, 0, –10, –5.5?

13.2: In a football league table, Arsenal, Blackburn and Chelsea all have the same number of points. Arsenal have 18 goals-for and 22 against, Blackburn have 32 for and 29 against, Chelsea have 25 for and 30 against. Work out the goal differences and put the teams in order in the table.

13.3: Make up situations about temperatures that are modelled by the additions: a) 4 + (–12); and b) (–6) + 10. Give the answers to the additions.

13.4: Give situations about bank balances that are modelled by the subtractions: a) 20 – (–5); b) (–10) – (–15); and c) (–10) – 20. Give the answers to the subtractions.

13.5: Find how to enter the integer, –42, on your calculator, in the middle of a calculation. Note how your calculator displays this integer.

13.6: Yesterday I was overdrawn at the bank by £187.85. Someone paid a cheque into my account and this morning I am £458.64 in credit. Model this situation with a subtraction. Use a calculator to find out how much the cheque was that was paid in.

Summary of teaching points

1. Use the number line and the ordinal aspect of number (numbers as labels for putting things in order) to introduce the concept of negative integers.
2. Use contexts such as temperatures, multistorey buildings, heights above and below sea level and bank balances to give meaning to positive and negative numbers.
3. Use problems with temperatures to explain additions with positive and negative integers: with the first number representing a starting point and the second a rise or fall.
4. To experience subtractions with positive and negative integers, use problems about the comparison of two temperatures, finding how much higher is one temperature than another, or the difference in temperature.
5. If necessary, extend this experience to situations with the inverse-of-addition structure, finding the change (up or down) from one temperature to another.
6. Use parallel examples about bank balances, credits and debits to provide further experience of the same structures as in 3, 4 and 5 above.
7. Do not talk about 'taking away' a negative number.
8. Make sure pupils know how to enter negative numbers on the basic calculators used in their school and that they know how they are displayed.

14

Fractions

Pupils should extend their understanding of the number system to include fractions. They should be taught to: understand fractions, locate them on a number line and use them to find fractions of shapes or quantities; understand simple equivalent fractions and simplify fractions by cancelling common factors; compare and order simple fractions by converting them to fractions with a common denominator, explaining their methods and reasoning.

In this chapter there are explanations of

- the different meanings of the fraction notation;
- some of the traditional language of fractions;
- the important idea of equivalent fractions;
- equivalent ratios and their use in scale drawings and maps;
- how to compare two simple fractions;
- how to add and subtract simple fractions;
- how to find a simple fraction of a quantity; and
- rational and irrational numbers.

I think of a fraction as representing a part of a whole. Is there any more to it than that?

Once again we encounter the special difficulty presented by mathematical symbols: that one symbol can represent a number of different kinds of situation in the real world. The mathematical notation used for a fraction might, in fact, be used in at least four different ways:

- To represent a part of a whole or a unit.
- To represent a part of a set.

- To model a division problem.
- As a ratio.

Consider, for example, the fraction three-eighths, which can be written either as $\frac{3}{8}$ or, more conveniently for word-processing, ⅜. The commonest interpretation of these symbols is illustrated by the diagrams in Figure 14.1. I find the most useful everyday examples are chocolate bars (rectangles) and pizzas (circles). One item (sometimes called the 'whole'), such as a bar of chocolate or a pizza, is somehow subdivided into eight equal sections, called 'eighths', and three of these, 'three-eighths', are then selected. Note that the word 'whole' does sound the same as 'hole'; this can be confusing for pupils in some situations. I recall one teacher tearing a sheet of paper into four quarters and then, in the course of her explanation, asking a child to show her 'the whole'; not surprisingly, the child kept pointing to the space in the middle. It's also not uncommon colloquially to hear someone talk about 'a whole half', as in 'I ate a whole half of a pizza'. Because of all this I prefer to talk about 'fractions of a unit', and to use the word 'whole' only as an adjective, for example, 'three-eighths of a whole pizza'.

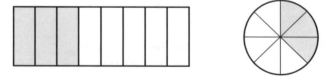

Figure 14.1   The shaded sections are three-eighths of the whole shape

This idea can then be extended to situations where a set of items is subdivided into eight equal subsets and three of these subsets are selected. For example, the set of 40 dots in Figure 14.2(a) has been subdivided into eight equal subsets (of 5 dots each) in Figure 14.2(b). The 15 dots selected in Figure 14.2(c) can therefore be described as three-eighths of the set of 40.

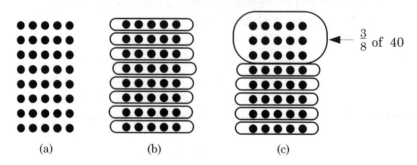

Figure 14.2   Three-eighths of a set of 40

But the fraction ⅜ can also be used to represent the division of 3 by 8. It might, for example, represent the result of sharing three bars of chocolate between eight people. Notice the marked difference here: in Figure 14.1, it was one bar of chocolate which was being subdivided; now we are talking about cutting up three bars. The actual process we would have to go through to solve this problem practically is not immediately obvious. One way of doing it is to lay the three bars side by side, as shown in Figure 14.3, and then to slice through all three bars simultaneously with a knife, cutting each bar into eight equal pieces. The pieces then form themselves nicely into eight equal portions. Figure 14.3 then shows that each of the eight people gets the equivalent of three-eighths of a whole bar of chocolate. (If you are doing this with pizzas you have to place them one on top of the other, rather than side by side, but otherwise the process is the same.) So what we see here is, first, that the symbols ⅜ can mean 'divide 3 units by 8' and, secondly, that the result of doing this division is 'three-eighths of a unit'. So the symbols ⅜ represent both an *instruction* to perform an operation and the *result* of performing it! We often need the idea that the fraction p/q means 'p divided by q' in order to handle fractions on a calculator. Simply by entering $p \div q$ we can express the fraction as a decimal.

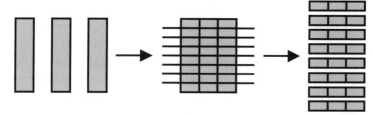

Figure 14.3   Three shared between eight

We have seen in Chapter 7 that one of the categories of problems modelled by division is where two quantities are compared by means of ratio. So, because the symbols ⅜ can mean 'three divided by eight', we can extend the meanings of the symbols to include 'the ratio of three to eight'. This is written sometimes as 3:8. For example, in Figure 14.4(a), when comparing the set of circles with the set of squares, we could say that 'the ratio of circles to squares is three to eight'. This means that for every three circles there are eight squares. Arranging the squares and circles as shown in Figure 14.4(b) shows this to be the case. The reason why we also use the fraction notation (⅜) to represent the ratio (3:8) is simply that another way of expressing the comparison between the two sets is to say that the number of circles is three-eighths of the number of squares.

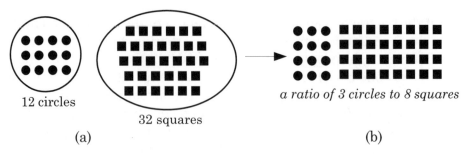

12 circles

32 squares

a ratio of 3 circles to 8 squares

(a)   (b)

Figure 14.4   A ratio of three to eight

What about numerators, denominators, vulgar fractions, proper and improper fractions, mixed numbers, and so on? Do I have to understand all these terms?

These are all important ideas associated with learning about fractions, but, in my view, it is quite acceptable to use more informal language to refer to them. For example, the *numerator* and the *denominator* are simply the top number and the bottom number in the fraction nota-tion. So, for example, in the fraction ⅜ the numerator is 3 and the denominator is 8. I prefer to call them simply the top number and the bottom number, but by all means use the technical terms if you wish! The phrase 'vulgar fraction', in which the word 'vulgar' actually means 'common' or 'ordinary', is certainly archaic. It was used to distinguish between the kinds of fractions discussed in this chapter, such as ⅜, written with a top number and a bottom number, and decimal fractions, such as 0.375, which are discussed in the next. (For those who are interested in the ways in which words shift their meaning, I have an arithmetic book dated 1886 in which the chapter on 'vulgar fractions' concludes with a set of 'promiscuous exercises'!)

The fraction notation for parts of a unit can also be used in a situation such as that shown in Figure 14.5, where there is more than one whole unit to be represented. Here there are, altogether, eleven-eighths of a pizza, written ¹¹⁄₈. Since eight of these make a whole pizza this quantity can be written as 1 + ⅜, which is normally abbreviated to 1⅜. This is sometimes called a *mixed number*. A fraction in which the top number is smaller than the bottom number, such as ⅜, is sometimes called a *proper fraction*, with a fraction such as ¹¹⁄₈ being referred to as an *improper fraction*. Proper fractions are therefore those that are less than 1, with improper fractions being those greater than or equal to 1. We could refer to the latter more informally as 'top-heavy fractions'.

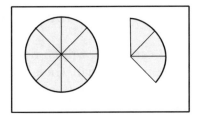

Figure 14.5   A fraction greater than 1

What is a rational number?

In Chapter 11, the term 'natural numbers' was introduced to describe the set of numbers that we use for counting: {1, 2, 3, 4, 5, 6, . . .}. In Chapter 13 we looked at the set of numbers that you get by extending this set to include negative numbers and zero: {. . ., –4, –3, –2, –1, 0, 1, 2, 3, 4, . . .}. This is referred to as the set of 'integers'. When we extend the set further to include fractions we get the set of *rational numbers*. The term *rational* derives from the idea that a fraction represents a *ratio*. The technical definition of a rational number is any number that is the ratio of two integers. In simple terms, this means all fractions, including decimal fractions, as well as all the integers themselves.

So, for example, ⅗ is a rational number because it is the ratio of 3 to 5, and 1.87 is a rational number because it is equal to ¹⁸⁷/₁₀₀, which is the ratio of 187 to 100. Here are some other rational numbers, showing how they can be expressed as ratios of integers:

¹⁴/₂₇ is a rational number. It is the ratio of 14 to 27.
2⅗ is a rational number. It is equal to ¹³/₅, which is the ratio of 13 to 5.
0.125 is a rational number. It is equal to ⅛, which is the ratio of 1 to 8.
12.5 is a rational number. It is equal to ²⁵/₂, which is the ratio of 25 to 2.
28 is a rational number. It is equal to ²⁸/₁, which is the ratio of 28 to 1.
–10 is a rational number. It is equal to ⁻¹⁰/₁, which is the ratio of –10 to 1.
0.6̇ (the recurring decimal 0.66666 . . .) is a rational number. It is equal to ⅔, which is the ratio of 2 to 3.

I should mention explicitly that all recurring decimals are actually rational numbers. Any recurring decimal can be obtained by dividing one integer by another integer. For example: 0.3̇ (0.333333 . . ., with the 3 recurring for ever) is 1 divided by 3; 0.2̇78̇ (i.e. 0.278278278 . . ., with the 278 recurring for ever) is obtained by dividing 278 by 999.

So, are there numbers that are not rational numbers?

There are real numbers that cannot be written down as exact fractions or decimals, and are therefore not rational. These are numbers like square roots or cube roots that do not work out exactly. For example, there is no decimal fraction that is exactly equal to $\sqrt{50}$. Using a calculator and the trial and improvement method explained in Chapter 12, we could conclude that the square root of 50 is somewhere between 7.07 and 7.08. If we went to further decimal places, we could decide that it lies somewhere between 7.0710678 and 7.0710679. But neither of these rational numbers is the square root of 50. Neither of them when multiplied by themselves would give 50 exactly: $(7.0710678)^2$ is just a bit less than 50 and $(7.0710679)^2$ is just a bit more than 50. And however many decimal places we went to we could never get a number that gave us 50 exactly when we squared it. But $\sqrt{50}$ is a real number! It represents a real length. For example, using Pythagoras's theorem (which is explained in Chapter 12), the length of the diagonal of a square of side 5 units would be $\sqrt{50}$ units. So this is a real length, but it is not a rational number. It is called an *irrational number*.

There are, of course, many numbers like this. All these square roots are irrational numbers, for example: $\sqrt{2}$, $\sqrt{3}$, $\sqrt{5}$, $\sqrt{6}$, $\sqrt{7}$, $\sqrt{8}$, $\sqrt{10}$, $\sqrt{11}$, $\sqrt{12}$, $\sqrt{13}$, $\sqrt{14}$, $\sqrt{15}$, $\sqrt{17}$, and so on. (Notice that $\sqrt{4}$, $\sqrt{9}$ and $\sqrt{16}$ are omitted from this list: they are rational numbers, since they work out exactly as 2, 3 and 4 respectively.)

And all these cube roots are irrational numbers: $\sqrt[3]{2}$, $\sqrt[3]{3}$, $\sqrt[3]{4}$, $\sqrt[3]{5}$, $\sqrt[3]{6}$, $\sqrt[3]{7}$, $\sqrt[3]{9}$, and so on. (Notice that $\sqrt[3]{8}$ is not included here, because it is exactly equal to 2 and is therefore rational.)

Another popular example of an irrational number – because it cannot be written exactly as a fraction or a decimal – is the number represented by the symbol π (pi: see Chapter 26).

Mathematicians call the set of all numbers that represent real lengths (which would include all rational and all irrational numbers) the set of *real numbers*. I know . . . you now want to ask me if there are any numbers that are not real numbers. If your appetite for number theory is really that insatiable, you will have to look elsewhere to find out how mathematicians use the idea of an *imaginary number* (like the square root of –1) to construct things called *complex numbers*.

What are equivalent fractions?

The concept of equivalence is one of the key ideas for pupils to grasp when working with fractions. Using the first idea of a fraction above, that it represents a part of a unit, it is immediately apparent from Figure 14.6, for example, that the fractions, three-quarters, six-eighths and nine-twelfths, all represent the same amount of chocolate bar. This kind of 'fraction chart' is an important teaching aid for explaining the idea of equivalence. Sequences of equivalent fractions follow a very straightforward pattern. For example, all these fractions are equivalent:

$$\tfrac{3}{5},\ \tfrac{6}{10},\ \tfrac{9}{15},\ \tfrac{12}{20},\ \tfrac{15}{25},\ \tfrac{18}{30},\ \tfrac{21}{35},\ \tfrac{24}{40},\ \text{and so on.}$$

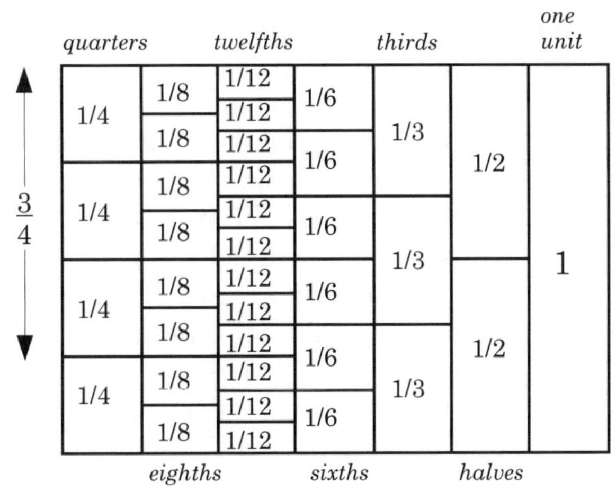

Figure 14.6   A fraction chart showing some equivalent fractions

The numbers on the top and bottom are simply the three-times and five-times tables, respectively. This means that, given a particular fraction, you can always generate an equivalent fraction by multiplying the top and the bottom by the same number; or, vice versa, by dividing by the same number. So, for example:

$\tfrac{4}{7}$ is equivalent to $\tfrac{36}{63}$ (multiplying top and bottom by 9); and
$\tfrac{40}{70}$ is equivalent to $\tfrac{4}{7}$ (dividing top and bottom by 10).

If we remember that the fraction notation can also be interpreted as meaning division of the top number by the bottom number, the principle above is another version of stating the constant ratio principle explained in Chapter 8: that you do not change the answer to a division calculation if you multiply or divide both numbers by the same thing. The same applies to ratios, of course: that if you multiply or divide two numbers by the same thing then the ratio stays the same.

This is an important method for simplifying fractions and ratios. For example, if I am comparing the price of two articles costing £28 and £32 by looking at the ratio of the prices, then the ratio 28:32 can be simplified to the ratio of 7:8 (dividing both numbers by 4). This means that one price is ⅞ (seven-eighths) of the other. Another example: if I am comparing a journey of 2.8 miles with one of 7 miles, then I could simplify the ratio, 2.8:7, by first multiplying both numbers by 10 (28:70) and then dividing both numbers by 14 (2:5), drawing the conclusion that one journey is ⅖ (two-fifths) of the other.

Often it is particularly useful to express a ratio as an equivalent ratio in which the first number is 1. For example, the ratio 2:5 used to compare the two journeys in the previous paragraph can be written as the equivalent ratio 1:2.5. This can then be interpreted as 'for every mile in the first journey you have to travel 2.5 miles in the second' or 'the second journey is 2.5 times longer than the first'. The commonest application of this kind of ratio is to scale-drawings and map scales. For example, if a scale drawing of the classroom represents a length of 2 metres by a length of 5 cm then the scale is the ratio of 5 cm to 2 metres, or, writing both lengths in centimetres, 5 cm to 200 cm. The ratio 5:200 can then be simplified to the equivalent ratio 1:40. This would be the conventional way of expressing the scale, indicating that each length in the original is 40 times the corresponding length in the scale drawing, or that each length in the scale drawing is ¹⁄₄₀ of the length of the original. Scale factors for maps are usually much larger than this, of course. For example, the Ordnance Survey Landranger maps of Great Britain use a scale of 1:50 000. This means that a distance of 1 cm on the map represents a distance of 50 000 cm in reality. Since 50 000 cm = 500 m = 0.5 km, then we conclude that each centimetre on the map represents ½ kilometre.

How do you compare one fraction with another?

The first point to notice here is that when you increase the bottom number of a fraction you actually make the fraction smaller, and vice versa. For example, ½ is greater than ⅓, which is greater than ¼, which is greater than ⅕, and so on. This is very obvious if the symbols are interpreted in concrete terms, as bits of pizzas or chocolate bars, for example. It is possible to get this wrong, of course, if you simply look at the numbers involved in the fraction notation without thinking about what they mean.

Then, second, there is no difficulty in comparing two fractions with the same bottom number. Clearly, five-eighths of a pizza (⅝) is more than three-eighths (⅜), for example.

Generally, to compare two fractions with *different* bottom numbers we may need to convert them to equivalent fractions with the *same* bottom number. This will have to be a common multiple of the two numbers. It might be (but does not have to be) the lowest common multiple (see Chapter 11). For example, which is greater, seven-tenths ($^7/_{10}$) of a chocolate bar or five-eighths ($^5/_8$)? The lowest common multiple of 10 and 8 is 40, so convert both fractions to fortieths:

$^7/_{10}$ is equivalent to $^{28}/_{40}$ (multiplying top and bottom by 4); and
$^5/_8$ is equivalent to $^{25}/_{40}$ (multiplying top and bottom by 5).

We can then see instantly that, provided you like chocolate, the seven-tenths is the better choice.

How do you add and subtract fractions?

To be honest I have to say that there are not many practical situations that genuinely require the addition or subtraction of fractions. In practice, most calculations, such as those arising from measurements, are done with decimals. Questions such as '$^1/_6$ of a class are 7 years of age and $^1/_2$ of the class are 8 years of age – what fraction of the class are 7 or 8 years of age?' do sound a bit contrived. However, just in case you find yourself in the situation where someone expects you to be able to do this kind of thing, here's how it's done.

To add or subtract two fractions: (a) change one or both of the fractions to equivalent fractions so that they finish up with the same bottom number – it's best to use the lowest common multiple for this; (b) add or subtract the top numbers; (c) if possible, cancel down to an equivalent fraction.

So to add $^1/_6$ and $^1/_2$, as in the example above, we would first change the $^1/_2$ to $^3/_6$, because 6 is the lowest common multiple of 6 and 2. Then we simply add up how many sixths there are all together ($1 + 3 = 4$) and finally cancel the $^4/_6$ to $^2/_3$.

$$^1/_6 + ^1/_2 = ^1/_6 + ^3/_6 = ^4/_6 = ^2/_3$$

Here's an example with subtraction: 'how much more is $^2/_3$ of a litre than $^1/_4$ of a litre? This time we change both fractions to twelfths, since 12 is the lowest common multiple of 3 and 4, to determine that the answer is $^5/_{12}$ of a litre:

$$^2/_3 - ^1/_4 = ^8/_{12} - ^3/_{12} = ^5/_{12}$$

What calculations with fractions do we have to do most often in everyday life?

The commonest everyday situations involving calculations with fractions are those where we have to calculate a simple fraction of a set or a quantity. For example, we might say, 'three-fifths of my class of 30 are boys'. If we see an article priced at £45 offered with one-third off, then the reduced price must be 'two-thirds of £45'. Or we might encounter fractions in measurements such as 'three-quarters of a litre' or 'two-fifths of a metre' and want to change these to millilitres and centimetres respectively. The process of doing these calculations is straightforward. For example, to find '⅗ of 30', first divide by the 5 to find one-fifth of 30, then multiply by the 3 to obtain three-fifths:

⅕ of 30 is 6, so ⅗ of 30 is 18.
⅓ of £45 is £15, so ⅔ of £45 is £30.
¼ of 1000 ml is 250 ml, so ¾ of 1000 ml (a litre) is 750 ml.
⅕ of 100 cm is 20 cm, so ⅖ of 100 cm (a metre) is 40 cm.

If the division and multiplication involved are difficult a calculator can be used. For example, if I am due to get three-sevenths of a legacy of £4500, then the calculation is performed on a calculator by entering: 4500, ÷ 7, × 3, =. The calculator display of 1928.5714 indicates that my entitlement is £1928.57. There is probably no need to go further than this in calculations with fractions in the primary school.

Self-assessment questions

14.1: Give examples where ⅘ represents: a) a part of a whole unit; b) a part of a set; c) a division using the idea of sharing; and d) a ratio.
14.2: Find as many different examples of equivalent fractions illustrated in the fraction chart in Figure 14.6 as you can.
14.3: Assuming you like pizzas, which would you prefer, three-fifths of a pizza (⅗) or five-eighths (⅝)? (Convert both fractions to fortieths.)
14.4: Put these fractions in order, from the smallest to the largest: (¾, ⅙, ⅓, ⅔, ⁵⁄₁₂).
14.5: Make up a problem about prices to which the answer is 'the price of A is three-fifths (⅗) of the price of B'.
14.6: Walking to work takes me 24 minutes, cycling takes me 9 minutes. Complete this sentence with an appropriate fraction: 'The time it takes to cycle is . . . of the time it takes to walk.'

14.7: Find: a) three-fifths of £100, without using a calculator; and b) five-eighths of £2500, using a calculator.

14.8: Which of these are rational numbers: (0.45, 23, ⅕, –10, √10)?

14.9: Which of these are irrational numbers: (√49, √20, ³√9, ³√27)?

Summary of teaching points

1. Introduce fraction notation as meaning a number of equal parts of a unit, making particular use of pizzas (circles) and chocolate bars (rectangles) in the explanation. In this interpretation, the fraction p/q means 'divide the unit into q equal parts and take p of these parts'.

2. When explaining fractions, be careful about using 'the whole' as a noun: try to use it only as an adjective, for example, 'a whole pizza'.

3. Extend the idea of a fraction as representing a number of equal parts of a unit to meaning a number of equal parts of a set, for example, two-thirds of a set of 12.

4. It is quite acceptable to use informal language such as top number, bottom number and top-heavy fraction, alongside formal language such as numerator, denominator and improper fraction.

5. Emphasize very strongly the idea of equivalent fractions. Children should make fraction charts like Figure 14.6 and find various examples of equivalent fractions.

6. Help children to see the pattern in sequences of equivalent fractions and use this to establish the idea that you can change one fraction into an equivalent fraction by multiplying (or dividing) the top and bottom numbers by the same thing.

7. Using simple examples with sharing pizzas and chocolate bars, establish the idea that p/q can also mean 'p divided by q'. For example, 'three pizzas shared between four people' is '3 divided by 4' and this results in ¾ of a pizza each.

8. Introduce children to the use of fractions to compare one quantity with another (i.e. finding the ratio) especially in the context of prices. For example, we can compare two prices of £9 and £12 by stating that one is three-quarters of the other.

9. Explain to children, with concrete illustrations, why making the bottom number larger makes the fraction smaller, and vice versa.

10. Introduce the procedure for finding which is the larger or which the smaller of two fractions, by changing them to equivalent fractions with the same bottom number.

11. Explain to children the procedure for finding a fraction of a quantity, by dividing by the bottom number and then multiplying by the top

number, applying this procedure to a range of everyday, practical contexts, and using a calculator where necessary.

12. There is more than enough involved in the important ideas associated with fractions listed above to introduce to primary-school children. There is no need to go any further into more complex calculations with fractions, such as multiplication and division of fractions.

15

Calculations with Decimals

Pupils should be taught to: add and subtract numbers involving decimals; multiply and divide decimals by 10 or 100; use written methods for short multiplication and division of numbers with decimals; recognize the equivalence between the decimal and fraction forms of one half, quarters, tenths, hundredths; use approximations and other strategies to check that answers are reasonable; know how to enter and interpret fractions on a calculator.

In this chapter there are explanations of

- the procedures for addition and subtraction with decimal numbers;
- the contexts that might give rise to the need for calculations with decimals;
- multiplication and division of a decimal number by an integer, in real-life contexts;
- the results of repeatedly multiplying or dividing decimal numbers by 10;
- how to deal with multiplication of two decimals;
- some simple examples of division involving decimals; and
- converting fractions to decimals and vice versa; and
- scientific notation.

Is there anything different about the procedures for addition and subtraction with decimals from those with whole numbers?

The procedures are effectively the same. Difficulties would arise only if you were to forget about the principles of place value outlined in Chapter 2. Provided you remember which digits are units, tens and hundreds, or tenths, hundredths, and so on, then the algorithms (and adhocorithms) employed for whole numbers (see Chapters 5 and 6)

149

work in an identical fashion for decimals, with the principle that 'one of these can be exchanged for ten of these' guiding the whole process. A useful tip with decimals, however, is to ensure that the two numbers in an addition or a subtraction have the same number of digits after the decimal point. If one has fewer digits than the other then fill up the empty places with zeros, acting as 'place-holders' (see Chapter 2). So, for example, 1.45 + 1.8 would be written as 1.45 + 1.80, 1.5 – 1.28 would be written as 1.50 – 1.28 and 10 – 4.25 would be written as 10.00 – 4.25. This makes the standard algorithms for addition and subtraction look just the same as when working with whole numbers, but with the decimal points in the two numbers lined up, one above the other, as shown in Figure 15.1.

```
    2.86        1.45        1.50       10.00
  + 4.04      + 1.80      - 1.28      -  4.25
  _____      _____      _____      _____

    (a)         (b)         (c)         (d)
```

Figure 15.1   Additions and subtractions with decimals

In practice, additions and subtractions like these with decimals would usually be employed to model real-life situations related to money or measurement. In Chapter 2, I discussed the convention of putting two digits after the decimal point when recording money in pounds. We saw also that when dealing with measurements of length in centimetres and metres, with a hundred centimetres in a metre, it is often a good idea to adopt the same convention, for example, writing 180 cm as 1.80 m, rather than 1.8 m. Similarly, when handling liquid volume and capacity, where we have 1000 millilitres in a litre, or mass, where we have 1000 grams in a kilogram, the convention would often be to write measurements in litres or kilograms with three digits after the point. This means that, if this convention is followed, the decimal numbers will arrive for the calculation already written in the required form, that is with each of the two numbers in the addition or subtraction having the same number of digits after the point, with zeros used to fill up empty places.

For example, the four calculations shown in Figure 15.1 might correspond to the following real-life situations:

(a) Find the total cost of two articles, costing £2.86 and £4.04 respectively.

(b) Find the total length of wall space taken up by a cupboard that is 1.45 m wide and a bookshelf that is 1.80 m wide.

(c) What is the difference in height between a girl who is 1.50 m tall and a boy who is 1.28 m tall?

(d) What is the change from a ten-pound note (£10.00) if you spend £4.25?

What about multiplications and divisions involving decimals?

I will discuss first the multiplication of a decimal number by a whole number. Once again, the key point is to think about the practical contexts that would give rise to the need to do multiplications of this kind. In the context of money we might need to find the cost of a number of articles at a given price. For example, find the cost of 12 rolls of sticky tape at £1.35 per roll. This problem in the real world is modelled by the multiplication, 1.35 × 12. On a calculator, we enter 1.35, ×, 12, =, read off the mathematical solution (16.2) and then interpret this as a total cost of £16.20.

But there is some potential to get in a muddle with the decimal point when doing this kind of calculation by non-calculator methods. So a useful tip is: if you can, avoid multiplying the decimal numbers altogether! In the example above this is easily achieved, simply by rephrasing the situation as 12 rolls at 135p per roll, hence writing the cost in pence rather than in pounds. We then multiply 135 by 12, by whatever methods we prefer (see Chapters 8 and 9), to get the answer 1620, interpret this as 1620p and, finally, write the answer as £16.20.

Almost all the multiplications involving decimals we have to do in practice can be tackled like this. Here's another example: find the length of wall space required to display eight posters each 1.19 m wide. Rather than tackle 1.19 × 8, rewrite the length as 119 cm, calculate 119 × 8 and convert the result (952 cm) back to metres (9.52 m).

The same principle applies when dividing a decimal number by a whole number. The context from which the calculation has arisen will suggest a way of handling it without the use of decimals. For example, a calculation such as 3.45 ÷ 3 could have arisen from a problem about sharing £3.45 between 3 people. We can simply rewrite this as the problem of sharing 345p between 3 people and deal with it by whatever division process is appropriate (see Chapters 8 and 9), concluding that each person gets 115p each. The final step is to put this back into pounds notation, as £1.15.

How do you explain the business about moving the decimal point when you multiply and divide by 10 or 100 and so on?

On a basic calculator, enter the following key sequence and watch carefully the display: 10, ×, 1.2345678, =, =, =, =, =, =, =. This procedure is making use of the constant facility, which is built into most basic calculators, to multiply repeatedly by 10. The results are shown in Figure 15.2(a). It certainly looks on the calculator as though the decimal point is gradually moving along one place at a time to the right. Now, without clearing your calculator, enter: ÷, 10, =, =, =, =, =, =, =. This procedure is repeatedly dividing by 10, thus undoing the effect of multiplying by 10 and sending the decimal point back to where it started, one place at a time. Because of this phenomenon we tend to think of the effect of multiplying a decimal number by 10 to be to move the decimal point one place to the right, and the effect of dividing by 10 to be to move the decimal point one place to the left. Since multiplying (dividing) by 100 is equivalent to multiplying (dividing) by 10 and by 10 again, this results in the point moving two places. Similarly multiplying or dividing by 1000 will shift it three places, and so on, for other powers of 10.

However, to understand this phenomenon rather than just observing it, it is more helpful to suggest that it is not the decimal point that is moving, but the digits. This is shown by the results displayed on the basis of place value, as shown in Figure 15.2(b). Each time we multiply by 10 the digits all move one place to the left. The decimal point stays where it is! To understand why this happens, trace the progress of one of the digits, for example the 3. In the original number it represents

(a) Results as displayed on a calculator	(b) Results displayed on the basis of place value
1.2345678	1.2345678
12.345678	12.345678
123.45678	123.45678
1234.5678	1234.5678
12345.678	12345.678
123456.78	123456.78
1234567.8	1234567.8
12345678.	12345678

Figure 15.2   The results of repeatedly multiplying by 10

3 hundredths. When we multiply the number by 10, each hundredth becomes a tenth, because ten hundredths can be exchanged for a tenth. This is, once again, the principle that 'ten of these can be exchanged for one of these', as we move right to left. So the 3 hundredths become 3 tenths and the digit 3 moves from the hundredths position to the tenths position. Next time we multiply by 10, these 3 tenths become three whole units, and the 3 shifts to the units position. Next time we multiply by 10, these 3 units become 3 tens, and so on. Because the principle that 'ten of these can be exchanged for one of these' as you move from right to left applies to any position, each digit moves one place to the left every time we multiply by 10. Since dividing by 10 is the inverse of multiplying by 10 (in other words, one operation undoes the effect of the other), clearly the effect of dividing by 10 is to move each digit one place to the right.

How does all this help when you have to multiply together two decimal numbers?

Imagine we want to find the area in square metres of a rectangular lawn, 3.45 m wide and 4.50 m long. The calculation required is: 3.45×4.50. For multiplications there is no particular value in carrying around surplus zeros, so we can rewrite the 4.50 as 4.5, giving us this calculation to complete: 3.45×4.5. This is a pretty difficult calculation. In practice, most people would sensibly do this on a calculator and read off the answer as 15.525 square metres. But it will be instructive to look at how to tackle it without a calculator. There are three steps involved:

1. Get rid of the decimals by multiplying each number by 10 as many times as necessary.
2. Multiply together the two integers.
3. Divide the result by 10 as many times in total as you multiplied by 10 in step 1.

So the first step is to get rid of the decimals altogether, using our knowledge of multiplying decimals repeatedly by 10, as follows:

$$3.45 \times 10 \times 10 = 345$$
$$4.5 \ \ \times 10 = 45$$

Hence, by doing '$\times$ 10' *three* times in total we have changed the multiplication into 345×45, a straightforward calculation with integers. The second step is to work this out, using whatever method is preferred (see

Chapters 8 and 9), to get the result 15 525. Finally, we simply undo the effect of multiplying by 10 three times, by dividing by 10 three times, shifting the digits three places to the right and producing the required result, 15.525.

To be honest, you don't really have to think in terms of multiplying and dividing by 10 like this, when doing an actual calculation, although you will probably not understand what you are doing without the explanation above. We can simply notice that the total number of times we have to multiply by 10 is determined by the total number of digits after the decimal points in the numbers we are multiplying. For example, in 3.45 × 4.5, there are two digits after the point in the first number and one in the second, giving a total of three: so we have to apply '× 10' three times in total to produce a multiplication of whole numbers. Then, when we apply '÷ 10' three times to our whole-number result, the effect is to shift three digits to positions after the decimal point. The upshot is that the total number of digits after the decimal points in the two numbers being multiplied is the same as the number of digits after the decimal point in the answer! So our procedure can be rewritten as follows:

1. Count the total number of digits after the decimal points in the numbers being multiplied.
2. Remove the decimal points from the two numbers and multiply them as though they were integers.
3. Put the decimal point back in the answer, ensuring that the number of digits after the point is the same as the total found in step 1.

For example:

1. Calculate 0.04 × 3.6 (three digits in total after the decimal points).
2. 4 × 36 = 144 (dropping the decimal points altogether).
3. 0.04 × 3.6 = 0.144 (with three digits after the decimal point).

Using this principle, Figure 15.3 shows how a whole collection of results can be deduced from one multiplication result with integers, using as examples: a) 4 × 36 = 144; and b) 5 × 44 = 220, to show that the procedure works just the same when there is a zero in the result. At an appropriate stage in the development of their work with decimals it can be instructive for pupils to use a calculator to compile various tables of this kind and to discuss the patterns which emerge.

Finally, in this section, we should remember when possible to check the reasonableness of our answers by using approximations. For example, 3.45 × 4.5 should give us an answer fairly close to 3 × 5 = 15. So the answer of 15.525 looks reasonable, whereas an answer of 1.5525 or 155.25 would suggest we had made an error with the decimal point.

×	36	3.6	0.36	0.036
4	144	14.4	1.44	0.144
0.4	14.4	1.44	0.144	0.0144
0.04	1.44	0.144	0.0144	0.00144
0.004	0.144	0.0144	0.00144	0.000144

×	44	4.4	0.44	0.044
5	220	22	2.2	0.22
0.5	22	2.2	0.22	0.022
0.05	2.2	0.22	0.022	0.0022
0.005	0.22	0.022	0.0022	0.00022

Figure 15.3 Multiplication tables for decimal numbers derived from (a) 4 × 36 = 144; and (b) 5 × 44 = 220

And what about dividing a decimal by a decimal?

Like the previous section, this is an area where the teacher's own level of skills should perhaps be noticeably higher than those they have to teach to their pupils, at least so that they can recognize quickly when pupils have made errors in using their calculators! I have four suggestions here for handling divisions by decimals:

1. In measuring contexts you can often work with whole numbers by changing the units appropriately.
2. You can often transform a division question involving decimals into a much easier equivalent calculation by multiplying both numbers by 10 or 100 or 1000.
3. You can always start from a simpler example involving the same digits and work your way gradually to the required result by multiplying and dividing by 10s.
4. Remember to check whether the answers are reasonable by using approximation.

The need to divide a decimal number by a decimal number might occur in a real-life situation with the inverse-of-multiplication division structure (see Chapter 7). This could be, for example, in the contexts of money or measurement. My first suggestion then is that in these cases we can usually recast the problem in units that dispense with the need for decimals altogether. For example, to find how many payments of £3.25 we need to make to reach a target of £52 (£52.00), we might at first be inclined to model the problem with the division, 52.00 ÷ 3.25. This would be straightforward if using a calculator. However, without a calculator we might get in a muddle with the decimal points. So what we could do is to rewrite the problem in pence, which gets rid of the decimal points altogether: how many payments of 325p do we need to reach 5200p? The calculation is now $5200 \div 325$, which can then be done by whatever method is appropriate. Similarly, to find how many portions of 0.125 litres we can pour from a 2.5-litre container, we could model the problem with the division, $2.500 \div 0.125$. But it's much less daunting if we change the measurements to millilitres, so that the calculation becomes $2500 \div 125$, with no decimals involved at all.

In fact, what we are doing here, in changing, for example, $52.00 \div 3.25$ into $5200 \div 325$, is multiplying both numbers by 100. This is using the principle established in Chapter 8, that you do not change the result of a division calculation if you multiply both numbers by the same thing. This is my second suggestion: that we can often use this principle when we have to divide by a decimal number.

For example, to find $4 \div 0.8$, simply multiply both numbers by 10, to get the equivalent calculation $40 \div 8$: so the answer is 5. Similarly, to find $2.4 \div 0.08$, multiply both numbers by 100, to get the equivalent calculation $240 \div 8$: so the answer is 30.

I find that an innocent-looking calculation like $0.46 \div 20$ can cause considerable confusion amongst students. Using the method suggested above, multiplying both numbers by 100 changes the question into the equivalent calculation $46 \div 2000$. But how do you deal with this? This is where my third suggestion comes to the rescue.

I will first make one observation about division: the smaller the divisor, the larger the answer (the quotient). Notice the pattern in the results obtained when, for example, 10 is divided by 2, 0.2, 0.02, 0.002, and so on:

$$
\begin{array}{lll}
10 \div 2 & = & 5 \\
10 \div 0.2 & = & 50 \\
10 \div 0.02 & = & 500 \\
10 \div 0.002 & = & 5000 \\
10 \div 0.0002 & = & 50\,000, \text{ etc.}
\end{array}
$$

Each time the divisor gets 10 times smaller the quotient gets 10 times bigger. This is such a significant property of division – which for some reason often surprises people – that it is worth drawing specific attention to it from time to time. It's easy enough to make sense of this property if you think of $A \div B$ as meaning 'how many Bs make A?' Is it not obvious that the smaller the number B, the greater the number of Bs that you can get from A?

And, of course, the reverse is true: the larger the divisor the smaller the answer. So we could construct a similar pattern for dividing 10 successively by 2, 20, 200, 2000, and so on:

$$
\begin{aligned}
10 \div 2 &= 5 \\
10 \div 20 &= 0.5 \\
10 \div 200 &= 0.05 \\
10 \div 2000 &= 0.005, \text{ etc.}
\end{aligned}
$$

Each time the divisor gets 10 times larger the answer gets 10 times smaller; in other words, it is divided by 10. So my third suggestion is that we can use these principles to handle a division like the $46 \div 2000$ above. Start with what you can do . . . $46 \div 2 = 23$. Then work step by step to the required calculation: $46 \div 20 = 2.3$, $46 \div 200 = 0.23$, $46 \div 2000 = 0.023$. Of course, you will not need to write all this down; it will be a mental process.

Here's another example: to calculate $0.05 \div 25$.
$0.05 \div 25$ is equivalent to $5 \div 2500$ (multiplying both numbers by 100).
$5 \div 2500$ is tricky, but I can manage $5 \div 2.5$ and then work gradually to
$$5 \div 2500.$$

$$
\begin{aligned}
5 \div 2.5 &= 2 \\
5 \div 25 &= 0.2 \\
5 \div 250 &= 0.02 \\
5 \div 2500 &= 0.002, \text{ so } 0.05 \div 25 = 0.002.
\end{aligned}
$$

Note: each time the divisor is multiplied by 10 (2.5, 25, 250, 2500) the quotient is divided by 10 (2, 0.2, 0.02, 0.002).

My final suggestion is to remember to check the reasonableness of the answers when possible by using approximations. For example, in working out how many payments of £3.25 are needed to reach £52 above we should expect the answer to be somewhere between 10 and 20, since £3 $\times$ 10 = £30 and £3 $\times$ 20 = £60. So if we get the answer to be 160 or 1.6 rather than 16 we've obviously made a mistake with the decimal point. Similarly, for the calculation $4 \div 0.8$, we would expect the answer to be fairly close to $4 \div 1$, which is 4. (In fact it should be greater than this, because the divisor is less than 1.) So, we are not surprised to get the answer 5. However, an answer of 0.5 or 50 would suggest again that we had made an error with the decimal point.

How do you change fractions into decimals, and vice versa?

Fractions such as tenths, hundredths and thousandths, where the de-nominator (the bottom number) is a power of ten, can be written dir-ectly as decimals. Here are some examples to show how this works:

$\frac{3}{10}$ = 0.3   (0.3 means 3 tenths)
$\frac{23}{10}$ = 2.3   (the 20 tenths make 2 whole units)
$\frac{3}{100}$ = 0.03   (0.03 means 3 hundredths)
$\frac{23}{100}$ = 0.23   (the 20 hundredths make 2 tenths)
$\frac{123}{100}$ = 1.23   (the 100 hundredths make 1 whole unit)
$\frac{3}{1000}$ = 0.003   (0.003 means 3 thousandths)
$\frac{23}{1000}$ = 0.023   (the 20 thousandths make 2 hundredths).

Then there are those fractions that we can readily change into an equivalent fraction (see Chapter 14) with a denominator of 10, 100 or 1000. For example, $\frac{1}{5}$ is equivalent to $\frac{2}{10}$ (multiplying top and bottom by 2), which, of course is written as a decimal fraction as 0.2. Similarly, $\frac{3}{25}$ is equivalent to $\frac{12}{100}$ (multiplying top and bottom by 4), which then becomes 0.12. Here are some further examples, many of which should be memorized:

$\frac{1}{2}$	is equivalent to	$\frac{5}{10}$	which as a decimal is 0.5
$\frac{4}{5}$	is equivalent to	$\frac{8}{10}$	which as a decimal is 0.8
$\frac{1}{4}$	is equivalent to	$\frac{25}{100}$	which as a decimal is 0.25
$\frac{3}{4}$	is equivalent to	$\frac{75}{100}$	which as a decimal is 0.75
$\frac{1}{20}$	is equivalent to	$\frac{5}{100}$	which as a decimal is 0.05
$\frac{7}{20}$	is equivalent to	$\frac{35}{100}$	which as a decimal is 0.35
$\frac{1}{50}$	is equivalent to	$\frac{2}{100}$	which as a decimal is 0.02
$\frac{3}{50}$	is equivalent to	$\frac{6}{100}$	which as a decimal is 0.06
$\frac{1}{25}$	is equivalent to	$\frac{4}{100}$	which as a decimal is 0.04.

Otherwise, to change a fraction into an equivalent decimal, recall that one of the meanings of the fraction notation is division (see Chapter 14). So all you have to do is to divide the top number by the bottom number, preferably using a calculator. Sometimes the result obtained will be an exact decimal, but often it will be a recurring decimal that has been truncated by the calculator (see Chapter 3).

The reverse process is to change a decimal into a fraction. First we recall that the decimal 0.3 means 'three-tenths', so it is clearly equivalent to the fraction ³⁄₁₀. Likewise, 0.07 means 'seven-hundredths' and is equivalent to the fraction ⁷⁄₁₀₀. Then to deal with, say, 0.37 (3 tenths and 7 hundredths), we have to recognize that the 3 tenths can be exchanged for 30 hundredths, which, together with the 7 hundredths, makes a total of 37 hundredths, which is the fraction ³⁷⁄₁₀₀. The only slight variation in all this is that sometimes the fraction obtained can be changed to an equivalent, simpler fraction, by dividing top and bottom numbers by the same number. Here are a few examples:

0.6 becomes ⁶⁄₁₀ which is equivalent to ³⁄₅
(dividing top and bottom by 2)

0.04 becomes ⁴⁄₁₀₀ which is equivalent to ¹⁄₂₅
(dividing top and bottom by 4)

0.45 becomes ⁴⁵⁄₁₀₀ which is equivalent to ⁹⁄₂₀
(dividing top and bottom by 5)

0.44 becomes ⁴⁴⁄₁₀₀ which is equivalent to ¹¹⁄₂₅
(dividing top and bottom by 4).

What is scientific notation?

The place value system is a very powerful and concise way of representing numbers, but it can be difficult to appreciate at a glance the values of very large (and very small) numbers. To help us in this there is a convention of separating the digits in very large numbers into groups of three, usually with a space. For example, the number 'twenty-three million, six hundred and forty-eight thousand and twenty-six' is correctly written as 23 648 026. Sometimes we might use commas to separate the groups of three digits, but this is no longer the accepted convention, partly because some countries use the comma to represent the decimal point.

Scientific notation (also called 'standard form') is a more sophisticated and very neat way of representing large numbers. Here's how it works.

Take, as an example, the number 37 600 000. To put this into scientific notation we first put the decimal point immediately after the first digit, reading from left to right. This gives us 3.76 (dropping the superfluous zeros, which are no longer needed as place-holders). We then indicate how many times we have to multiply this by 10 to get it back to the original number. In this case this is 7 times, because the decimal point has moved 7 places. So our number is written as 3.76×10^7, meaning 3.76 multiplied by 10 seven times. Here are some other examples of large numbers written in scientific notation:

$$5600 = 5.6 \times 10^3$$
$$6\,102\,000 = 6.102 \times 10^6$$
$$400\,000\,000\,000\,000 = 4 \times 10^{14} \text{ (see self-assessment question 11.11)}$$

Scientific notation can also be used to represent very small numbers. For example, the number 0.000003 would be written 3×10^{-6}. The negative power of 10 indicates how many times the 3 has to be *divided* by 10 to get the given number. Here are some other examples:

$$0.00056 \quad = 5.6 \times 10^{-4}$$
$$0.000001 \quad = 1 \times 10^{-6}$$
$$0.000000801 = 8.01 \times 10^{-7}$$

Scientific notation enables you quickly to compare the sizes of large or small numbers, because the most significant part of the number is the power of ten. So, for example, I can spot at a glance that 1.2×10^8 is greater than 9.8×10^7; and that 1.8×10^{-6} is greater than 8.9×10^{-7}. This notation would not usually be introduced in a primary school, but it is included here because primary teachers may need to understand the notation when accessing statistical or scientific data involving large or small numbers.

Self-assessment questions

15.1: Complete the solution of the problems (a), (b), (c) and (d) modelled by the additions and subtractions in Figure 15.1.

15.2: Remembering that there are 1000 millilitres in a litre and 1000 grams in a kilogram, suggest real-life questions which would be modelled by: a) 1.500 – 0.125, in the context of liquid volume and capacity; and b) 1.120 + 2.500, in the context of weighing. Answer your questions without using a calculator.

15.3: Pose a problem in the context of money that is modelled by 3.99×4. Solve your problem without using a calculator.

15.4: Pose a problem in the context of length that might be modelled by $4.40 \div 8$. Solve your problem without using a calculator.

15.5: Given that $4 \times 46 = 184$, find: a) 4×4.6; b) 0.4×46; c) 0.04×0.046.

15.6: Given that $4 \times 45 = 180$, find: a) 4×4.5; b) 0.4×45; and c) 0.04×0.045.

15.7: What is the value of $(0.01)^2$? State a question about area that might be modelled by this calculation.

15.8: Find: a) $2 \div 0.5$ (hint: multiply both numbers by 10); b) $5.5 \div 0.11$ (hint: multiply both numbers by 100).

15.9: You know that $2 \div 4 = 0.5$, so what is: a) $2 \div 0.04$? b) $2 \div 4000$? c) $0.02 \div 4$?

15.10: Express these fractions as equivalent decimals: a) $^{17}\!/_{100}$; b) $^3\!/_5$; c) $^7\!/_{20}$; d) $^2\!/_3$ (use a calculator); and e) $^1\!/_7$ (use a calculator).

15.11: Express these decimals as fractions: a) 0.09; b) 0.79; and c) 0.15.

15.12: The populations of three states are given as 2.4×10^5, 1.2×10^6, and 9.8×10^5. Put these in order of size from largest to smallest.

15.13: Use approximations to spot the errors that have been made in placing the decimal points in the answers to the following calculations: a) $2.8 \times 0.95 = 0.266$; b) $12.05 \times 0.08 = 9.64$; c) $27.9 \div 0.9 = 3.1$.

Summary of teaching points

1. Try to locate calculations with decimals in realistic contexts where the decimals represent money or measurements.
2. Emphasize the importance of having the same number of digits after the decimal point when adding or subtracting money or measurements written in decimal notation. Explain to children about putting in extra zeros as place-holders where necessary.
3. Show how the principle of 'one of these can be exchanged for ten of these' works when adding or subtracting with decimals in the same way as when working with integers.
4. Realistic multiplication and division problems with decimals involving money or measurements can often be recast into calculations with whole numbers by changing the units (for example, pounds to pence, metres to centimetres). Teach children how to do this.
5. Base your explanation of multiplication and division of decimal numbers by 10 (and 100 and 1000) on the principle of place value. Talk about the digits moving, rather than the decimal point.
6. Allow pupils to explore repeated multiplications and divisions by 10 with a calculator, making use of the constant facility.
7. Not many primary pupils will get on to multiplying two decimal numbers together by non-calculator methods. For those who do, show how this can be done by getting rid of the decimal point and putting it back after the multiplication has been done. Explain the procedure in terms of multiplying repeatedly by 10, but teach them the trick of counting the digits after the points as well.

8. Show the more able pupils how to simplify divisions with decimals by multiplying both numbers by 10, 100, 1000, and so on, as appropriate.

9. Emphasize the principle that the smaller the number you divide by, the larger the answer, and let pupils explore this with sequences of divisions on a calculator.

10. Remember that in practice most people do calculations with decimals with a calculator, so be reasonable in the demands put upon pupils for non-calculator methods.

11. Emphasize the importance of checking the reasonableness of an answer to a calculation by using approximations.

12. Pupils should explore equivalences between fractions and decimals, using calculators where necessary.

13. Encourage pupils to learn by heart some of the common equivalences, such as $\frac{1}{2} = 0.5$, $\frac{1}{4} = 0.25$, $\frac{3}{4} = 0.75$, $\frac{1}{5} = 0.2$, $\frac{2}{5} = 0.4$.

16

Proportions and Percentages

Pupils should be taught to: solve simple problems involving ratio and direct proportion; understand that 'percentage' means 'the number of parts per 100' and that it can be used for comparisons; find percentages of whole number quantities, using a calculator where appropriate; recognize approximate proportions of a whole and use simple fractions and percentages to describe them, explaining their methods and reasoning.

In this chapter there are explanations of

- how to solve simple proportion problems;
- the meaning of the term *per cent*;
- the use of percentages to express proportions of a quantity or of a set;
- *ad hoc* and calculator methods for evaluating percentages;
- the usefulness of percentages for comparing proportions;
- equivalences between fractions, decimals and percentages;
- the meaning of percentages greater than 100; and
- how to calculate a percentage of a given quantity or number, using *ad hoc* and calculator methods.

How do you solve proportion problems?

Consider the following five problems, all of which have exactly the same mathematical structure:

1. A recipe for 6 people requires 12 eggs. Adapt it for 8 people.
2. A recipe for 6 people requires 4 eggs. Adapt it for 9 people.
3. A recipe for 6 people requires 120 g of flour. Adapt it for 7 people.
4. A recipe for 8 people requires 500 g of flour. Adapt it for 6 people.
5. A recipe for 6 people requires 140 g of flour. Adapt it for 14 people.

163

These have the classic structure of a problem of direct proportion. Such a problem involves four numbers, three of which are known and one of which is to be found. The structure can be represented by the four-cell diagram shown in Figure 16.1, in which it is assumed that the three numbers *w*, *x* and *y* are known and the fourth number *z* is to be found.

Variable A   Variable B

w	*x*
y	*z* ?

Figure 16.1   The structure of a problem of direct proportion

The problems always involve two 'variables', which I have called variable *A* and variable *B* in Figure 16.1. For example, in problem (1) above, variable *A* would be the number of people and variable *B* would be the number of eggs. The numbers *w* and *y* are values of variable *A*, and the numbers *x* and *z* are values of variable *B*. So, for example, in problem (1) above *w* = 6 and *y* = 8, *x* = 12 and *z* is to be found. (See Figure 16.2(a).) In situations like the recipe problems above we say that the two variables

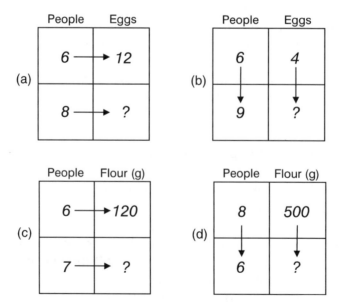

Figure 16.2   Solving the recipe problems

are 'in direct proportion', meaning that the ratio of variable A to var B (for example, the ratio of people to eggs) is always the same. 1. means that the ratio $w:x$ must be equal to the ratio $y:z$. It is also true that the ratio $w:y$ is equal to the ratio $x:z$. As a consequence, when it comes to solving problems of this kind you can work with either the left-to-right ratios or the top-to-bottom ratios, depending on the numbers involved. It is important to note therefore that the most efficient way of solving one of these problems will be determined by the numbers involved, as is illustrated in Figure 16.2(a), (b), (c) and (d).

Recipe problem (1) (Figure 16.2a)
Here I am attracted immediately by the simple relationship between 6 and 12. Double 6 gives me 12. So, I work from left to right, doubling the 8, to get 16. Answer: 16 eggs.

Recipe problem (2) (Figure 16.2b)
This time it's the relationship between the 6 and the 9 that attracts me. Halving 6 and multiplying by 3 gives 9. So, I work from top to bottom, and do the same thing to the 4, halving it and multiplying by 3, to get 6. Answer: 6 eggs.

Recipe problem (3) (Figure 16.2c)
The left to right relationship is the easier to work with here: multiplying 6 by 20 gives 120. So, do the same to the 7, to get 140. Answer: 140 g of flour.

Recipe problem (4) (Figure 16.2d)
I think it's easier to use the ratio of 8 to 6 than 8 to 500. So I'll work from top to bottom, going from 8 people to 4 to 2, and then to 6. Now, 8 people need 500 g, so 4 people need 250 g, so 2 people need 125 g. Adding the results for 4 people and 2 people, 6 people need 375 g.

These informal, *ad hoc* approaches are the ways in which most people solve the problems of ratio and proportion that they encounter in everyday life, including problems involving percentages such as those discussed below. We should encourage their use by our pupils. The four-cell diagrams used in Figures 16.1 and 16.2 provide a useful starting point for organizing the data in a structured way that makes the relationships between the numbers more transparent. However, sometimes there is no easy or obvious relationship between the numbers in the problem. In such a case we may call on a calculator to help us in using the method shown below:

Recipe problem (5)
6 people require 140 g
So, 1 person requires 140 ÷ 6 = 23.333 g   (using a calculator)
So, 14 people require 23.333 × 14 = 326.662 g   (using a calculator)
Answer: approximately 327 g.

What does 'per cent' mean?

The term *per cent* means 'for each hundred'. The Latin root *cent*, meaning 'a hundred', is used in many English words, such as 'century', 'centurion', 'centigrade' and 'centipede'. We use the concept of *per cent* first and foremost to describe a proportion of a quantity or of a set. So, for example, if there are 300 pupils in a school and 180 of them are girls, we might describe the proportion of girls as 'sixty per cent' (written as 60%) of the school population. This means simply that there are 60 girls for each 100 pupils. If on a car journey of 200 miles a total of 140 miles is single carriageway, we could say that 70% (seventy per cent) of the journey is single carriageway, meaning 70 miles for each 100 miles. In effect, we have here the structure shown in Figure 16.1 for a direct proportion problem, but where one of the numbers must be 100, as shown in Figure 16.3.

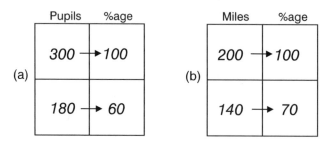

Figure 16.3   Percentage seen as direct proportion

What we are doing in these examples is also just what we did with fractions in Chapter 14, when we used them to represent a part of a unit or a part of a set. The concept of a percentage is simply a special case of a fraction, with 100 as the bottom number. So 60% is an abbreviation for $^{60}/_{100}$ and 70% for $^{70}/_{100}$.

How do you express a proportion as a percentage?

In the examples above it was fairly obvious how to express the proportions involved as 'so many per hundred'. This is not always the case. The following examples demonstrate a number of approaches to expressing a proportion as a percentage, using *ad hoc* methods, when the numbers can be related easily to 100. The trick is to find an equivalent proportion for a population of 100, by multiplying or dividing by appropriate numbers.

1. In a school population of 50, there are 30 girls. What percentage are girls? What percentage are boys?
   30 girls out of 50 pupils is the same proportion as 60 out of 100.
   So, 60% of the population are girls.
   This means that 40% are boys. (Since the total population must be 100%.)

2. In a school population of 250, there are 130 girls. What percentage are girls? What percentage are boys?
   130 girls out of 250 pupils is the same proportion as 260 out of 500.
   260 girls out of 500 pupils is the same as 52 per 100 (dividing 260 by 5).
   So, 52% of the population are girls.
   This means that 48% are boys. (52% + 48% = 100%)

3. In a school population of 75, there are 30 girls. What percentage are girls? What percentage are boys?
   30 girls out of 75 pupils is the same proportion as 60 out of 150.
   60 girls out of 150 pupils is the same proportion as 120 out of 300.
   120 girls out of 300 pupils is the same as 40 per 100 (dividing 120 by 3).
   So, 40% of the population are girls, and therefore 60% are boys.

4. In a school population of 140, there are 77 girls. What percentage are girls?
   77 girls out of 140 pupils is the same proportion as 11 out of 20 (dividing by 7).
   11 girls out of 20 pupils is the same proportion as 55 per 100 (multiply by 5).
   So, 55% of the population are girls, and therefore 45% are boys.

When the numbers do not relate so easily to 100 as in these examples, the procedure is more complicated and is best done with the aid of a calculator:

5. In a school population of 140, there are 73 girls. What percentage are girls? What percentage are boys?
   73 girls out of 140 pupils means that $^{73}/_{140}$ are girls.

The equivalent proportion for a population of 100 pupils is $^{73}/_{140}$ of 100.

Work this out on a calculator. (Key sequence: 73, ÷, 140, x, 100, =.)

Interpret the display (52.14285): just over 52% of the population are girls.

This means that just under 48% are boys.

Most calculators have a percentage key (labelled %) which enables this last example to be done without any complicated reasoning at all. On my calculator, for example, I could use the following key sequence: 73, ÷, 140, %. This makes finding percentages with a calculator very easy indeed.

Why are percentages used so much?

They certainly are used extensively, in newspapers, in advertising, and so on. We are all familiar with claims such as '90% of cats prefer Kit-tymeat' and '20% of 7-year-olds cannot do subtraction'. There is certainly no shortage of material in the media for us to use with our pupils to make this topic relevant to everyday life. The convention of always relating everything to 100 enables us to make comparisons in a very straightforward manner. It is much easier, for example, to compare 44% with 40%, than to compare $^{4}/_{9}$ with $^{2}/_{5}$. This is why percentages are used so much: they provide us with a standard way of comparing various proportions.

Consider this example. School A spends £190 300 of its annual budget of £247 780 on teaching-staff salaries. School B is larger and spends £341 340 out of an annual budget of £450 700. It is very difficult to take in figures like these. The standard way of comparing these would be to express the proportions of the budget spent on teaching-staff salaries as percentages. Using a calculator, I find that School A spends about 76.80% on salaries (key sequence: 190300, ÷, 247780, %), whereas School B spends about 75.74% on salaries (key sequence: 341340, ÷, 450700, %). Now I can make a direct comparison: School A spends about £76.80 in every £100, School B spends about £75.74 in every £100.

There are other occasions, however, when the tendency always to put proportions into percentage terms seems a bit daft. For example, I come from a family of 3 boys and 1 girl. I could say that 75% of the children in my family are boys. I suppose there's no harm in this, but remember that what this is saying is effectively: '75 out of every 100 children in my family are boys'!

How do percentages relate to decimals?

In the previous chapter we saw how a decimal such as 0.37 means 37 hundredths. Since 37 hundredths also means 37 per cent, we can see a direct relationship between decimals with two digits after the point and percentages. So, 0.37 and 37% are two ways of expressing the same thing. Here are some other examples: 0.50 is equivalent to 50%, 0.05 is equivalent to 5%, 0.42 is equivalent to 42%. It really is as easy as that: you just move the digits two places to the left, because effectively what we are doing is multiplying the decimal number by 100. It's just like changing pennies into pounds and vice versa. This works even if there are more than two digits, for example, 0.125 = 12.5% and 1.01 = 101%.

This means that we have effectively three ways of expressing proportions of a quantity or of a set: using a fraction, using a decimal or using a percentage. It is useful to learn by heart some of the most common equivalences, such as the following:

Fraction	Decimal	Percentage
½	0.5 (0.50)	50%
¼	0.25	25%
¾	0.75	75%
⅕	0.2 (0.20)	20%
⅖	0.4 (0.40)	40%
⅗	0.6 (0.60)	60%
⅘	0.8 (0.80)	80%
¹⁄₁₀	0.1 (0.10)	10%
³⁄₁₀	0.3 (0.30)	30%
⁷⁄₁₀	0.7 (0.70)	70%
⁹⁄₁₀	0.9 (0.90)	90%
¹⁄₂₀	0.05	5%
⅓	0.33 (approximately)	33% (approximately)

Knowledge of these equivalences is useful for estimating percentages. For instance, in example (2) above, 130 out of 250 pupils were girls. This is just over half the population, so I would expect the percentage to be just a bit more than 50% (it is 52%). A proportion of 145 girls out of 450 pupils is a bit less than a third, so I would expect a percentage of around 33% (it is about 32.22%).

Also, because it is so easy to change a decimal into a percentage, and since we can convert a fraction to a decimal (see Chapter 15) just by dividing the top number by the bottom number, using a calculator, this gives us another direct way of expressing a fraction or a proportion as a percentage. For example, 23 out of 37 corresponds to the fraction $^{23}/_{37}$. On a calculator enter: 23, ÷, 37, =. This gives the approximate decimal equivalent, 0.6216216. Since the first two decimal places correspond to the percentage, we can just read this straight off as 'about 62%'. If we wish to be more precise, we could include a couple more digits, such as 62.16%. (See Chapter 10 for a discussion of rounding.)

So, in summary, we now have these four ways of expressing a proportion of '*A* out of *B*' as a percentage:

1. Use *ad hoc* multiplication and division to change the proportion to an equivalent number out of 100.
2. Work out $^{A}/_{B} \times 100$, using a calculator, if necessary.
3. Just enter on to a calculator: *A*, ÷, *B*, % (but note that calculators may vary in the precise key sequence to be used).
4. Use a calculator to find $A \div B$ and read off the decimal answer as a percentage, by shifting all the digits two places to the left.

How can you have a hundred and one per cent?

Since 100% represents the whole quantity being considered, or the whole population, it does seem a bit odd at first to talk about percentages greater than 100. Football managers are well known for abusing mathematics in this way, for example, by talking about their team having to give a hundred and one per cent – meaning, presumably, everything they have plus a little more.

However, there are perfectly correct uses of percentages greater than 100, not for expressing a proportion of a whole unit but for comparing two quantities. Just as we use fractions to represent the ratio of two quantities, we can also use percentages in this way. So, for example, if in January a window-cleaner earns £500 and in February he earns only £400, one way of comparing the two month's earnings would be to say that February's were 80% of January's. The 80% here is simply an equivalent way of saying four-fifths (⅘). If then in March he was to earn £600 then we could quite appropriately record that March's earning were 120% of January's. This is equivalent to saying 'one and a fifth' of January's earnings.

How do you calculate a percentage of a quantity?

The most common calculation we have to do with percentages is to find a percentage of a given quantity, particularly in the context of money.

In cases where the percentage can be converted to a simple equivalent fraction, there are often very obvious *ad hoc* methods of doing this. For example, to find 25% of £48, simply change this to ¼ of £48, which is £12. Then when the quantity in question is a nice multiple of 100, we can often find easy ways to work out percentages. First, let us note that, for example, 37% of 100 is 37. So, if I had to work out 37% of £600, we could reason that, since 37% of £100 is £37, we simply need to multiply £37 by 6 to get the answer required, namely, £222.

It is also possible to develop *ad hoc* methods for building up a percentage, using easy components. One of the easiest percentages to find is 10% and most people intuitively start with this. (Note, however, that the fact that 10% is the same as a tenth makes it a very special case: 5% is not a fifth, 7% is not a seventh, and so on. Because we often start with 10% and make so much use of it, teachers should make a special point of explaining that this connection works *only* with 10%.) So to find, say, 35% of £80, I could build up the answer like this:

10% of £80 is £8
so   20% of £80 is £16 (doubling the 10%)
and   5% of £80 is £4 (halving the 10%)
Adding the 10%, 20% and 5% gives me the 35% required: £28.

It is often the case that 'intuitive' approaches to finding percentages, such as this one, are neglected in schools, in favour of more formal procedures. This is a pity, since success with this kind of manipulation all contributes to greater confidence with numbers generally.

When the numbers are too difficult for such methods as these, then we should turn to a calculator. For example, to find 37% of £946, we need to find $\frac{37}{100}$ of 946. This can be evaluated on a calculator. An appropriate key sequence is: 37, ÷, 100, ×, 946, =. This gives the result, 350.02, so we conclude that 37% of £946 is £350.02. Personally, I use a more direct method on the calculator. Since 37% is equivalent to 0.37, I just enter the key sequence: 0.37, ×, 946, =. There is another way, of course, using the percentage key. On my calculator the appropriate key sequence is: 946, ×, 37, %.

What about percentage increases and decreases?

One of the most common uses of percentages is to describe the size of a change in a given quantity, by expressing it as a proportion of the starting value. We are all familiar with percentage increases in salaries, for example. So if your monthly salary of £1500 is increased by 5%, to find your new salary you would have to find 5% of £1500 (£75) and add this to the existing salary. There is a more direct way of doing this: since your new salary is the existing salary (100%) plus 5%, it must be 105% of the existing salary. So you could get your new salary by finding 105% of the existing salary, that is, by multiplying by 1.05 (remember that 105% = 1.05 as a decimal).

Similarly, if an article costing £200 is reduced by 15%, then to find the new price we have to find 15% of £200 (£30) and deduct this from the existing price, giving the new price as £170. More directly, we could reason that the new price is the existing price (100%) less 15%, so it must be 85% of the existing salary. Hence we could just find 85% of £200, for example, by multiplying 200 by 0.85.

The trickiest problem is when you are told the price after a percentage increase or decrease and you have to work backwards to get the original price. For example, if the price of an article has been reduced by 20% and now costs £44, what was its original price? This problem is represented in Figure 16.4. The £44 must be 80% of the original price. We have to find what is 100% of that original price. It's fairly easy now to get from 80% (£44) to 20% (£11) and then to 100% (£55).

%age	Price (£)
80	44
100	?

Figure 16.4   If 80% is £44 find 100%

There is an interesting phenomenon related to percentage increases and decreases which often puzzles people. If you apply a given percentage increase and then apply the same percentage decrease, you do not get back to where you started! For example, the price of an article is £200. The price is increased one month by 10%. The next month the price is decreased by 10%. What is the final price? Well, after the 10% increase the price has gone up to £220. Now we apply the 10% decrease to this. This is a decrease of £22, not £20, because the percentage change always applies to the existing value. So the article finishes up costing £198.

Self-assessment questions

16.1: If you can exchange 70 guilders for £20, what would be the equivalent cost in pounds of an article costing 42 guilders?

16.2: A rise in temperature of 9 °F is equivalent to a rise of 5 °C. What is the equivalent in °C of a rise of 45 °F?

16.3: A department store is advertising '25% off' for some items and 'one-third off' for others. Which is the greater reduction?

16.4: Use *ad hoc* methods to find what percentage of pupils in a year group achieve level 5 in a mathematics test, if there are: a) 50 pupils in the year group and 13 achieve level 5; b) 300 in the year group and 57 achieve level 5; c) 80 in the year group and 24 achieve level 5; and d) 130 in the year group and 26 achieve level 5. In each case, state what percentage do not achieve level 5.

16.5: On a page of an English textbook there are 1249 letters, of which 527 are vowels. In an Italian text it is found that there are 277 vowels in a page of 565 letters. Use a calculator to determine approximately what percentage of letters are vowels in each case.

16.6: Change: a) $\frac{3}{20}$ into a percentage; and b) 65% into a fraction.

16.7: Use informal, intuitive methods to find: a) 30% of £120; and b) 17% of £450.

16.8: The price of a television costing £275 is increased by 12% one month and decreased by 12% the next. What is the final price? Use a calculator, if necessary.

16.9: The price of a television licence is increased by 14% to £171. How much was it before the increase?

16.10: A shop is advertising a stereo system for £600. But the manager tells you that there must be 20% tax added to this price. However, he is also offering 10% discount. Which would you prefer the manager to apply first? The tax or the discount?

Summary of teaching points

1. Use the four-cells diagram to make clear the structure of direct proportion problems and encourage pupils to use the relationships between the given three numbers to find the fourth number.

2. Explain the meaning of *per cent* as 'for each hundred' and show how percentages are used to describe a fraction of a quantity or of a set.

3. Encourage pupils to find examples of percentages used in newspapers and advertising and discuss with them what is being claimed.

4. Encourage the use of *ad hoc* methods for expressing a proportion as a percentage, using numbers that relate easily to 100.
5. Allow pupils to use calculators to express more difficult proportions as percentages, showing them the various different ways of doing this.
6. Emphasize the equivalence between fractions and percentages.
7. Show pupils how simple it is to change a percentage into an equivalent decimal and vice versa, by moving the digits two places.
8. Encourage pupils to memorize common equivalences between fractions, decimals and percentages.
9. Encourage pupils to use informal, intuitive methods for finding a percentage of a quantity, particularly building up a percentage using easy proportions such as 10% and 5%.
10. Let pupils use calculators for the more difficult examples of finding a percentage of a quantity, and explain to them some of the different ways of doing this.
11. Emphasize that 10% being equivalent to one-tenth is a special case.
12. Be aware that not all calculators follow the same key sequence for expressing a proportion as a percentage or for calculating percentages of a quantity.

17

Handling Data

Pupils should be taught to: select and use handling-data skills when solving problems in other areas of the curriculum, in particular science; decide how best to organize and present findings; use the precise mathematical language and vocabulary for handling data; solve problems involving data; interpret tables, lists and charts used in everyday life; construct and interpret frequency tables, including tables for grouped discrete data; represent and interpret discrete data using graphs and diagrams, including pictograms, bar charts and line graphs, then interpret a wider range of graphs and diagrams, using ICT (information communication technology) where appropriate; recognize the difference between discrete and continuous data; draw conclusions from statistics and graphs and recognize when information is presented in a misleading way.

In this chapter there are explanations of

- the four stages of handling data: collecting, organizing, representing, interpreting;
- the use of tallying and frequency tables for collecting and organizing data;
- the differences between discrete data, grouped discrete data and continuous data;
- the representation of discrete and grouped discrete data in block graphs;
- the misleading effect of suppressing zero in a frequency graph; and
- other ways of representing data: set diagrams, pictograms, pie charts and line graphs.

What do pupils have to learn about handling statistical data?

Essentially there are four stages involved in handling data: collecting it, organizing it, representing it and interpreting it. (*Note*: I adopt the

175

current usage of *data* as a singular noun, meaning 'a collection of information'.) Pupils should therefore have experience of all four of these stages.

They should learn how to collect data as part of a purposeful enquiry,
setting out to answer specific questions that they might raise. This might
involve the skills associated with designing simple questionnaires. For
example, as part of a geography-focused project on transport, they
might decide to collect data about how pupils travel to school and seek
to make comparisons between, say, pupils in a rural school and those in
a city school. A useful technique here is that of *tallying*, based on counting in fives. Data should then be organized in a *frequency table*. Figure
17.1 shows both these processes for the information collected from a
Year 5 class in a rural school.

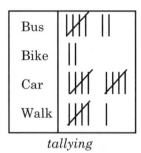

tallying		How we travel	Number of pupils

How we travel	Number of pupils
Bus	7
Bike	2
Car	10
Walk	6
Total	25

tallying   *frequency table*

Figure 17.1   Using tallying and a frequency table

Various kinds of graphs and diagrams can then be used to represent
the data, before the final step of interpreting it. To involve pupils in this
important step of interpretation, I have found three approaches useful
in the classroom:

1. Pupils just write about what the graph tells them, particularly in
   relation to the questions and issues that prompted the collection of
   the data.
2. Pupils write sentences about what the graph tells us, incorporating
   key words, such as 'most', 'least', 'more than', 'less than'.
3. Pupils make up a number of questions that can be answered from the
   graph, to pose to each other.

What is discrete data?

The word *discrete* means 'separate'. Discrete data is information about a
particular population (such as the children in a class), which automatically

sorts the members of the population into quite distinct, separate subsets. The information about travelling to school, shown in Figure 17.1, is a good example of discrete data, since it sorts the pupils automatically into four separate, distinct subsets: those who come by bus, by car, by bicycle or on foot. Other examples of this kind of discrete data that pupils might collect, organize, display and interpret would include: favourite television pro- gramme, chosen from a list of six possible programmes; daily newspaper taken at home, including 'none'; and month in which they were born.

In each case the question asked (for example, how did you travel to school today?) identifies a *variable* (for example, means of transport) and the answer determines a *value* for the variable (for example, bus, car, bike, on foot). Separate subsets are formed for each individual value taken by the variable. The number in each subset is called the *frequency*. Sometimes the variable is numerical, rather than just descriptive; for example, pupils might be asked how many children are there in their family (the possible values of this variable are 1, 2, 3, 4, . . .), or what size shoes they wear, or how many pets they have. Initially, we should use variables that have no more than a dozen values, otherwise we finish up with too many subsets to allow any meaningful interpretation. We can then display the data in a conventional *block graph*.

There are two important stages in the development of this type of graph. In Figure 17.2(a) each square is shaded individually, as though each square represents one child. In interpreting the graph the pupil can count the number of squares, as though counting the number of chil- dren in each subset, so there is no need for a vertical axis. (In an earlier stage still, children would write their names on squares of gummed paper which would be arranged in columns, so that the individual con- tribution of each child can be identified.)

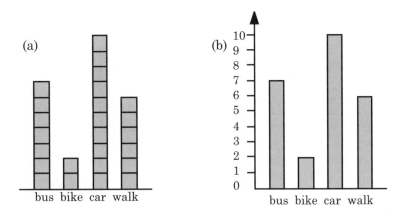

Figure 17.2   Two stages in the use of block graphs

Figure 17.2(b) is based on a more sophisticated idea. Now, the individual contributions are lost and it is the height of the column that indicates the frequency, rather than the number of squares in the column. We read off this frequency by relating the tops of the columns to the scale on the vertical axis, where, it should be noted, the numbers label the points on the axis, not the spaces between them. We have progressed from counting to measurement. This is an important step because, even though we may still use squared paper to draw these graphs, we now have the option of using different scales on the vertical axis, appropriate to the data: for example, with larger populations we might take one unit on the vertical scale to represent 10 people. Notice that, in Figure 17.2, I have used the convention, sometimes used for discrete data, of leaving gaps between the columns; this is an appropriate procedure because it conveys pictorially the way in which the variable sorts the population into discrete subsets. In order to present an appropriate picture of the distribution of the data, it is essential that the columns in a block graph be drawn with equal widths.

There is a further important point to make about using block graphs to represent frequencies, illustrated by the graphs shown in Figure 17.3. This was produced prior to a general election to show the numbers of votes gained by three political parties (which I have called A, B and C) in the previous general election. The graph in Figure 17.3(a) was the version put out by our local Party A candidate to persuade us that we would be wasting our vote by voting for Party C. By not starting the frequency axis at zero a totally false picture is presented of the relative standing of Party C compared with A and B. Because the purpose of drawing a graph is to give us an instant overview of the relationships within the data, this

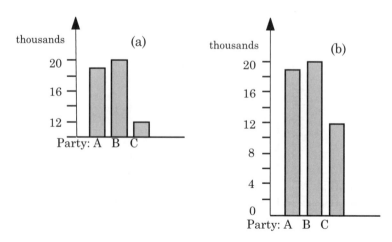

Figure 17.3   Suppression of zero

procedure (called *suppression of zero*) is nearly always inappropriate or misleading and should be avoided. The graph in Figure 17.3(b), properly starting the vertical axis at zero, presents a much more honest picture of the relative share of the vote.

So what is meant by 'grouped discrete data'?

Discrete data, like that in the examples above, is the simplest kind of data to handle. Sometimes, however, there are just too many values of the variable concerned for us to sort the population into an appropriate number of subsets. So the data must first be organized into groups. For example, a group of Year 5 pupils were asked how many writing implements (pencils, pens, felt-tips, etc.) they had with them one day at school. The responses were as follows: 1, 2, 2, 3, 4, 4, 5, 5, 5, 6, 6, 8, 8, 8, 9, 9, 10, 10, 11, 13, 14, 14, 14, 15, 15, 18, 19, 25, 26, 32. Clearly, there are just too many possibilities here to represent this data in a block graph as it stands. The best procedure, therefore, is to group the data, for example, as shown in Figure 17.4. Notice that the range of values in the subsets (0–4, 5–9, 10–14, 15–19, etc.) should be the same in each case, that the groups should not overlap, that they must between them cover all the values of the variable, and that groups with zero frequency (like 20–24 in Figure 17.4) should not be omitted from the table or from the graph. Of course, the data could have been grouped in other ways, producing either more subsets (for example, 0–1, 2–3, 4–5, and so on: 17 groups), or fewer (for example, 0–9, 10–19, 20–29, 30–39). When working with *grouped discrete data* like this we should aim for between five

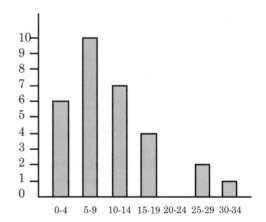

no.of pens etc	frequency
0-4	6
5-9	10
10-14	7
15-19	4
20-24	0
25-29	2
30-34	1

Figure 17.4 Handling grouped discrete data

and a dozen groups: more than a dozen, we have too much information to take in; less than five, we have lost too much information.

What other kind of data is there apart from discrete?

Discrete data contrasts with what is called *continuous data*. This is the kind of data produced by a variable that can theoretically take any value on a continuum. For example, if we were collecting data about the waist sizes of a group of adults, the measurements could come anywhere on a tape measure from, say, 50 cm to 120 cm. They are not just restricted to particular, distinct points on the scale. For example, the waist measurement for one individual might be about 62.5 cm. If he or she put on some weight and the measurement increases to about 64.5 cm, then we know that the waist size would increase continuously from one measurement to the next, on the way taking every possible value in between; it would not suddenly jump from one value to the other! This is a characteristic of a continuous variable. The contrast with a discrete variable like, for example, the number of pets you own, is clear. If you have three pets and then get a fourth, you suddenly jump from three to four, without having to pass through 3.1 pets, 3.2 pets, and so on. Measurements of length, mass, volume and time intervals are all examples of continuous data.

   Having said that, we always have to record measurements 'to the nearest something' (see the discussion on rounding in Chapter 10). The effect of this is immediately to change the values of the continuous variable into a set of discrete data! For example, we might measure waist size to the nearest centimetre. This now means that our data is restricted to the following, separate, distinct values: 50 cm, 51 cm, 52 cm, and so on. This means that, in practice, the procedure for handling this kind of data – produced by recording a series of measurements to the nearest something – is no different from that for handling discrete data with a large number of potential values, by grouping it as explained above. It is therefore an appropriate activity for primary-school children. For example, pupils can collect data about: their heights (to the nearest centimetre); their masses (to the nearest tenth of a kilogram); the circumferences of their heads (to the nearest millimetre); the volume of water they can drink in one go (to the nearest tenth of a litre); the time taken to run 100 metres (to the nearest second); and so on. Each of these is technically a continuous variable, but by being measured to the nearest something it generates a set of discrete data, which can then be grouped appropriately and represented in a graph. The only difference I would suggest is that we should reflect the fact that the data originated from a continuous variable by drawing the columns in the graph with no gaps between them, as shown in Figure 17.5. Any further development of handling of continuous data than this would be beyond the scope of primary-school mathematics.

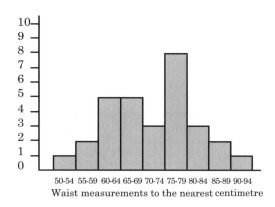

waist measurements to nearest centimetre	frequency
50 - 54	1
55 - 59	2
60 - 64	5
65 - 69	5
70 - 74	3
75 - 79	8
80 - 84	3
85 - 89	2
90 - 94	1

Figure 17.5   A graph derived from a continuous variable

What other ways are there of representing data?

Figure 17.6 shows two other ways of representing the data used in Figure 17.1. The most elementary method, picture (a), is a *set diagram*, with the actual names of the pupils written in the various subsets. Then in picture (b), a *pictogram*, the names have been replaced by pictures, organized in neat rows and columns. The pictogram is clearly only a small step from a block graph, with the pictures replaced by individual shaded squares. It

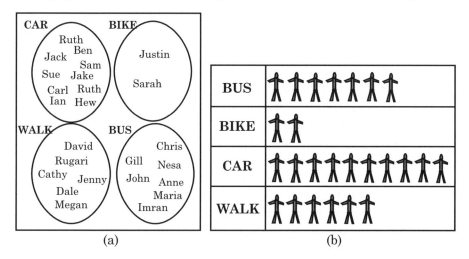

(a)   (b)

Figure 17.6   A set diagram and a pictogram

is also possible with larger populations to use pictograms where each icon (picture) represents a number of individuals rather than just one.

Much more sophisticated is the *pie chart*, shown in Figure 17.7. Here it is the angle of each slice of pie that represents the proportion of the population in each subset. It is usual practice to write these proportions as percentages (see Chapter 16) within the slice itself, if possible.

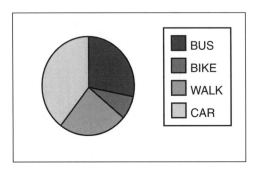

Figure 17.7   A pie chart

Pie charts are really only appropriate for discrete data with a small number of subsets, say, six or less. They are often used to show what proportions of a budget are spent in various categories. The mathematics for producing a pie chart can be quite complicated for primary-school children, unless the data is chosen very carefully. For example, to determine the angle for the slice representing travel by bus, in Figure 17.7, we would have to divide 360 degrees by 25 to determine how many degrees per person in the population, then multiply by 7. Using a calculator, the key sequence is: 360, ÷, 25, ×, 7, = (answer 100.8, which is about 101 degrees). This angle then has to be drawn using a protractor. Fortunately, this can all be done nowadays by a computer. If the data in question is entered on a database or on a spreadsheet then usually there is available a choice of a block graph, a pie chart or a line graph (see below) at the press of a button. Many simple examples of these kinds of programs are available for use in primary schools. This certainly means that primary-school children should learn how to interpret pie charts – but it also means that they do not really need to learn how to draw them for themselves.

The other type of graph used sometimes for representing statistical data is the *line graph*. An example of a line graph is shown in Figure 17.8. This shows the number of pupils on a primary-school roll at the beginning of each school year for a number of years. For statistical data, a line graph is really only appropriate where the variable along the horizontal axis is 'time'. In this example, the movement of the line, up and down, gives a picture of how the number on roll is changing over time. It would be useful for showing, for example, the average midday temperature over a series of months, the number of pupils absent each day one week, the number of pupils who have completed their mathematics work by various numbers of minutes past ten o'clock, and so on. A line graph would therefore be totally inappropriate as a means of presenting discrete data such as that relating to travelling to school in Figure 17.1, and fairly inappropriate for all the other examples of statistical data used in this chapter.

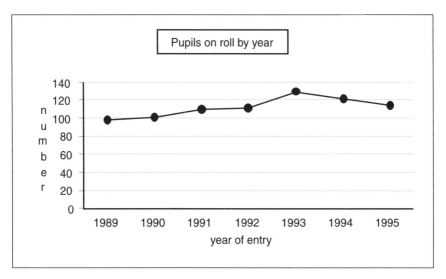

Figure 17.8   A line graph

Self-assessment questions

17.1: Make up two questions that can be answered from the graphs shown in each of: a) Figure 17.2; b) Figure 17.4; and c) Figure 17.5.

17.2: Which of these variables are discrete? Which would generate discrete data; which should be grouped? Which are continuous? a) The time it takes a person to count to a thousand; b) your height; c) the number of living grandparents; d) the amount of money in coins in a person's possession; e) a person's favourite kind of music chosen from a list of ten possibilities; f) the number of A-levels a person has passed; and g) the mass of the classroom guinea pig recorded each Monday morning for a term.

17.3: Which of the examples in Question 17.2 would be best represented in a pie chart? Which would be best represented in a line graph?

17.4: For example (d) in question 17.2, the data collected from a group of students ranged from zero to £4.59. How would you choose to group this data in order to represent it in a bar chart?

17.5: (a) In a class of 36 pupils, 14 come to school by car. What angle would be needed in the slice of a pie chart to represent this information? (b) What would it be for 14 pupils out of a class of 33?

Summary of teaching points

1. Pupils should have experience of all four stages of handling data: collecting, organizing, representing, interpreting.
2. Motivation is higher when the data is collected by the pupils themselves, higher still when it is collected to answer some questions they have posed themselves and even higher when it is about themselves!
3. The skills of handling data and pictorial representation are best taught through purposeful enquiries related to topics focusing on other areas of the curriculum, such as geography, history or science.
4. Teach the technique of tallying and encourage pupils to use it when collating data.
5. Pupils should first handle discrete data with non-numerical variables (for example, means of travel to school), then discrete data using numerical variables (for example, number of pets owned). Use examples with no more than a dozen subsets.
6. Introduce pupils to set diagrams and pictograms as ways of representing discrete data.
7. Block graphs are introduced first by sticking on or shading individual squares, the number of which represents the frequency, and then by columns, the heights of which represent the frequency.
8. Later pupils can learn to interpret pie charts: these are best used when there is only a small number of subsets.
9. Pupils should progress to handling discrete data with so many values that the data has to be organized into subsets covering a range of values.
10. Finally they can deal with continuous variables, such as measurements of length, mass, time and volume, by recording measurements to the nearest something and thus converting the values of the variable to discrete data, which can then be grouped appropriately.
11. Pupils should use database and spreadsheet programs to organize data and to generate graphs (particularly block graphs and pie charts) for them to interpret.

12. Encourage pupils to collect examples of graphs and tables of data from the press and advertising and discuss whether they are helpful or misleading.
13. Introduce line graphs for statistical data or other measurements related to the passing of time.

18

Comparing Sets of Data

Pupils should be taught to: use the precise mathematical vocabulary for handling data; know that mode is a measure of average and that range is a measure of spread; use the ideas of average and spread to describe and compare data sets.

In this chapter there are explanations of

- the idea of an average as a representative figure for a set of data;
- three measures of average: the mean, the median and the mode;
- quartiles and the five-number-summary of a distribution;
- range and inter-quartile range as measures of spread;
- box-and-whisker diagrams;
- percentiles and deciles; and
- the concept of average speed.

I thought an average was what you get by adding up a set of numbers and dividing by the number in the set. Is there more to it than that?

The process outlined in the question posed here produces one kind of average figure, called the *mean* (or, to use its full title, the *arithmetic mean*). The purpose of finding an average is to produce a *representative figure* for a set of numerical data. The mean is just one way of doing this which is appropriate in many circumstances. But it is not the only way. Sometimes it makes more sense to use other kinds of average, in particular, the *median* and the *mode*. The important purpose shared by all three of these measures of average is to find a suitable way of obtaining one number that can represent the whole set of numbers. This 'average' figure will then enable us: 1) to make comparisons between different sets of data, by comparing their means, medians or modes; and 2) to make sense of individual numbers in a set by relating them to these averages.

In the discussion below we will use these different kinds of average to consider the marks out of 100 gained by two groups of pupils (Group A, 14 pupils; Group B, 11 pupils) in the same mathematics and English tests, as follows:

Group A: Mathematics 23, 25, 46, 48, 48, 49, 53, 60, 61, 61, 61, 62, 69, 85
Group B: Mathematics 36, 38, 43, 43, 45, 47, 60, 63, 69, 86, 95

Group A: English   45, 48, 49, 52, 53, 53, 53, 53, 54, 56, 57, 58, 59, 62
Group B: English   45, 52, 56, 57, 64, 71, 72, 76, 79, 81, 90

Can you explain the logic behind the process of finding the mean?

To find the mean value of a set of numbers three steps are involved: 1) find the sum of all the numbers in the set; 2) divide by the number of numbers in the set; and 3) round the answer appropriately, if necessary (see Chapter 10).

For example, to find the mean score of Group A above in mathematics: 1) the sum of the scores is 751; 2) divide 751 by 14, using a calculator to get 53.642857; and 3) round this to, say, one decimal place, to determine the mean score to be about 53.6. The logic behind using this as a representative figure is that the total marks obtained by the group would have been the same if all the pupils had scored the mean score (allowing for the possibility of a small error introduced by rounding). I imagine the process to be one of pooling. All the pupils put all their marks into a pool, which is then shared out equally between all 14 of them. This is an application of the concept involved in division structures associated with the word 'per' (see Chapter 7): we are finding the 'marks per student', assuming an equal sharing of all the marks awarded between them. An example that illustrates this well would be to find the mean amount of money that a group of people have in their possession. This could be done by putting all their money on the table and then sharing it out again equally between the members of the group. This is precisely the process that is modelled by the mathematical procedure for finding the mean.

We can now use this procedure to make comparisons. For example, to compare Group A with Group B in mathematics, we could compare their mean scores. Group B's mean score is about 56.8 (625 ÷ 11). This would lend some support to an assertion that, on the whole, Group B (mean score 56.8) has done better in the test than Group A (mean score 53.6).

We can also use average scores to help make sense of individual scores. For example, Cathy in Group B scored 60 in mathematics and 64 in English. Reacting naively to the raw scores, we might conclude that she did better in English than in mathematics. But by comparing the marks with the mean scores for her group leads to a different interpretation: Cathy's mark for mathematics (60) is above the mean (56.8), whilst the higher mark she obtained for English (64) is actually below the mean for her group (which works out to be 67.5). This would lend some support to the view that Cathy has done better in mathematics than in English.

What is the median?

The *median* is simply the number that comes in the middle of the set when the numbers are arranged in numerical order. Finding this average figure is much easier therefore than calculating the mean, especially when you are dealing with a very large population with a large number of possible values for the variable being considered. It is very common, for example, for government education statistics to use medians as representative, average figures. The only complication arises when there is an even number of elements in the set, because then there is not a middle one. So the process of finding the median is as follows:

1. Arrange all the numbers in the set in order from smallest to largest.
2. If the number of numbers in the set is odd, the median is the number in the middle.
3. If the number of numbers in the set is even, the median is the mean of the two numbers in the middle, in other words, halfway between them.

If you are not sure how to decide where the middle of a list is situated, here's a simple rule for finding it: if there are n items in the list, the position of the middle one (the median) is 'half of (n + 1)'. For example, with 11 items in the list the position of the median is half of 12, which is the sixth item. With 83 items in the list, the position of the median would be half of 84, which is the forty-second item. If n is even, this formula still tells you where to find the median. For example, with 50 items, the formula gives the position of the median as half of 51, which is 25½: we interpret this to mean 'halfway between the twenty-fifth and twenty-sixth items'.

So, for example, for Group B mathematics, with a set of 11 pupils, the median is the sixth mark when the marks are arranged in order; hence the median is 47. For Group A mathematics, with a set of 14, the median comes halfway between the seventh and eighth marks, which is halfway between 53 and 60; hence the median is 56.5.

Interestingly, if we use the median rather than the mean as our measure of average we would draw a different conclusion altogether when comparing the two groups: that on the whole Group A (median mark of 56.5) has done rather better than Group B (median mark of 47)!

Although the median is often used for large sets of statistics, it sometimes has advantages over the mean when working with a small set of numbers as well, as in these examples. The reason for this is that the median is not affected by one or two extreme values, such as the 95 in Group B. For a small set of data, a score much larger than the rest, like this one, can increase the value of the mean quite significantly and produce an average figure that does not represent the group in the most appropriate way. To take an extreme case, imagine that in a test nine pupils in a group score 1 and the other pupil scores 100: this data produces a mean score of 10.9 and a median of 1! There is surely no argument here with the view that the median 'represents' the performance of the group as a whole more appropriately. All this simply serves to illustrate the fact that most sets of statistics are open to different interpretations – which is why I have used the phrase 'lend some support to . . .' when drawing conclusions from the data in these examples.

Returning to our pupil Cathy, who scored 60 for mathematics and 64 for English, we can compare her performance with the median scores for her group, of 47 and 71 respectively. These statistics again lend support to the assertion that she has done better in mathematics than in English.

What is the mode and when would you use it?

The mode is simply the number in the set that occurs most frequently. For example, for Group A mathematics, the mode (or the modal mark) is 61, because this occurs three times, which is more than any other number in the set. For Group B mathematics, the mode is 43. This is actually a pretty daft way of determining representative marks for these sets of data. The mode is really only of any use as a measure of average when you are dealing with a large set of data and when the number of different values in the set of data is quite small. A good example of the use of a mode would be when discussing an 'average' family. In the UK, the modal number of children in a family is two, because more families have two children than any other. So if I were to write a play featuring an 'average' family, there would be two children in it. Clearly the mode is more use here than the mean, since '2.4 children' would be difficult to cast. Like the mean and the median, the mode enables us to make useful comparisons between different sets, when it is an appropriate and meaningful measure of average; for example, when comparing social factors in, say, parts of China, some countries in Africa and European states, the modal number of children per family would be very significant statistics to consider.

What is a five-number summary?

To describe a set of numerical data and to get a feel for how the numbers in the set are distributed, a *five-number summary* is often used. First, we list all the numbers in the set in order from smallest to largest. This enables us to find five significant numbers that help us to describe the distribution and to compare it with another set of data. Two of these significant numbers are simply the minimum and maximum values, the first and last numbers in the list. The third one is the median, which has been explained above.

The other two are the *lower quartile* (LQ) and the *upper quartile* (UQ). The lower quartile, the median and the upper quartile are three numbers that divide the list into four quarters. Just as the *median* is the midpoint of the set, the lower and upper quartiles are a quarter and three-quarters of the way along the list respectively. So, for the mathematics scores of Group B considered above,

36, 38, 43, 43, 45, 47, 60, 63, 69, 86, 95,

the median is the sixth score (47), the lower quartile is the third score (43) and the upper quartile is the ninth score (69).

Group B is a convenient size for discussing quartiles because it is fairly easy to decide where the quarter-points of the list are situated. Group A is not so straightforward. There is a similar rule to that for the median for deciding where the lower and upper quartiles come. For completeness I will explain it, but you really do not have to be able to do this! The position of the lower quartile is a quarter of $(n + 1)$ and that of the upper quartile is three-quarters of $(n + 1)$. So, for group B, with 11 items, the positions of the LQ and UQ are a quarter and three-quarters of 12, namely positions 3 and 9 in the list. However, for Group A, with 14 scores in the list, the position of the lower quartile would be a quarter of 15, which is 3¾. This means that it comes three-quarters of the way between the third and fourth scores, (46 and 48) which is 47.5. The position of the upper quartile is three-quarters of 15, which is 11¼. This means that it comes a quarter of the way between the eleventh and twelfth scores (61 and 62), which is 61.25.

I should say that this kind of fiddling around deciding precisely where the quartiles are located between particular items in a list is not necessary in practice when you are dealing with large sets of data. Anyway, the reader's requirements will be only to understand the idea of a quartile when it is met in government statistics, not to be able to calculate them for awkward sets of data.

The five-number summaries for Groups A and B for their scores for mathematics are therefore as follows:

	Group A	Group B
Min	23	36
LQ	47.5	43
Median	56.5	47
UQ	61.25	69
Max	85	95

This is a fairly standard way of presenting data from two populations for comparison. Teachers may well encounter government data about educational performance presented in this form. For example, the performance of primary schools in mathematics in two local education authorities (LEA X and LEA Y) might be compared by the following five-number-summaries based on data from the national test for 11-year-olds for mathematics.

	LEA X	LEA Y
Min	26	23
LQ	47	48
Median	65	73
UQ	84	93
Max	96	100

The variable used here is the percentage of pupils in each school in the LEA gaining level 4 in the mathematics test. For example, the upper quartile of 84 for LEA X means: if the schools in LEA X are listed in order from the school with the lowest percentage of pupils achieving level 4 to the school with the highest percentage, then the school that is three-quarters of the way along the list had 84% of pupils achieving level 4. Glancing at these summaries we can see that there is very little difference between the results of the bottom quarter (from the minimum to the lower quartile) of the schools in the two LEAs. But the other results for LEA Y are markedly better than LEA X, with a higher median and a higher upper quartile. The comparison shows that the 'average' and higher-performing schools in LEA Y are doing better than those in LEA X.

What are measures of spread?

Returning to the test scores for Groups A and B given at the start of this chapter, let us compare Group A's marks for mathematics (mean score 53.6) with their marks for English (mean score 53.7). By looking just at the means (53.6 and 53.7) we might conclude that the sets of marks for the two subjects were very similar. Looking at the actual data it is clear that they are not. The most striking feature is that the mathematics marks are more widely spread and the English marks are relatively closely clustered together. Statisticians have various ways of measuring the degree of 'spread' (sometimes called 'dispersion') in a set of data. The reader may have heard, for example, of the 'standard deviation'. These measures of spread have a similar purpose to the measures of average: they enable us to compare sets of data and to make sense of individual items of data. For primary-school work we would only introduce the simplest measure of spread, the *range*. This is as simple as it sounds: the range is just the difference between the largest and the smallest values in the set. So, for example, when comparing Group A's mathematics and English scores we would note that, although they have about the same mean scores, the range for mathematics is 62 marks (85 – 23), whereas the range for English is only 17 marks (62 – 45). Clearly the mathematics marks are more spread out.

However, one or two exceptionally high or low scores will result in the range not being a good indication of how spread out is *most* of the data in the set – it might therefore give a false impression when comparing two sets of data. So it is better to use what is called *the inter-quartile range*. This is simply the difference between the quartiles. Since this measure excludes the top quarter and the bottom quarter of the data in the set it is not affected by the odd extreme value and gives a better indication of the spread of most of the data. In the data given above for comparing LEA X and LEA Y, the inter-quartile range for the data for LEA X is 37 (84 – 47), whereas the inter-quartile range for LEA Y is 45 (93 – 48). This indicates that there is a greater spread of percentages of pupils achieving level 4 in mathematics in the schools in LEA Y than in LEA X.

What is a box-and-whisker diagram?

A box-and-whisker diagram (also called a box plot or a box-and-whisker plot) is a simple way of putting the numerical information given in a five-number summary into a pictorial form. The basic ingredients of a box-and-whisker diagram for a set of data are shown in Figure 18.1.

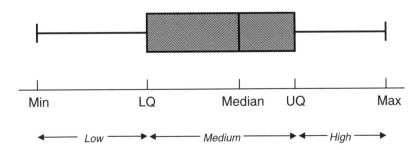

Figure 18.1   A box-and-whisker diagram

The 'box' part contains the middle 50% of the population, and therefore stretches from the lower quartile to the upper quartile. A line is usually drawn within the box to show the position of the median. The two 'whiskers' emerging from the ends of the box show the range of scores achieved by the bottom and top quarters, so they stretch from the lower quartile to the minimum, and from the upper quartile to the maximum. In this way, the diagram shows very clearly the range of values of three important subsets within the data set. We can think of these loosely as 'low' (the left-hand whisker), 'medium' (the box) and 'high' (the right-hand whisker). For example, if we collected data about the heights of male schoolteachers, those represented by the left-hand whisker would be 'short teachers', those in the box would be 'teachers of medium height' and those in the right-hand whisker would be 'tall teachers'. Note that the distance between the two ends of the whiskers represents the range of values in the set, and the length of the box represents the inter-quartile range.

Figure 18.2 shows box-and-whisker plots for the data for LEAs X and Y given above. The diagrams enable the reader at a glance to compare the performances of the two LEAs. The comparisons made verbally above can now be seen visually. The left-hand whiskers represent the schools with relatively low percentages of pupils achieving level 4 in mathematics; the right-hand whiskers represent the schools with relatively high percentages of pupils achieving level 4 in mathematics; and the boxes represent the schools in the middle 50%.

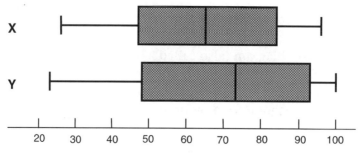

Figure 18.2   Comparing two data sets with box-and-whisker diagrams

Note that in Figures 18.1, 18.2 and 18.3 (see self-assessment questions) the box-plots have been drawn horizontally. They could just as well have been drawn vertically.

What are percentiles and deciles?

The process of identifying quartiles and the median involves listing all the data in the set in numerical order and then dividing the set into four parts (quarters), with equal numbers of items in each part. With larger populations it is common practice to divide the list into a hundred equal parts. The values used to separate these hundred parts are called *percentiles*. Note that the word 'percentile' is sometimes abbreviated to '%ile'.

If you read that the ninetieth percentile score in a test administered to a large number of pupils is 58, this means that the bottom 90% of pupils scored 58 or less and the top 10% of pupils scored 58 or more. Similarly, if you read that the twentieth percentile score was 26, this means that the bottom 20% of the pupils scored 26 or less and that the top 80% of pupils scored 26 or more.

It follows therefore that the lower quartile can also be referred to as the twenty-fifth percentile, the median as the fiftieth percentile and the upper quartile as the seventy-fifth percentile.

Sometimes reports will divide the set into ten equal parts, using what are called the *deciles*. The ninetieth percentile, for example, can also be called the ninth decile, and so on.

The raw percentage scores in a numeracy test administered to a sample of 450 teacher-trainees are presented in terms of percentiles as follows:

10th %ile	58%
20th %ile	60%
30th %ile	63%
40th %ile	65%

50th %ile	70%
60th %ile	78%
70th %ile	84%
80th %ile	88%
90th %ile	92%

This example is included deliberately because it can be confusing when the numbers in the set of data are themselves percentages, as in this case. Readers should not get confused between the *percentiles*, which refer to percentages of the number of items in the set, and the *percentage scores*, which are the actual items of data in the set. The following are examples of observations that could be made from this data:

- a trainee scoring 94% on the numeracy test is in the top 10% in this sample;
- a trainee scoring 64% on the test is well below average, with more than 60% of others doing better than this;
- the median score on the test was 70%;
- the top half of the sample scored 70% or more on the test;
- the bottom 30% of the sample scored 63% or less on the test;
- the top 20% of trainees scored 88% or more on the test;
- the seventh decile score was 84%; and
- the lower quartile was somewhere between 60% and 63%.

How does the idea of 'average speed' fit in with the concept of an average?

In the UK, pupils' first experience of speed is usually the speed of a vehicle, measured in 'miles per hour'. It is therefore a bit perverse for us to use 'kilometres per hour' when discussing speed in primary schools, as occurs in many primary mathematics schemes, since this is mostly unrelated to the children's experience. Note that average speed gives us another example of that important little word, 'per'. The idea of average speed derives from the concept of a mean. Over the course of a journey in my car, my speed will be constantly changing; sometimes it will even be zero. When we talk about the average speed for a journey, it is as though we add up all the miles covered during various stages of the journey and then share them out equally 'per hour'. This uses the same idea of 'pooling' which was the basis for calculating the mean of a set of numbers. So if my journey covers 400 miles in total and takes 8 hours, the average speed is 50 miles per hour (400 ÷ 8). The logic here is that if

I had been able to travel at a constant speed of 50 miles in each hour, then the journey would have taken the same time (8 hours). So the average speed (in miles per hour) is the total distance travelled (in miles) divided by the total time taken (in hours). We can then extend this definition of average speed to apply to journeys where the time is not a whole number of hours; for example, for a journey of 22 miles in 24 minutes (0.4 hours) the average speed is 22 ÷ 0.4, which is 55 miles per hour. And, of course, the same principle applies whatever units are used for distance and time; for example, if the toy car takes 5 seconds to run down a ramp of 150 centimetres, the average speed is 30 centimetres per second (150 ÷ 5).

Self-assessment questions

18.1: Compare the mean and median scores for English for Groups A and B, using the data given at the start of this chapter. Which group did better for English on the whole?

18.2: Find the mean score for English for the two groups combined. Is the mean score of the two groups combined equal to the mean of the two separate mean scores?

18.3: Find the median scores and the ranges for English and mathematics for the two groups combined.

18.4: John, in Group A, scored 49 for mathematics. How does this score compare with the performance of Group A as a whole?

18.5: Compile a frequency table for the numbers of letters in the last one hundred words in this chapter (ignoring numbers). What is the modal number of letters per word?

18.6: Toy car P travels 410 centimetres in 6 seconds; toy car Q travels 325 centimetres in 5 seconds. Which had the greater average speed?

18.7: On a car journey of 400 miles I average a speed of 40 miles per hour: how long does the journey take? On the way back I average a speed of 50 miles per hour: how long does the return journey take? Now (be careful!), what is the average speed for the whole journey, there and back?

18.8: The following table shows percentages of pupils reaching level 2 or above in a national test for reading, in schools with more than 20% and up to 35% of pupils eligible for free school meals:

95th %ile	UQ	60th %ile	median	40th %ile	LQ	5th %ile
94	83	78	76	72	67	52

St Anne's primary school has 24% of pupils eligible for free school meals, so it comes into this group. In the reading test, 69% of their pupils achieved level 2 or above. How well did they do compared with schools in this group?

18.9: Primary schools with 8% or less pupils eligible for free school meals (group A) are compared with primary schools with more than 50% eligible for free school meals (group E) in relation to the performances of pupils in the national reading test. Figure 18.3 is a box-and-whisker diagram showing the comparison: a) Just by glancing at the diagram, what is your impression of the comparative performances of the two groups of schools in the reading test? b) What is the median percentage of pupils for schools in group A achieving level 2 or above for reading? c) What is the highest percentage of pupils achieving level 2 or above for schools in group E? d) What is the median percentage of pupils for schools in group E achieving level 2 or above for reading? e) What is the lowest percentage of pupils achieving level 2 or above for schools in group A? f) Based on this evidence, which of group A or group E has the greater range of achievement in reading? g) Compare the inter-quartile ranges for the two groups.

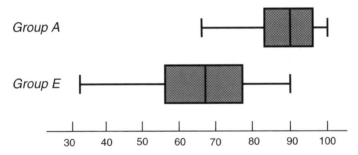

Figure 18.3   Percentages of pupils achieving level 2 or above in a reading test

Summary of teaching points

1. The idea of an average is appropriately introduced to pupils towards the upper end of the primary range. Explain to pupils the idea of an average being a representative figure for a set of numbers, enabling us to make comparisons between different sets.
2. Explain the idea of the mean, first using the example of pooling money and sharing it out equally, then extending it to other examples.
3. Emphasize that the median is just the one in the middle when the numbers are arranged in order, but point out how to deal with a set with an even number of numbers.

4. Introduce pupils to the idea of using the mode as a measure of average when appropriate, for example, when dealing with a large set of numbers with a limited range of possible values.
5. Show pupils, using examples of sets with approximately the same mean but very different spreads, the importance of looking at the range of values when comparing sets of numbers.
6. Pupils should use and apply these concepts to make comparisons between sets of data and to make sense of individual items of data, using information they have collected themselves in the course of purposeful enquiries.
7. Useful sources of data for applying these concepts are: the pupils themselves (their ages, their heights, distance of home from school, children in their family, and so on), the weather, sport, science experiments (repeating a measurement several times and recording a mean value) and most geography-focused topics (particularly for making comparisons between different areas).
8. Pupils must learn that conclusions drawn from statistics, such as averages, can be uncertain or even misleading.
9. To inform their own teaching and assessment of pupils' standards and progress, teachers will need to understand government statistics presented in terms of medians, quartiles, percentiles and deciles, and the use of box-and-whisker diagrams.

19

Probability

Pupils should be taught to: explore doubt and certainty and develop an understanding of probability through classroom situations; discuss events using a vocabulary that includes the words 'equally likely', 'certain'.

In this chapter there are explanations of

- the meaning of probability as a measurement applied to events;
- some of the language we use to indicate probability subjectively;
- the use of a numerical scale from 0 to 100%, or from 0 to 1, for measuring probability;
- estimating probability from statistical data;
- estimating probability from data obtained by repeating an experiment a large number of times;
- estimating probability by using theoretical arguments based on symmetry and equally likely outcomes;
- the use of two-way tables for identifying all the possible equally likely outcomes from an experiment involving two independent events;
- mutually exclusive events; and
- rules for combining probabilities for independent and mutually exclusive events.

What is probability?

First, we should recognize that in mathematics probability is a measurement, just like any other measurement such as length or mass. Second, it is a measurement that is applied to *events*. But what it is about an event that is being measured is surprisingly elusive. My view is that what we are measuring is how strongly we believe that the event will happen. We describe this level of belief with words ranging from 'impossible' to 'certain' and compare our assessment of different events by talking about one being 'more likely' or 'less likely' than another. This strength of belief is determined by different kinds of *evidence* that we may assemble.

Sometimes this evidence is simply the accumulation of our experience, in which case our judgement about how likely one event may be compared with others is fairly *subjective*. For example, one group of students wrote down some events that might occur during the following 12 months and ranked them in order from the least likely to the most likely as follows:

1. It will snow in Norwich during July.
2. Norwich City will win the FA Cup.
3. Steve will get a teaching post.
4. There will be a general election in the UK.
5. Someone will reach the summit of Mount Everest.

When they were then told that Steve had an interview at a school the following week for a post for which he was ideally suited, this extra piece of evidence had an immediate effect on their strength of belief in event (3) and they changed its position in the ranking.

By using 'more likely than' and 'less likely than', this activity is based on the ideas of comparison and ordering, always the first stages of the development of any aspect of measurement. The next stage would be to introduce some kind of measuring scale. For measuring probability, this can be done at first using everyday language. For example, we might judge that event (1) is 'almost impossible', event (2) is 'fairly unlikely' and event (5) is 'almost certain'. When we feel that an event is as likely to happen as not to happen, we say that 'the chances are evens'. To introduce a numerical scale, we can think of awarding marks out of 100 for each event, with 0 marks for an event we believe to be impossible, 100 marks for an event we judge to be certain, and 50 marks for 'evens'. For example, purely subjectively, the students in the group awarded 1 mark for event (1), 5 marks for event (2), 50 marks for event (4) and 99 marks for event (5). Event (3) started out at 40, but moved to 75 when the new evidence was obtained.

If these marks out of 100 are now thought of as percentages and converted to decimals (see Chapter 16 for how to do this), we have the standard scale used for measuring probability, ranging from 0 (impossible), through 0.5 (evens), to 1 (certain). For example, our subjective assessment of the probabilities of events (2) and (5) are 0.05 and 0.99 respectively.

How can you measure probability more objectively?

There are three ways of collecting evidence that can be used for a more objective estimate of probability:

1. We can collect statistical data and use the idea of relative frequency.
2. We can perform an experiment a large number of times and use the relative frequency of different outcomes.
3. We can use theoretical arguments based on symmetry and equally likely outcomes.

The first of these is used extensively in the world of business, such as in insurance or marketing, where probabilities are often assessed by gathering statistical data. For example, to determine an appropriate premium for a life insurance policy for a person such as myself, an insurance company would use the probabilities that I might live to 60, to 70, to 80, and so on. To determine these probabilities they could collect statistical data about university lecturers of my age living in East Anglia and find what proportion of these survive to various ages. If it is found that out of 250 cases, 216 live to 70, then this evidence would suggest that a reasonable estimate for the probability of my living to this age is 86.4% (216 ÷ 250) or, as a decimal, 0.864. Since it is normally impractical to obtain data from the entire population, this application of probability is usually based on evidence collected from a *sample*. For example, what is the probability that a word chosen at random from a page of text in this book will have four letters in it? To answer this we could use the last hundred words of the previous chapter as a sample. Since 12 of these words have four letters, the *relative frequency* of four-letter words in the sample is 12%. So an estimate for the probability, based on this evidence, would be 0.12. In general, the larger the sample, the more reliable is the relative frequency as an estimate of the probability.

The second procedure for obtaining objective estimates for probabilities applies the same idea, but to an *experiment*, often the kind of thing that can be experienced in a classroom. Now the 'event' in question is an *outcome* of the experiment. For example, the experiment might be to throw three identical dice simultaneously. The outcome we are interested in is that the score on one of them should be greater than the sum of the scores on the other two. What is the probability of this outcome? A useful experience for pupils is to make a subjective estimate of the probability, based purely on intuition, and then to perform the experiment a large number of times, recording the numbers of successes and failures. For example, they might make a subjective estimate that the chances of this happening would be a bit less than evens, so the probability is, say, about 0.40. Then the dice are thrown, say, 200 times and it is found that the number of successes is 58. Hence the relative frequency of successes is 29% (58 ÷ 200) and so the best estimate for the probability, based on this evidence, would be 0.29.

For some experiments, however, we can consider all the possible outcomes *theoretically* and make estimates for probability using an argument based on *symmetry*. Experiments with coins and dice lend themselves to this kind of argument. The simplest argument would be about tossing one coin. There are only two possible outcomes, heads and tails. Given the symmetry of the coin, there is no reason to assume that one outcome is more or less likely than the other. So we would conclude that the probability of a head is 0.5 and the probability of a tail is 0.5. Notice that the sum of the probabilities of all the possible outcomes must be 1. This represents 'certainty': we are certain that the coin will come down either heads or tails. Similarly, if we throw a conventional, six-faced die, there are six possible outcomes, all of which, on the basis of symmetry, are equally likely. We therefore determine the probability of each number turning up to be one-sixth, or about 0.17 (1 ÷ 6 = 0.1666666 on a calculator). We can also determine the probability of events that are made up of various outcomes. For example, there are two scores on the die that are multiples of three, so the probability of throwing a multiple of three would be two-sixths, or about 0.33 (2/6 = 1/3 = 0.3333333 on a calculator).

So the procedure for determining the probability of a particular event by this theoretical approach is:

1. List all the possible equally likely outcomes from the experiment, being guided by symmetry, but thinking carefully to ensure that the outcomes listed really are equally likely.
2. Count up in how many of these outcomes the event in question occurs.
3. Divide the second number by the first.

For example, to find the probability that a card drawn from a conventional pack of playing cards will be less than 7:

1. There are 52 equally likely outcomes from the experiment, i.e. 52 possible cards that can be drawn.
2. The event in question (the card is less than 7) occurs in 24 of these.
3. So the probability is 24 ÷ 52, or about 0.46.

It is important to remember at this stage what I said at the beginning of this chapter about the meaning of probability. It is a measure of how strongly you believe an event will happen. So when I say the probability of a coin turning up heads is 0.5, I am making a statement about how strongly I believe that it will come up heads. This kind of theoretical probability, provided the argument based on symmetry was valid, does not change from one outcome to the next. So the result of one trial does not affect the probabilities of what will happen in the next. If I have just thrown a head, the probability of the next toss being a head is still 0.5. If I have just thrown 20 tails in succession, the probability of the next one being a head is still 0.5. (Of course, there might be something peculiar about the coin, but I am assuming that it is not bent or weighted in any way that might distort the results.) What the probability does tell me, however, is that *in the long run*, if you go on tossing the coin long enough, you will see the relative frequency of heads (and tails) gradually getting closer and closer to 50%. This does not mean that with a thousand tosses I would *expect* 500 of each; in fact, that would be very surprising! But I would expect the proportion of heads to be about 50% and getting closer to 50% the more experiments I perform. It is therefore important for pupils actually to do such experiments a large number of times, obtain the relative frequencies of various outcomes for which they have determined the theoretical probability and observe and discuss the fact that the two are not usually exactly the same. There is a wonderfully mystical idea here: that in an experiment with a number of equally likely possible outcomes we have no way of predicting what will be the outcome of any given experiment, but we can predict with confidence what will happen in the long run! (This for me seems to provide a mathematical model for resolving the theological paradox of free will and predestination.)

How do you deal theoretically with tossing two coins or throwing two dice?

We do have to be careful when arguing theoretically about possible outcomes to ensure that they are really all equally likely. For example, one class of pupils decided there were three possible outcomes when you toss two coins – two heads, two tails, one of each – and determined the probabilities to be one-third for each. Then performing the experiment 1000 times between them (40 times each for 25 pupils) they found that two heads turned up 256 times, two tails turned up 234 times and one of each turned up 510 times. So the relative frequencies were 25.6%, 23.4% and 51%, obviously not getting close to the 'theoretical' 33.3%. The problem is that these three outcomes are *not equally likely*. Calling the two coins A and B, we can identify *four* possible outcomes: A and B both heads, A head and B tail, A tail and B head, A and B both tails. So the theoretical probabilities of two heads, two tails and one of each are 0.25, 0.25 and 0.50 respectively.

In this example, the outcome of tossing coin A and the outcome of tossing coin B are technically called *independent events*. This means simply that what happens to coin B is not affected in any way by what happens to coin A, and *vice versa*. With experiments involving two independent events, such as two coins being tossed or two dice being thrown, a useful device for listing all the possible outcomes is a two-way table. Figure 19.1(a) is such a table, showing the four possible outcomes from tossing two coins. Figure 19.1(b) similarly gives all 36 possible outcomes, shown as total scores in the table, when two dice are thrown. From this table we can discover, for example, that the probability of scoring seven (7 occurs 6 times out of 36: $^6/_{36}$ = 0.17 approximately) is much higher than, say, scoring eleven (11 occurs 2 times out of 36: $^2/_{36}$ = 0.06 approximately).

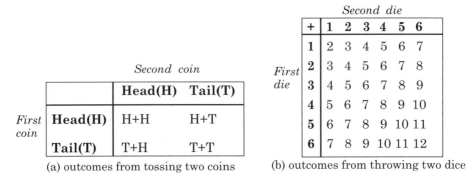

Figure 19.1   *Two-way tables for an experiment with two independent events*

An important principle in probability theory is that the probability of both of two independent events occurring is obtained by multiplying the probabilities of each one occurring. For example, if I toss a coin the probability of obtaining a head is 0.5. If I throw a die the probability of scoring an even number is 0.5. So, if I toss the coin and throw the die simultaneously, the probability of getting a head *and* an even number is $0.5 \times 0.5 = 0.25$. This principle can be expressed as a generalization as follows:

If the probabilities of two independent events A and B are *p* and *q* then the probability of both A and B occurring is $p \times q$.

What are mutually exclusive events?

Events that cannot possibly occur at the same time are said to be *mutually exclusive*. For example, if I throw two dice, getting a total score of 7 and getting a total score of 11 are two mutually exclusive outcomes – since you cannot score both 7 and 11 simultaneously. However, getting a total score of 7 and getting a total score that is odd are not mutually exclusive events, since clearly you can do both at the same time. The reader should note that mutually exclusive events are definitely not independent, because if one occurs then the other one cannot.

A second important principle of probability theory is that the probability that one or other of two mutually exclusive events occurring is the sum of their probabilities. So, for example, the probability of scoring 7 or 11 when I throw two dice is the sum of $6/36$ (the probability of scoring 7) and $2/36$ (the probability of scoring 11), that is, $8/36$, or 0.22, approximately. This principle can be expressed as a generalization as follows:

> If the probabilities of two mutually exclusive events A and B are p and q then the probability of either A or B occurring is $p + q$.

If you list a set of mutually exclusive events that might occur in a particular experiment that cover all possible outcomes then the sum of all their probabilities must equal 1. For example, in throwing two coins we could identify these three mutually exclusive events: two heads (probability 0.25), two tails (probability 0.25), one head and one tail (probability 0.5). The sum of these probabilities is $0.25 + 0.25 + 0.5 = 1$.

Self-assessment questions

19.1: What would be the most appropriate way to determine the probability that: a) a drawing-pin will land point-up when tossed in the air; b) a person aged 50–59 years in England will have two living parents; and c) the total score when two dice are thrown is an even number?

19.2: What is the probability that a word chosen at random in this book will have fewer than six letters in it? Use the sample of data collected in question 18.5 in the previous chapter to make an estimate for this.

19.3: If I throw a regular dodecahedron die (with 12 faces, numbered 1 to 12): a) what is the probability that I will score a number with two digits? b) what is the probability that I will score a number with one digit?

19.4: See Figure 19.1(b). When two conventional dice (with six faces, numbered one to six) are thrown, what is the probability of: a) Scoring a multiple of 3? b) Scoring a multiple of 4? c) Scoring a number that is a multiple of 3 or 4 or both?

19.5: I throw two conventional dice. Write down an outcome that has a probability of 0 and another outcome that has a probability of 1.

19.6: If you draw a card at random from a pack of playing cards, the probability that the card will be an ace is $\frac{1}{13}$. The probability that it will be a black card is $\frac{1}{2}$. Are these two outcomes independent? Are they mutually exclusive? What is the probability of getting a black ace?

19.7: If a shoe is tossed in the air the probability of it landing the right way up is found by experiment to be 0.35. The probability that it will land upside down is found to be 0.20. Are these two events independent? Are they mutually exclusive outcomes? What is the probability of the shoe landing either the right way up or upside down? The only other possible outcome is that it lands on one of its sides; what is the probability of this?

19.8: Statistics show that the probability of a male teacher age 30 being alive on his sixty-fifth birthday is 0.8 and the probability of his being alive on his seventy-fifth birthday is 0.5. Are these two events independent? Are they mutually exclusive outcomes? What is the probability of both these events occurring?

Summary of teaching points

1. Introduce probability by getting pupils to write down events that might occur in the next 12 months and then to rank them in order from least likely to most likely. Use this to introduce some of the language of probability, particularly 'more likely than' and 'less likely than'.

2. Pupils should describe events that might occur with such labels as 'impossible', 'nearly impossible', 'not very likely', 'evens', 'fairly likely', 'almost certain', 'certain'.

3. Introduce the idea of measuring probability on a numerical scale, by subjectively assigning points out of 100 (i.e. percentage scores) to various events that might occur; then use these to introduce the probability scale from 0 to 1, by changing the percentages to decimals.

4. Pupils can be introduced to the idea of relative frequency, expressed as a percentage and as a decimal, using statistical data they have gathered themselves, as part of a purposeful enquiry.

5. Then explain to them how to apply the idea of relative frequency to the outcomes of experiments, interpreting these as estimates of probability.

6. Give pupils opportunities to compare their intuitive estimates of probabilities of various outcomes from an experiment with the estimates of probabilities obtained by repeating the experiment a large number of times.
7. In using theoretical arguments based on symmetry, emphasize the importance of identifying equally likely outcomes.
8. Let pupils compare probabilities determined theoretically with the results of performing experiments a large number of times.
9. Emphasize the idea that probability does not tell you anything about what will happen next, but predicts what will happen in the long run.
10. One obvious application of probability is to betting and lotteries. Be aware that some parents will hold strong views about gambling, so handle this subject in a way that is sensitive to different perspectives on the morality and acceptability of gambling as a pastime.

20

Algebra

Pupils should be taught to: understand and investigate general statements; search for pattern in their results; recognize and describe number patterns and use these to make predictions; make general statements, using words to describe a functional relationship, and test these; recognize, represent and interpret simple number relationships, constructing and using formulae in words then symbols; understand brackets to determine the order of operations; use patterns and relationships to explore simple algebraic ideas.

In this chapter there are explanations of

- the difference in the meaning of letters used as abbreviations in arithmetic and as used in algebra;
- the idea of a letter representing a variable;
- some other differences between arithmetic thinking and algebraic thinking;
- precedence of operators;
- ways of introducing pupils to the idea of a letter as a variable;
- the important role played by tabulation;
- the ideas of sequential and global generalization;
- independent and dependent variables;
- the meaning of the word 'mapping' in an algebraic context; and
- the usefulness of the trial-and-improvement method for solving equations arising from problems.

What do the letters used in algebra, like 'x' and 'y', actually mean?

To answer this important question I will start by posing two problems, using letters as symbols. The reader is invited to write down his or her answers to these two problems before reading on:

- Problem 1: You can get 10 francs to the pound. You have P pounds. You exchange this money for F francs. What is the relationship between P and F?
- Problem 2: S is the number of students in a school. T is the number of teachers. There are 20 times as many students as teachers. Write down an equation using S and T.

Most people write down $10F = P$ for Problem 1 (or $10F = 1P$ or $P = 10F$ or $1P = 10F$, which are all different ways of saying the same thing). The correct answer is actually $F = 10P$. Figure 20.1(a) shows various values for P and F. For example, if I have 1 pound ($P = 1$) I can exchange this for 10 francs ($F = 10$); if I have 2 pounds ($P = 2$) I can exchange this for 20 francs ($F = 20$); similarly, when $P = 3$, $F = 30$, and so on. The table makes it clear that whatever number is chosen for P (1, 2, 3, . . .) the value of F is ten times this number (10, 20, 30, . . .). This is precisely what is meant by the algebraic statement, $F = 10P$. Even people who are apparently quite well qualified in mathematics get this the wrong way round when this problem is given to them, so it is instructive to analyse the thinking which leads to this misunderstanding. What those who write down $10F = P$ are thinking, of course, is that they are writing a statement that is saying '10 francs make a pound'. The F and P are being used as abbreviations for 'franc' and 'pound'. This is, of course, how we use letters in *arithmetic*, when they are actually abbreviations for fixed quantities or measurements. When we write 10p or 5 m the p stands for 'a penny' and the m stands for 'a metre'. But this is precisely what the letters do *not* mean in *algebra*. They are not abbreviations for measurements. They do not represent 'a thing' or an object. They are *variables*. The letter P in Problem 1 stands for 'whatever number of pounds you choose'. It does not stand for a pound, but for the *number* of pounds.

No. of pounds	No. of francs		No. of teachers	No. of students
P	**F**		**T**	**S**
1	10		1	20
2	20		2	40
3	30		3	60
4	40		4	80
5	50		5	100
(a)			(b)	

Figure 20.1   Tabulating values for Problems 1 and 2

So, in Problem 2, the relationship between S and T is *not* $20S = T$. Those who write this down think that what they are saying is, '20 students for 1 teacher'. Here they are thinking that the S stands for 'a student' and T stands for 'a teacher'. Again, we see the same misunderstanding. S and T are not abbreviations for a student and a teacher. They stand for 'the number of students' and 'the number of teachers'. They are variables. T can be any number and whatever number is chosen, S is 20 times this. So the relationship is $S = 20T$. This means 'the number of students is 20 times the number of teachers' or, referring to the tabulation of values in Figure 20.1, 'the number in column S is 20 times whatever number is in column T'.

It is understandable that so many people get the algebraic statements in these problems the wrong way round. First, the choice of P, F, S, T as letters to represent the variables in the problems is actually unhelpful (deliberately, I have to admit). Using the first letters of the words 'pound', 'franc', 'student' and 'teacher' does rather suggest that they are abbreviations for these things. (Fewer people get these relationships the wrong way round if other letters are used for the variables, such as N and M.) Then, so many of us have been subjected to explanations in 'algebra lessons' that reinforce this misconception that the letters stand for things. For example, it does not help to explain $2a + 3a = 5a$ by saying '2 apples plus 3 apples makes 5 apples'. This again makes us think of a as an abbreviation for apples. What this statement means is: whatever number you choose for a, then 'a multiplied by 2' plus 'a multiplied by 3' is the same as 'a multiplied by 5'.

Are there other differences between arithmetic and algebra in the way symbols are used that I should be aware of?

The distinction between the meaning of letters used in algebra (as variables) and in arithmetic (as abbreviations) is undoubtedly one of the most crucial differences between these two branches of mathematics. But there are a number of other significant differences of which teachers should be aware:

- The use of the equals sign.
- The need to recognize the mathematical structure of a problem.
- The distinction between solving a problem and representing it.
- The need to recognize 'precedence of operators'.

Surely the equals sign always means the same thing, doesn't it?

What the equals sign means strictly in mathematical terms is not the same thing necessarily as the way it is interpreted in practice. When doing arithmetic, that is manipulating numbers, pupils mostly think of the equals sign as an instruction to do something with some numbers, to perform an operation. They see '3 + 5 =' and respond by doing something: adding the 3 and the 5 to get 8. So, given the question, $3 + \square = 5$, many younger pupils put 8 in the box; they see the equals sign as an instruction to perform an operation on the numbers in the question, and naturally respond to the '+' sign by adding them up. Pupils also use the equals sign simply as a device for connecting the calculation they have performed with the result of the calculation. It means simply, 'This is what I did and this is what I got . . .' Given the problem, 'You have £28, earn £5 and spend £8, how much do you have now?' pupils will quite happily write something like: $28 + 5 = 33 - 8 = 25$. This way of recording the calculation is mathematically incorrect, because $28 + 5$ does not equal $33 - 8$. But this is not what the pupil means, of course. What is written down here represents the pupil's thinking about the problem, or the buttons he or she has pressed on a calculator to solve it. It simply means something like, 'I added 28 and 5, and got the answer 33, and then I subtracted 8 and this came to 25'. In algebra, however, the equals sign must be seen as representing *equivalence*. It means that what is written on one side 'is the same as' what is written on the other side. Of course, it has this meaning in arithmetic as well: $3 + 5 = 8$ does mean that $3 + 5$ is the same as 8. But pupils rarely use it to mean this; their experience reinforces the perception of the equals sign as an instruction to perform an operation with some numbers. In algebraic statements it is the idea of equivalence that is strongest in the way the equals sign is used. For example, when we write $p + q = r$, this is not actually an instruction to add p and q. In fact, we may not have to do anything at all with the statement. It is simply a statement of equivalence between one variable and the sum of two others.

What is different about arithmetic and algebra in relation to recognizing the mathematical structure of a problem?

In arithmetic, pupils often succeed through adopting informal, intuitive, context-bound approaches to solving problems. Often they do this without having to be aware explicitly of the underlying mathematical structure. For example, many pupils will be able to solve, 'How much for 10 grams of chocolate if you can get 2 grams per penny?' without recognizing the formal structure of the problem as that of division. But even with a calculator, they may then be unable to solve the same problem with more difficult numbers: 'How much for 75 grams of chocolate if you can get 1.35 grams per penny?' The corresponding algebraic problem is a generalization of all problems with this same structure: 'How much for A grams of chocolate if you can get B grams per penny?' It is often no use in trying to explain this just putting in some simple numbers for A and B and asking what you do to these numbers to answer the question, because the pupils do not recognize the existence of a division structure here at all. The primitive, intuitive thinking about the arithmetic problem with simple numbers does not make the mathematical structure explicit in a way that supports the algebraic generalization, $A \div B$. It is partly because of this that I have put so much stress on the *structures* of addition, subtraction, multiplication and division in Chapters 4 and 7, and encouraged the frequent use of the question, 'what is the calculation you enter on a calculator to answer this?' as a device for making the mathematical structure explicit.

Can you explain the distinction between solving a problem and representing it?

The discussion above leads to a further significant difference between arithmetic and algebra. Given a problem to solve in arithmetic involving more than one operation, the question we ask ourselves is, 'What sequence of operations is needed to *solve* this problem?' In algebra, the question is, 'What sequence of operations is needed to *represent* this problem?' For example, consider this problem:

● Problem 3: A plumber's call-out charge is £15; then you pay £12 an hour. How many hours' work would cost £75?

The arithmetic thinking might be: $75 - 15 = 60$, then $60 \div 12 = 5$. This is the sequence of operations required to *solve* the problem. But the algebraic approach would be to let N stand for the number of hours (which is therefore a variable and can take any value) and then to write down: $12N + 15 = 75$. This is the sequence of operations that *represents* the problem. (Then to solve the problem we have to find the value of N that makes this algebraic equation true.) It is quite possible, therefore, that the two approaches, as illustrated here, result in the use of inverse operations. To solve the problem we think: subtraction, then division; but to represent the problem algebraically we think: multiplication, then addition. It is this kind of difference in the thinking involved which makes it so difficult for many pupils to make generalized statements using words or algebraic symbols, even of the simplest kind.

What is meant by 'precedence of operators'?

An expression like $3 + 5 \times 2$ is potentially ambiguous. If you do the addition first the answer is 16. But if you do the multiplication first the answer is 13. Which is correct? Well, if you enter this calculation as it stands on to the kind of basic calculator used in primary schools (using the key sequence: 3, +, 5, x, 2, =), you get 16. The calculator does the operations in the order they are entered. However, if you use a more advanced, scientific calculator, with the same key sequence, you will probably get the answer 13. These calculators use what is called an *algebraic operating system.* (As do many computer applications, such as spreadsheet programs.) This means that they adopt the convention of giving precedence to the operations of multiplication and division. So, when you enter $3 + 5$, the calculator waits to determine whether there is a multiplication or a division following the 5; if there is, this is done first. If you actually mean to do the addition first you would have to use brackets to indicate this: for example, $(3 + 5) \times 2$. (This can also be written as $2(3 + 5)$, with the multiplication sign omitted but understood.)

Now this convention of precedence of operators is always applied strictly in algebra and is essential for avoiding ambiguity, particularly because of the way symbols are used in algebra to represent problems not just to solve them. So, for example, $A + B \times C$ (which is usually written $A + BC$, with the understanding that BC means $B \times C$) stands for 'B multiplied by C, add A'; whereas to represent 'A added to B, then multiply by C' we would write $(A + B) \times C$. (This is usually written $C(A + B)$.) But in arithmetic – and therefore in number work in primary schools – we do not actually need this convention. The calculations we have to do should always arise from a practical context which will naturally determine the order in which the various operations have to be performed, so there is not usually any ambiguity. Since the basic calculators we use in primary schools deal with operations in the order they arrive, there is little point in giving pupils calculations like $3 + 5 \times 2$ and insisting that this means you do the multiplication first. But as soon as we get into using algebra to express generalizations, we need this convention for precedence of operators, so pupils have to learn to recognize it and to use brackets as necessary to override it.

How can the idea of a letter being a variable be introduced to pupils?

The central principle in algebra is the use of letters to represent *variables* which enable us to express *generalizations*. Pupils should therefore first encounter the use of letters as algebraic symbols for this purpose. The most effective way of doing this is through the tabulation of number patterns in columns, with the problem being to express the pattern in the numbers, first in words and later in symbols. A useful game in this context is What's My Rule?

Figure 20.2 shows some examples of this game. In each case the pupils are challenged to say what is the rule that is being used to find the numbers in column B and then to use this rule to find the number in column B when the number in column A is 100. In example (a), pupils usually observe first that the rule is 'adding 2'. Here they have spotted what I refer to when talking to children as the 'up-and-down rule'. When talking to teachers I call it the *sequential generalization*. This is the pattern that determines how to continue the sequence. Asking what answer do you get when the number in A is 100, or some other large number, makes us realize the inadequacy of the sequential generalization. We need a 'left-to-right rule': a rule which tells us what to do to the numbers in A to get the numbers in B. This is the *global generalization*. Pupils towards the top end of the primary range can usually determine that when the number in A is 100, the number in B is 201, and this helps them to recognize that the rule is 'double and add 1'. Later this can be expressed algebraically as $B = A \times 2 + 1$, or $B = 2A + 1$. This clearly uses the idea of letters as variables, expressing generalizations. The statement means essentially, 'The number in column B is whatever number is in column A multiplied by 2, add one'. Similarly, in Figure 20.2(b), the sequential generalization, 'add 4', is easily spotted; more difficult is the global generalization, 'multiply by 4 and subtract 1', although again working out what is in B when 100 is in A helps to make this rule explicit. This leads to the algebraic statement, $B = A \times 4 - 1$, or $B = 4A - 1$. In these kinds of examples, where A is chosen and a rule is used to determine B, A is called an *independent variable* and B a *dependent variable*.

This experience of tabulation and finding generalizations to describe the patterns that emerge occurs very often in *mathematical investigations*, particularly those involving a sequence of geometric shapes, such as those discussed in Chapter 12. For example, an investigation into the pattern in the triangle numbers shown in Figure 12.5 could lead to the generalization that the nth triangle number, which is the sum of $1 + 2 + 3 + 4 + 5 + \ldots + n$, is equal to $\frac{1}{2}n(n + 1)$. The reader is invited to confirm this in self-assessment question 20.8 below.

A	B
1	3
2	5
3	7
4	9
5	11
6	13
7	15
8	17
9	19
10	21
100	?

(a)

A	B
1	3
2	7
3	11
4	15
5	19
6	23
7	27
8	31
9	35
10	39
100	?

(b)

A	B
1	3
2	8
3	13
4	18
5	23
6	28
7	33
8	38
9	43
10	48
100	?

(c)

A	B
1	99
2	98
3	97
4	96
5	95
6	94
7	93
8	92
9	91
10	90
100	?

(d)

Figure 20.2 What's My Rule?

Figure 20.3 provides another example: the problem is to determine how many children can sit around various numbers of tables, arranged side by side, if six children can sit around one table. The number of tables here is the independent variable and the number of children the dependent variable. With 2 tables we can seat 8 children; with 3 tables we can seat 10. These results are already tabulated. The tabulation can

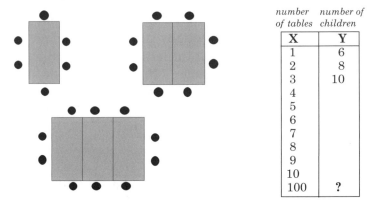

number of tables	number of children
X	Y
1	6
2	8
3	10
4	
5	
6	
7	
8	
9	
10	
100	?

Figure 20.3 An investigation leading to a generalization

then be completed for other numbers of tables, the sequential generalization can be articulated, the answer for 100 tables can be predicted and finally the global generalization can be formulated, first in words and then in symbols, with X, representing the independent variable, that is, the number of tables, and Y the dependent variable, that is, the number of children. This is left as an exercise for the reader, in question 20.6 below.

So what is a mapping?

In the examples of tabulation used above there have always been the following three components: a set of input numbers (the values of the independent variable), a rule for doing something to these numbers and a set of output numbers (the values of the dependent variable). These three components put together – input set, rule, output set – constitute what is sometimes called a *mapping* or a *functional relationship*.

This is an all-pervading idea in algebra. In fact, most of what we have to learn to do in algebra fits into this simple structure. Sometimes we are given the input and the rule and we have to find the output: this is substituting into a formula. Then sometimes we are given the input and the output and our task is to find the rule: this is the process of generalizing (as in the examples of tabulation above). Then, finally, we can be given the output and the rule and be required to find the input: this is the process of solving an equation. That just about summarizes the whole of algebra!

Is solving equations something to introduce in primary schools?

As a formal algebraic process, I would not usually introduce solving equations in primary schools, especially since the techniques involved can so easily reinforce the idea that the letters stand for 'things', or even specific numbers, rather than variables. What is appropriate, however, is to introduce pupils to the algebraic thinking involved in solving problems through the *trial-and-improvement* approach (see Chapter 12). These can be purely numerical problems that cannot be solved by a simple arithmetic procedure, such as finding square roots and cube roots, as explained in Chapter 12, or they can be practical problems. Problems about area and perimeter are particularly useful here. In Figure 20.4, the problem posed is: 'What should be the length of the side of a square lawn if the area of the whole garden is to be 200 square metres?'

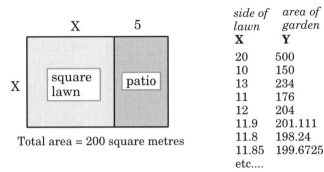

side of lawn X	area of garden Y
20	500
10	150
13	234
11	176
12	204
11.9	201.111
11.8	198.24
11.85	199.6725
etc....	

Total area = 200 square metres

Figure 20.4   A problem solved by trial and improvement

The width of the patio is fixed as 5 metres. This is approached by trying various inputs (for the side of the square) and using an appropriate rule to determine the outputs (the corresponding area of the garden). One possible rule is 'add 5 to the side of the square and multiply by the side of the square'. Expressing this in symbols: the area = $X(X + 5)$. So we are actually solving the equation, $X(X + 5) = 200$. The first trial is $X = 20$. This gives an area of 500, which is too large. Next we try 10, which gives an area of 150, which is too small. So we try something in between, say, $X = 13$. This gives an area of 234, too large . . . and so on, until we get an answer to whatever level of accuracy we require.

The calculations here can be done with a calculator, as they have been in the table in Figure 20.4. Alternatively, this kind of problem provides a good application of a computer spreadsheet package. Figure 20.5 shows how this might work. In column A are entered the various trials used for the values of X. *Formulas* are entered into the cells in column B which calculate automatically the areas for the corresponding garden. Figure 20.5(a) shows what a typical spreadsheet might look like on the computer screen, with the areas in column B given to one decimal place. The solution found here is that a side of length 11.86 m gives the required area of 200 square metres. The beauty of using a spreadsheet is that the formula for the area has to be entered only once. This can be explained with Figure 20.5(b), which reveals the formulas that have been entered in the spreadsheet to produce the numbers in Figure 20.5(a). We first enter the appropriate formula in cell B2. This is '= A2*(A2 + 5)'. We then simply instruct the computer to fill this formula down the column – all spreadsheet packages have a simple procedure for doing this – and the computer automatically modifies the formula for each row, as shown. Then we can enter our various trials in column A and home in on the solution. The reader is encouraged to explore the use of spreadsheets for solving mathematical problems like this one.

	A	B
1	X: Side of square (m)	Area of garden (m^2)
2	20	500.0
3	10	150.0
4	13	234.0
5	11	176.0
6	12	204.0
7	11.8	198.2
8	11.9	201.1
9	11.88	200.5
10	11.87	200.2
11	11.86	200.0

	A	B
1	X: Side of square (m)	Area of garden (m^2)
2	20	= A2*(A2+5)
3	10	= A3*(A3+5)
4	13	= A4*(A4+5)
5	11	= A5*(A5+5)
6	12	= A6*(A6+5)
7	11.8	= A7*(A7+5)
8	11.9	= A8*(A8+5)
9	11.88	= A9*(A9+5)
10	11.87	= A10*(A10+5)
11	11.86	= A11*(A11+5)

(a)   (b)

Figure 20.5   Using a spreadsheet to solve X(X + 5) = 200

The point about solving equations this way is that the letter involved (*X* standing for the side of the square) is genuinely perceived as a variable – and our task is to find the value of this independent variable which generates the required value for the dependent variable. This is much more sophisticated and powerful than the idea that '*X* stands for an unknown number'. I remember being told this at school and spending a whole year doing things like 2*X* + 3*X* = 5*X*, all the time believing that the teacher actually knew what this unknown number was and that one day he would tell us.

Self-assessment questions

20.1: The length of a garden is *F* feet. Measured in yards, it is *Y* yards long. What is the relationship between *F* and *Y*? (There are three feet in one yard.) What criticism could you make of this question?

20.2: If I buy *A* apples at 10p each and *B* bananas at 12p each, what is the meaning of: a) *A* + *B*; b) 10*A*; c) 12*B*; and d) 10*A* + 12*B*? What criticism could you make of this question?

20.3: The first 5 rides in a fair are free. The charge for all the other rides is £2 each. If Jenny has £12 to spend, how many rides can she have? What are the arithmetic steps you used in answering this question? How would you *represent* the problem algebraically, using *N* to stand for the number of rides?

20.4: What answer would you get if you entered 25 – 5 × 3 on to: a) a basic calculator; and b) a scientific calculator using an algebraic operating system?

20.5: For each of Figure 20.2(c) and 20.2(d), write down: a) the sequential generalization; b) the value of B when A is 100; c) the global generalization in words; and d) the global generalization in symbols (B = . . .).

20.6: Complete the tabulation of results in Figure 20.3. Then write down: a) the sequential generalization; b) the number of children if there are 100 tables; c) the global generalization in words; and d) the global generalization in symbols (Y = . . .). Now repeat this investigation with the tables arranged end to end, rather than side by side.

20.7: I choose a number, double it, add 3 and multiply the answer by my number. The result is 3654. What is my number? Use a calculator and the trial-and-improvement method to answer this. What equation have you solved?

20.8: List the first 10 triangle numbers: 1, 3, 6, 10, and so on. Now double these to get 2, 6, 12, 20, and so on. Express each of these numbers as products of two factors, starting with 1×2, 2×3, 3×4. Hence obtain a generalization for the nth triangle number (the sum of the first n natural numbers). What is the one-hundredth triangle number (i.e. the sum of all the natural numbers from 1 to 100)?

Summary of teaching points

1. Use the What's My Rule? game to introduce pupils to algebraic thinking through making generalizations, first in words, then in symbols.
2. Reinforce this with tabulated results from investigations, where pupils can find patterns in the sequence of numbers obtained.
3. Use this procedure: tabulate results in an orderly fashion; articulate the sequential generalization (the up-and-down rule); predict the result for a big number, such as 100; articulate the global generalization (the left-to-right rule) in words; check this on some results you know; and express the global rule in symbols.
4. Avoid the fruit-salad approach to explaining algebraic statements, for example, referring to $3a + 5b$ as '3 apples and 5 bananas', or anything that reinforces the ideas that the letters stand for objects or specific numbers.
5. Emphasize the idea that a letter in algebra stands for 'whatever number is chosen', i.e. a variable.
6. Reinforce through your own language the idea that the equals sign means 'is the same as', even in the early stages of recording the results of calculations.

7. Use the question, 'What is the calculation you would enter on a calcula-tor to solve this problem?', to help make the underlying structures of problems explicit (see summaries in Chapters 4 and 7).
8. Do not worry about precedence of operators when doing number work: the context giving rise to the calculation will determine the ap-propriate sequence of operations.
9. But make this principle explicit when algebraic notation is introduced, explaining the different systems used by various calculators, and show-ing the need for brackets when some rules are written algebraically.
10. Use trial-and-improvement methods, with a calculator or a spreadsheet, to solve equations arising from practical or numerical problems, to reinforce the idea of a variable.

21

Coordinates and Linear Relationships

Pupils should be taught to: read or plot coordinates in the first quadrant, then in all four quadrants; locate and draw shapes using coordinates in the first quadrant, then in all four quadrants.

In this chapter there are explanations of

- how the coordinate system enables us to specify location in a plane;
- axis, *x*-coordinate and *y*-coordinate, origin;
- the meaning of 'quadrant' in the context of coordinates;
- the difference between the coordinate system for labelling points in a plane and other systems which label spaces;
- some of the ways in which the coordinate system enables us to connect algebraic and geometric relationships;
- how to plot an algebraic relationship as a graph; and
- linear relationships, including those where one variable is directly proportional to another.

What is meant by 'coordinates in the first quadrant'?

The coordinate system is a wonderfully simple but elegant device for specifying location in two dimensions. Two number lines are drawn at right angles to each other, as shown in Figure 21.1. These are called *axes* (plural of *axis*). Of course, the lines can continue as far as we wish at either end. The point where the two lines meet (called the *origin*) is taken as the zero for both number lines. The vertical line is called the *y*-axis, and the horizontal line the *x*-axis. Then any point in the plane can be specified by two numbers, called its *coordinates*. The *x*-coordinate of a point is the distance moved along the *x*-axis, and the *y*-coordinate is the distance moved vertically, in order to get from the origin to the point in question. For example, to reach the point P shown in Figure 21.1 we would move 3 units along the x-axis and then 4 units vertically, so the x-coordinate of P is 3 and the y-coordinate is 4. We then state that the coordinates of P are (3,4). The convention is always to give the x-coordinate first and the y-coordinate second.

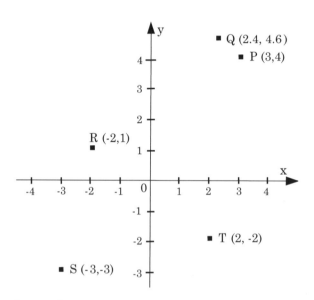

Figure 21.1   The coordinate system

The axes divide the plane into four sections, called *quadrants*. The first quadrant consists of all the points that have a positive number for each of their two coordinates. The points P and Q in Figure 21.1 are in the first quadrant. The point R (–2,1) is in the second quadrant, S (–3, –3) in the third quadrant and T (2, –2) in the fourth quadrant.

The beauty of this system is that we can now refer specifically to any point in the plane. And, of course, we are not limited to integers, as is shown by the point Q, with coordinates (2.4, 4.6). We can also use the coordinate system to describe the movement from one point to another. For example, from R to P is a movement of 5 units in the x-direction and 3 units in the y-direction; from T to S is a movement of –5 in the x-direction and –1 in the y-direction.

An important feature of this system is that it is the *points* in the plane which are labelled by the coordinates, not the *spaces*. This is a similar point to that made in Chapter 17, with reference to Figure 17.2(b), where the numbers on the vertical axis labelled the points on the scale, not the spaces between them. This is an important teaching point, because there are a number of situations that pupils will encounter which use coordinate systems based on the idea of labelling the spaces – for example, a number of board games and computer games, city street-maps, and computer spreadsheets. A common system employed in these and other similar examples is to use the labels for the columns (for example, A, B, C . . .) and the labels for the rows (for example, 1, 2, 3 . . .) to specify individual cells or squares (for example, B3). So, moving from this kind of labelling of spaces to the labelling of points is an important and significant step in the development of the idea of a coordinate system.

How do coordinates help to understand number relationships and geometry?

The system described above is sometimes called the *Cartesian coordinate system*. It takes its name from René Descartes (1596–1650), a prodigious French mathematician, who first made use of the system to connect geometry and algebra. He discovered that by interpreting the inputs and outputs from an algebraic mapping (see Chapter 20) as coordinates, and then plotting these as points, you could generate a geometric picture of the relationship. Then by the reverse process, starting with a geometric picture drawn on a coordinate system, you can generate an algebraic representation of the geometric properties. At primary-school level, we can only just touch on these massive mathematical ideas, so a couple of simple examples will suffice here.

First, we can take any simple algebraic relationship of the kind considered in Chapter 20 and explore the corresponding geometric picture. The convention is to use the x-axis for the independent variable. For example, the table shown in Figure 20.2(a) is generated by the algebraic rule, $B = 2A + 1$. In this case, A is the independent variable and is appropriately represented by the x-axis, and B is represented by the y-axis. So the conventional way of expressing the relationship, using the variables x and y for A and B, would be $y = 2x + 1$. The pairs of values in the table can be written as coordinates, as follows: (1, 3), (2, 5), (3, 7), and so on. When these are plotted, as shown in Figure 21.2(a), it is clear that they lie on a straight line. These points can then be joined up and the line continued indefinitely, as shown in Figure 21.2(b). This straight line is a powerful geometric image of the way in which the two variables are related. An algebraic rule like $y = 2x + 1$ which produces a straight-line graph is sometimes called a *linear relationship*. We can use the straight-line graph to read off related values of x and y other than those plotted; for example, the arrow in Figure 21.2(b) shows that when $y = 8$, $x = 3.5$. What we have done here is to find the value of the variable x for which $2x + 1 = 8$; in other words, we have *solved the equation $2x + 1 = 8$*. This can be an early introduction to the important mathematical method of solving equations by drawing graphs and reading off values.

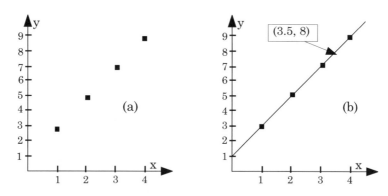

Figure 21.2   The rule y = 2x + 1 represented by coordinates

Exploring the graphs of different algebraic rules leads us to recognize a linear relationship as one in which the rule is simply a combination of multiplying or dividing by a fixed number and addition or subtraction. For example, all these rules are linear relationships:

divide by 6 and add 4	$(y = {}^x/_6 + 4)$
multiply by 7 and subtract 5	$(y = 7x - 5)$
multiply by 3 and subtract from 100	$(y = 100 - 3x)$
add 1 and multiply by 2	$(y = 2(x + 1))$

There are, of course, relationships that are non-linear. These are other kinds of rules, for example, those involving squaring (for example, multiply the input by itself) and other powers (cubes, and so on) which produce sets of coordinates that do not lie on straight lines. These are beyond the scope of this book.

The simplest kind of linear relationship is where y is *directly proportional* to x (see Chapter 16). This means that the ratio of y to x is constant, or, to put it another way, y is obtained by multiplying x by a constant factor. Examples of this kind of relationship abound in everyday life. If a bottle of wine costs £3, x is the number of bottles I buy and y

is the total cost in pounds, then the rule for finding y is 'multiply x by 3' or $y = 3x$. This rule generates the coordinates, (1, 3), (2, 6), (3, 9), and so on, and, including the possibility that I do not buy any bottles (0, 0). As shown in Figure 21.3, this rule produces a straight-line graph which, noting again the significance of the (0, 0) possibility, passes through the origin. Any rule of this kind, in which y is directly proportional to x, such as $y = 7x$, $y = 0.5x$, $y = 2.75x$, will produce a straight-line graph passing through the origin. An interesting point for discussion in the example above relates to the fact that the number of bottles bought is a 'discrete' variable (see Chapter 17): you cannot buy 3.6 bottles, for example. This means that the points on the line between the whole number values do not actually have any meaning. By contrast, if x had been the number of litres of petrol being bought at £3 per litre (price used for demonstration purposes only), then the rule would have been the same, $y = 3x$, but this time x would be a continuous variable and all the points on the straight-line graph in the first quadrant would have meaning. For example, when x is 3.6, y is 10.8, corresponding to a charge of £10.80 for 3.6 litres of petrol.

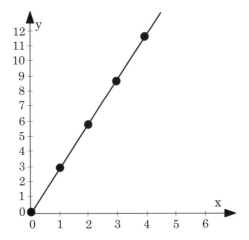

Figure 21.3   The variable y is directly proportional to x

This provides us with a practical method for solving direct proportion problems. For example, most conversions from one unit of measurement to another provide examples of two variables that are directly proportional and will therefore generate a straight line graph passing through the origin. Consider exchanging pounds for Dutch guilders, for example, where the exchange rate is given as 3.6 guilders to the pound.

A quick bit of mental arithmetic tells us that 36 guilders is equivalent to £10. Plotting this as the point with coordinates (36, 10) and drawing the straight line through this point and the origin produces a standard conversion graph, as shown in Figure 21.4. This can then be used to do other conversions. The arrows, for example, show a) how you would convert 45 guilders to £12.50, and b) £15 to 54 guilders. All problems of direct proportion, such as those tackled by arithmetic methods in Chapter 16, can also be solved by this graphical method (see, for example, self-assessment question 21.7 below).

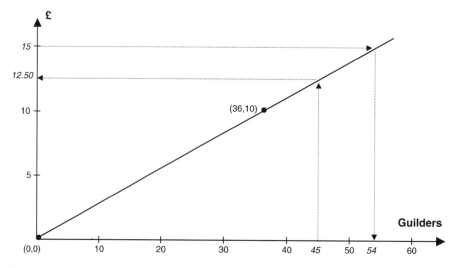

Figure 21.4   Conversion graph for guilders and pounds, where 36 guilders = £10

Can you give an example of how coordinates might be used to investigate a geometric property?

Using coordinates we can easily communicate a geometric shape, made up of straight lines, to someone else. For example, I could ask a class of pupils to plot the points (1, 2), (3, 2), (3, 6) and (1, 6) and to join these points up in the order given, to produce the rectangle ABCD in Figure 21.5. The corners A, B, C and D are called the *vertices* of the rectangle (each one is a *vertex*). Similarly, rectangle PQRS is produced by plotting (5, 2), (9, 4), (8, 6) and (4, 4). An interesting question is now raised: what rules or numerical patterns determine the coordinates of the four vertices of a rectangle? For example, we might notice that the movement from P to S (–1 in the *x*-direction, 2 in the *y*-direction) is the same as that from Q to R; and similarly for S to R and P to Q. A particularly interesting rule relates the coordinates of opposite vertices. I will leave readers to discover this for themselves (see question 21.4 below). In this way we can analyse geometric properties, such as the characteristics of a rect-angle, by means of algebraic relationships. It is the potential for explor-ing the connection between algebraic and geometric relationships which makes the coordinate system such a fundamental part of mathe-matics at every level.

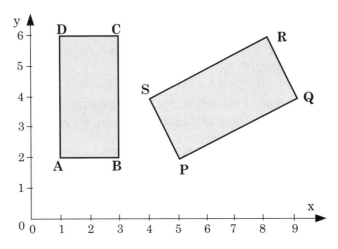

Figure 21.5   Using coordinates to draw rectangles

Self-assessment questions

21.1: A knight's move in chess is two steps horizontally (left or right) and one step vertically (up or down), or two steps vertically and one step horizontally. Starting at (3, 3), which points can be reached by a knight's move? Plot them and join them up.

21.2: On squared paper, plot some of the points corresponding to each of the tables (b), (c) and (d) in Figure 20.2. Are the algebraic rules here linear relationships?

21.3: Give an example of a variable which is directly proportional to each of the following independent variables: a) the number of boxes of eggs bought, with six eggs in each; b) the number of pounds exchanged at a bank for some foreign currency; and c) the bottom number in a set of equivalent fractions.

21.4: Plot the three points, (1, 2), (0, 3) and (3, 6), on squared paper. Join them up in this order and find the fourth point needed to complete a rectangle. Looking at this example and the two rectangles in Figure 21.5, what is the rule connecting the coordinates of opposite vertices of a rectangle? Use this rule to determine the fourth vertex of a rectangle, if the first three vertices are (4, 4), (5, 8), (13, 6). Check your answer by plotting the points and joining them up.

21.5: Plot these points and join them up in order to form a rectangle: A (0, 0), B (4, 0), C (4, 3) and D (0, 3). Now keep A and B fixed, but change C and D by adding 1 to each of their x-coordinates. What happens to the shape? Repeat this procedure and produce another shape. And again. The shapes you are making are all examples of parallelograms. What rules can you find for connecting the coordinates of the four vertices of a parallelogram? Use these rules to find the fourth vertex if the first three are (1, 1), (4, 2) and (4, 4).

21.6: Use Figure 21.2(b) to solve the equation $2x + 1 = 6$.

21.7: Use the fact that 11 stone is about the same as 70 kilograms to draw a conversion graph for stones and kilograms. Convert your personal weight from one to the other.

21.8: Draw a graph representing the linear relationship between temperatures in °F and in °C, given that 0°C is 32°F and 100°C is 212°F. (Plot the points (0, 32) and (100, 212) and join them with a straight line.) Use the graph to convert a) 82°F to°C, b) 16°C to°F.

Summary of teaching points

1. The use of coordinates to specify the location of points in a plane, rather than spaces, as in street-maps, is a significant point to be explained to pupils carefully.

2. Give pupils experience of activities where they use the coordinate system to describe movements from one point to another.

3. There is actually no need to limit primary-school pupils' experience of coordinates to the first quadrant, since the principles are the same in the other quadrants and these provide some useful experience of interpreting and applying negative numbers.

4. Pupils should interpret tables of values obtained by exploring algebraic relationships (as in Chapter 20) as sets of coordinates, plot these and discuss the results.

5. Pupils should investigate whether or not a particular relationship produces a straight-line graph when plotted as coordinates.

6. When a real-life relationship produces a straight-line graph, pupils should discuss whether or not the points between those plotted have meaning.

7. Show pupils how a relationship where one variable is directly proportional to another can be shown as a straight-line graph passing through the origin.
8. Give pupils the opportunity to analyse simple properties of geometric shapes such as rectangles and parallelograms, by looking for patterns and rules in the coordinates of their vertices.

22

Measurement

Pupils should be taught to: recognize the need for standard units of length, mass and capacity, choose which ones are suitable for a given task, and use them to make sensible estimates in everyday situations; convert one metric unit to another; know the rough metric equivalents of imperial units still in daily use; recognize that measurement is approximate; read the time from analogue and digital 12- and 24-hour clocks; use units of time – seconds, minutes, hours, days, weeks – and know the relationships between them.

In this chapter there are explanations of

- the distinction between mass and weight;
- the distinction between volume and capacity;
- two aspects of the concept of time: time interval and recorded time;
- the role of comparison and ordering as a foundation for measurement;
- the principle of transitivity in the context of measurement;
- some principles of inequalities, using the signs < and >;
- conservation of length, mass and liquid volume;
- non-standard and standard units;
- the idea that all measurement is approximate;
- the difference between a ratio scale and an interval scale;
- SI and other metric units of length, mass and time, including the use of prefixes;
- the importance of estimation and the use of reference items; and
- imperial units still in use and their relationship to metric units.

What is the difference between mass and weight?

There is a real problem here about the language we use to describe what we are measuring when, for example, we put a book in one pan of a balance and equalize it with, say, 200 grams in the other. Colloquially, most people say that what we have found out is that the book *weighs* 200 grams, or that its *weight* is 200 grams. This is technically incorrect. What we have discovered is that the book *weighs the same as* a mass of 200 grams, or that the *mass* of the book is 200 grams. This conflict between everyday language usage and the scientifically correct usage is not resolved simply by using the two words, mass and weight, interchangeably.

The units we use for weighing, such as grams and kilograms, or pounds and ounces, are actually units for measuring the mass of an object, not its weight. The mass is a measurement of the quantity of matter there is in the object. Note that this is not the same thing as the amount of space it takes up – that is, the *volume* of the object. A small lump of lead might have the same mass as the 200-gram book, but it would take up much less space, because the molecules making up the piece of lead are much more tightly packed together than those in the book. The problem with this concept of mass is that we cannot actually experience it directly. I cannot see the mass of the book, feel it or perceive it in any way. When I hold the book in my hand what I experience is the weight of the book. The weight is the force exerted on the book by the pull of gravity. I can feel this, because I have to exert a force myself to hold the book up. Of course, the weight and the mass are directly related: the greater the mass, the greater the weight, and therefore the heavier the object feels when I hold it in my hand. However, the big difference between the two is that, whereas the mass of an object is invariant, the weight changes depending on how far you are from the centre of the earth (or whatever it is that is exerting the gravitational pull on the object). We are all familiar with the idea that an astronaut's weight changes in space, or on the Moon, because the gravitational pull being exerted on the astronaut is less than it is on the earth's surface. In some circumstances, for example when in orbit, this gravitational pull can effectively be cancelled out and the astronaut experiences 'weightlessness'. The astronaut can then place a book on the palm of his or her hand and it weighs nothing. On the Moon's surface the force exerted on the book by gravity, that is, the weight of the book, is about one-sixth of what it was back on the earth's surface. But throughout all this the mass of the astronaut and the mass of the book remain unchanged. The book is still 200 grams, as it was on Earth, even though its weight has been changing constantly. (So a good way of losing weight is to go to the Moon, but this does not affect your waist size because what you really want to do is to lose mass!)

An important point to note is that the balance-type weighing devices do actually measure mass. We put the book in one pan, balance it with a mass of 200 grams in the other pan, and because the book 'weighs the same as' a mass of 200 grams we conclude that it also has a mass of 200 grams. Note that we would get the same result using the balance on the Moon. However, the pointers on spring-type weighing devices, such as many kitchen scales and bathroom scales, actually respond directly to weight. This means that they would give a different reading if we took them to the Moon, for example. But, of course, they are calibrated for use on the Earth's surface, so when I stand on the bathroom scales and the pointer indicates 72 kilograms I can rely on that as a measurement of my mass. On the Moon it would point to 12 kilograms; this would just be totally wrong.

Because weight is a force, it should be measured in the units of force. The standard unit of force in the metric system is the *newton*, appropriately named after Sir Isaac Newton (1642–1727), the mathematical and scientific genius who first articulated this distinction between mass and weight. A newton is defined as the force required to increase the speed of a mass of 1 kilogram by 1 metre per second every second. A newton is actually about the weight of a small apple and a mass of a kilogram has a weight of nearly 10 newtons. You probably don't need to know this, although you may come across spring-type weighing devices with a scale graduated in newtons.

One way to introduce the word 'mass' to primary-school pupils is to refer to those plastic or metal things we use for weighing objects in a balance as 'masses' (rather than 'weights'). So we would have a box of 10-gram masses and a box of 100-gram masses, and so on. Then when we have balanced an object against some masses, we can say that the object weighs the same as a mass of so many grams, as a step towards using the correct language, that the mass of the object is so many grams.

Can you explain the distinction between volume and capacity?

The volume of an object is the amount of three-dimensional space that it occupies. By historical accident, liquid volume and solid volume are conventionally measured in different units, although the concepts are exactly the same. Liquid volume is measured in litres and millilitres, and so on, whereas solid volume would have to be measured in units such as cubic metres and cubic centimetres. In the metric system the units for liquid and solid volume are related in a very simple way: 1 millilitre is the same volume as 1 cubic centimetre; or 1 litre is the same volume as 1000 cubic centimetres (see Figure 22.1).

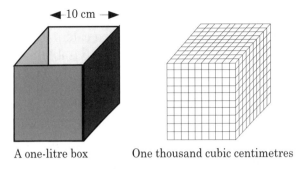

A one-litre box   One thousand cubic centimetres

Figure 22.1   A litre is the same volume as 1000 cubic centimetres

Only containers have *capacity*. The capacity of a container is the maximum volume of liquid that it can hold. Hence capacity is measured in the same units as liquid volume. For example, if a wine glass holds 180 millilitres of wine when filled to the brim then its capacity is 180 millilitres.

What about measuring time?

There are two quite different aspects of time that pupils have to learn to handle. First there is the idea of a *time-interval*. This refers to the length of time occupied by an activity, or the time that passes from one instant to another. Time-intervals are measured in units such as seconds, minutes, hours, days, weeks, years, decades, centuries, millennia.

Then there is the idea of *recorded time*, the time at which an event occurs. To handle recorded time, we use the various conventions for reading the time of day, such as o'clocks, a.m. and p.m., the 24-hour system, together with the different ways of recording the date, including reference to the day of the week, the day in the month and the year. So, for example, we might say that the meeting starts at 1530 on Monday, 7 October 2002, using the concept of 'recorded time', and that it is expected to last for 90 minutes, using the concept of 'time-interval'.

Time is one aspect of measurement that has not gone metric, so the relationships between the units (60 seconds in a minute, 60 minutes in an hour, 24 hours in a day, and so on) are particularly challenging. This makes it difficult, for example, to use a subtraction algorithm for finding the time intervals from one time to another. I strongly recommend that problems of this kind are done by an *ad hoc* process of adding-on. For example, to find the length of time of a journey starting at 10.45 a.m. and finishing at 1.30 p.m., reason like this: 15 minutes to 11 o'clock, then 2 hours to 1 o'clock, then a further 30 minutes, making a total of 2 hours and 45 minutes. Setting this out as a formal subtraction would be highly inadvisable. But representing it as a calculation on a number-line as shown in Figure 22.2 would be highly advisable.

Learning about time is also complicated by the fact that the hands on a conventional dial-clock go round twice in a day; it would have been so much more sensible to go round once a day! Because of the association of a circle with 12 hours on a clock face, I always avoid using a circle to represent a day. For example, I would avoid a pie chart for 'how I spend a day' or a circular diagram showing the events of a day. For this last illustration I would recommend a diagram like the one shown in Figure 22.3. Pupils can add to this pictures or verbal descriptions of what they are doing at various times of day.

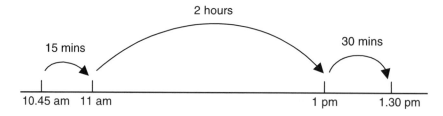

Figure 22.2   Finding the time-interval from 10.45 a.m. to 1.30 p.m. on a number-line

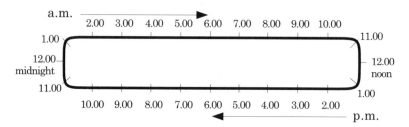

Figure 22.3   A picture of a day

Then there are the added complications related to the variety of watches and clocks that pupils may use, as well as the range of ways of saying the same time. For example, as well as being able to read a conventional dial-clock and a digital display in both 12-hour and 24-hour versions, pupils have to learn that the following all represent the same time of day: twenty to four in the afternoon, 3.40 p.m., 1540 (also written sometimes as 15:40 or 15.40). Incidentally, the colloquial use of, for example, 'fifteen hundred' to refer to the time 1500 in the 24-hour system is an unhelpful abuse of mathematical language. It reinforces the misunderstanding, mentioned in Chapter 2, of thinking that '00' is an abbreviation for 'hundred'. I prefer the BBC World Service convention:

'The time is fifteen hours.' A couple of further small points relate to noon and midnight. First, note that 'a.m.' and 'p.m.' are abbreviations for *ante meridian* and *post meridian*, meaning 'before noon' and 'after noon', respectively. This means that 12 noon is neither a.m. nor p.m. It is just 12 noon. Similarly, 12 o'clock midnight is neither a.m. nor p.m. Then, in the 24-hour system, midnight is the moment when the recorded time of day starts again, so it is not 2400, but 0000, 'zero hours'.

What principles are central to teaching measurement in the primary age range?

Some of the central principles in learning about measurement relate to the following headings: 1) comparison and ordering; 2) transitivity; 3) conservation; 4) non-standard and standard units; 5) approximation; 6) a context for developing number concepts; and 7) the meaning of zero.

First, the foundation of all aspects of measurement is direct comparison, putting two and then more than two objects (or events) in order according to the attribute in question. The language of comparison, discussed in relation to subtraction in Chapter 4, is of central importance here. Two objects are placed side by side and pupils determine which is the longer, which is the shorter. Two items are placed in the pans of a balance and pupils determine which is the heavier, which is the lighter. Water is poured from one container to another to determine which holds more, which holds less. Two pupils perform specified tasks, starting simultaneously, and observe which takes a longer time, which takes a shorter time. No units are involved at this stage, simply direct comparison leading to putting two or more objects or events in order.

Recording the results of comparison and ordering can be an opportunity to introduce the *inequality signs* (< and >). So, for example, 'A is longer than B' can be recorded as $A > B$, and 'B is shorter than A' as $B < A$. This introduces in a practical context an important principle of inequalities that can be expressed formally as follows:

$$\text{If } A > B, \text{ then } B < A.$$
$$\text{If } A < B, \text{ then } B > A.$$

An important mathematical principle here is that of *transitivity*. In Chapter 11 we saw that this mathematical property applied to the relationships 'is a multiple of' (illustrated in Figure 11.1) and 'is a factor of' (illustrated in Figure 11.3). The principle of transitivity is shown in Figure 22.4. If we know that A is related to B (indicated by an arrow) and B is related to C, the question is whether A is related to C as a logical consequence. With some relations (such as 'is a factor of') it does follow logically and we can draw in the arrow connecting A to C. In other cases it does not. For example, the relationship 'is a mirror image of' can be applied to a set of shapes: if shape A is a mirror image of shape B, and B is a mirror image of shape C, then it is *not* true that A must automatically be a mirror image of C. So this is not a transitive relationship. We can now see that whenever we compare two objects (or events) using a measuring attribute such as their lengths, their masses, their capacities or the length of time (for events), then we are again making use of a transitive relationship.

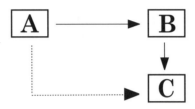

Figure 22.4   The transitive property

The arrow used in Figure 22.4 could represent any one of the measuring relationships used to compare two objects or events, such as: 'is longer than', 'is lighter than', 'holds more than' or 'takes less time than'. In each case, because A is related to B and B is related to C, then it follows logically that A is related to C. This principle is fundamental to ordering a set of more than two objects or events: once we know A is greater than B and B is greater than C, for example, it is this principle which allows us not to have to check A against C. Grasping this is a significant step in the development of a pupil's understanding of measuring.

The transitive property of measurement can be expressed formally using inequality signs as follows:

$$\text{If } A > B \text{ and } B > C \text{ then } A > C.$$
$$\text{If } A < B \text{ and } B < C \text{ then } A < C.$$

Next we should note the principle of *conservation*, another fundamental idea in learning about measurement of length, mass and liquid volume. Pupils meet this principle first in the context of conservation of number. They have to learn, for example, that if you rearrange a set of counters in different ways you do not alter the number of counters. Similarly, if two objects are the same length, they remain the same length when one is moved to a new position: this is the principle of conservation of length.

Conservation of mass is experienced when pupils balance two lumps of Plasticene, then rearrange each lump in some way, such as breaking one up into small pieces and moulding the other into some shape or other, and then check that they still balance. Conservation of liquid volume is the one that catches many pupils out. When they empty the water from one container into another, differently shaped container, as shown in Figure 22.5, by focusing their attention on the heights of the water in the containers, pupils often lose their grip on the principle that the volume of water has actually been unchanged by the transformation.

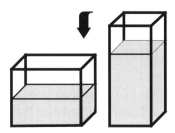

Figure 22.5   Conservation of liquid volume

Fundamental to the idea of measuring is the use of a 'unit'. The use of non-standard units to introduce to pupils the idea of measuring in units is a well-established tradition in primary-school mathematics teaching. For example, they might measure the length of items of furniture in spans, the length of a wall in cubits (a cubit is the length of your forearm), the mass of a book in conkers, the capacity of a container in eggcups. Many adults make use of non-standard units of length in everyday life, especially, for example, when making rough-and-ready measurements for practical jobs around the house and garden. The value of this approach is that children get experience of the idea of measuring in units through familiar, unthreatening objects first, rather than going straight into the use of mysterious things called millilitres and grams, and so on. Also, it is often the case that the non-standard unit is a more appropriate size of unit for early measuring experiences. For example, most of the things around the classroom the pupils might want to weigh will have a mass of several hundred grams. The gram is a very small mass for practical purposes to begin with, and the kilogram is far too large; conkers and glue-sticks are much more appropriate sizes of units for measuring mass in the early stages. Eventually, of course, we must learn that there is a need for a standard unit. The experience of working with non-standard units often makes this need explicit, as, for example, when two pupils measure the length of the hall in paces and get different answers.

The next major principle of measurement is that nearly all measurements are *approximate*. If you are measuring length, mass, time or capacity, all you can ever achieve is to make the measurement to the nearest something, depending on the level of accuracy of your measuring device. The principle of measuring to the nearest something and the associated language (see Chapter 10 for a discussion on rounding) should be introduced to primary-school pupils from the earliest stages. Even when measuring in non-standard units they will encounter this idea, as, for example, when determining that the length of the table is 'nearly 9 spans' or 'about 9 spans' or 'between 8 and 9 spans'.

Then we should stress the central importance of measurement experiences as a context for developing number concepts. Throughout this book I have used measurement problems and situations to reinforce ideas such as place value (Chapter 2), the various structures for the four operations (Chapters 4 and 7) and calculations with decimals (Chapter 15).

Finally in this section, a comment on the meaning of zero. Measurements such as length, mass, liquid volume and capacity, and time-intervals, are examples of what are called *ratio scales*. These are scales where the ratio of two quantities has a real meaning. For example, if a child is 90 cm tall and an adult is 180 cm tall, we can legitimately compare the two heights by means of ratio, stating that the adult is twice as tall as the child. Similarly, we can compare masses, capacities and time intervals by ratio. However, recorded time is not like this: it would make no sense to compare, say, 6 o'clock with 2 o'clock by saying that one is three times the other. This is an example of what is called an *interval scale*. Comparisons can only be made by reference to the difference (the interval) between two measurements, for example, saying that 6 o'clock is 4 hours later than 2 o'clock. Of course, you can compare the measurements in a ratio scale by reference to difference (for example, the adult is 90 cm taller than the child), but the point about an interval scale is that you cannot do it by ratio, you can only use difference. Temperature measured in degrees centigrade (or Fahrenheit) is another example of an interval scale. It would be meaningless to assert that 15 °C is three times as hot as 5 °C; the two temperatures should be compared by their difference. The interesting mathematical point here is that the thing that really distinguishes a ratio scale from an interval scale is that in a ratio scale the zero means *nothing*, but in an interval scale it does not. When the recorded time is 'zero hours', time has not disappeared. When the temperature is 'zero degrees', there is still a temperature out there and we can feel it! But a length of 'zero metres' is no length; a mass of 'zero grams' is nothing; a bottle holding 'zero millilitres' of wine is empty; a time-interval of 'zero seconds' is no time at all.

What metric units and prefixes do I need to know about?

There is an internationally accepted system of metric units called *SI units* (Système International). This system specifies one base unit for each aspect of measurement. For length the SI unit is the *metre*, for mass it is the *kilogram* (not the gram), for time it is the *second*. There is not a specific SI unit for liquid volume, since this would be measured in the same units as solid volume, namely cubic metres. However, the *litre* is a standard unit for liquid volume and capacity that is used internationally. Other units can be obtained by various prefixes being attached to these base units. There is a preference for those related to a thousand: for primary-school use this would be just *kilo* (*k*), meaning 'a thousand', and *milli* (*m*), meaning 'a thousandth'. So, for example, throughout this book we have used kilograms (kg) and grams (g), where 1 kg = 1000 g, and litres (l) and millilitres (ml), where 1 litre = 1000 ml. Note that the symbol used for litre (l) can be confused in print with the numeral 1, so to it is often better to write the word in full. Similarly we can have kilometres (km) and metres (m), with 1 km = 1000 m, and metres and millimetres (mm), with 1 m = 1000 mm. These are the only uses of the prefixes kilo and milli likely to be needed in the primary school. For practical purposes we will need other prefixes, especially *centi* (*c*), meaning 'a hundredth'. This gives us the really useful unit of length, the centimetre (cm), where 1 m = 100 cm. We might also find it helpful, for example when explaining place value and decimals with length (see Chapter 2), to use the prefix *deci* (*d*), meaning 'a tenth', as in decimetre (dm), where 1 m = 10 dm. We might also note that some wine bottles are labelled 0.75 litres, others are labelled 7.5 dl (decilitres), others 75 cl (centilitres) and others 750 ml (millilitres). These are all the same amount of wine.

I grew up using mainly imperial units. How can I get better at thinking metric?

Take every opportunity to practise *estimation* of lengths, heights, widths and distances, liquid volume and capacity, and mass. In the supermarket, take note of which items are sold by mass (although they will call it weight) and which by volume; estimate the mass or volume of items you are purchasing and check your estimate against what it says on the packet or the scales. This all helps significantly to build up confidence in handling less familiar units.

One way of becoming a better estimator is to learn by heart the sizes of some specific *reference items*. Pupils should be encouraged to do this for length, mass and capacity, and then to relate other estimates to these. Here are some that I personally use:

- A child's finger is about 1 cm wide.
- The pupils' rulers are 30 cm long.
- A sheet of A4 paper is about 21 cm by 30 cm.
- The distance from my nose to my outstretched finger-tip is about one metre (100 cm).
- The classroom door is about 200 cm or 2 m high.
- The mass of an individual packet of crisps is 30 g.
- The mass of a standard packet of tea is 125 g.
- The mass of a standard-size tin of baked beans is about 500 g (including the tin).
- A standard can of drink has a capacity of 330 ml.
- A wine bottle holds 750 ml of wine.
- Standard cartons of milk or fruit juice are 1 litre (1000 ml).
- A litre of water has a mass of a kilogram (1000 g).

What imperial units are still important?

The attempt to turn the UK into a fully metricated country has not been entirely successful. A number of popular units of measurement stubbornly refuse to go away. For example, many people still find temperatures given in degrees Fahrenheit to be more meaningful than those in centigrade (properly called celsius). (See self-assessment question 21.8 for converting between the two scales.) The prime candidate for survival would seem to be the *mile*: somehow I cannot imagine in the foreseeable future all the road signs and speed limits in the UK being converted to kilometres. Because pupils cannot possibly have practical experience of measuring distances in kilometres to compensate for the lack of experience of this metric unit in everyday life, it makes sense for any work we do in primary schools related to journeys and average speeds (see Chapter 18) to be done in miles and miles per hour.

For those who wish to relate miles to kilometres the most common equivalence used is that 5 miles is about 8 kilometres. A simple method for doing conversions is to read off the corresponding speeds on the speedometer in a car, most of which are given in both miles per hour and kilometres per hour. For example, you can read off that 30 miles is about 50 km, 50 miles is about 80 km, 70 miles is about 110 km. There is also an intriguing connection between this conversion and a sequence of numbers called the *Fibonacci sequence*, named after Leonardo

Fibonacci, a twelfth/thirteenth-century Italian mathematician: 1, 2, 3, 5, 8, 13, 21, 34, 55, 89, etc. The sequential generalization here is to add the two previous numbers to get the next one. So, for example, the next number after 89 is 144 (55 + 89). Now, purely coincidentally, it happens that one of these numbers in miles is approximately the same as the next one in kilometres. For example, 2 miles is about 3 km, 3 miles is about 5 km, 5 miles is about 8 km, 8 miles is about 13 km, and so on. This works remarkably well to the nearest whole number for quite some way! (See question 22.1 below.)

Other common measurements of length likely to survive through everyday usage, together with an indication of the kinds of equivalences that might be useful to learn, are:

- the inch (about the width of an adult thumb, about 2.5 cm);
- the foot (about the length of a standard class ruler or a sheet of A4 paper, that is, about 30 cm); and
- the yard (a bit less than a metre, about 91 cm).

Units of mass still used occasionally and unofficially in the market or delicatessen are:

- the ounce (about the same as a small packet of crisps, that is, about 30 g);
- the pound (getting on for half a kilogram, about 450 g).

Many people still like to weigh themselves in stones: a stone is a bit more than 6 kg (about 6.35 kg). I find it useful to remember that 11 stone is about 70 kg: see self-assessment question 21.7 in the previous chapter. And, for those who enjoy this kind of thing, a hundredweight is just over 50 kg, and a metric tonne (1000 kg) is therefore just a little more than an imperial ton (20 hundredweight).

Gallons have disappeared from the petrol station, but still manage to survive in common usage; for example, people still tell me how many miles per gallon their car does, even though petrol is almost universally sold in litres. My car, incidentally, does 9 miles to the litre. A gallon is about 4.5 litres. Given the drinking habits of the British public, another contender for long-term survival must be the pint. I have noticed that many primary-school pupils refer to any carton of milk as 'a pint of milk', regardless of the actual volume involved. A pint is just over half a litre (568 ml).

Conversion between metric and imperial units can be done using the methods described in Chapter 16 for direct proportion problems or using conversion graphs as described in Chapter 21.

Self-assessment questions

22.1: Given that 1 mile is 1.6093 km, use a calculator to find how far the rule for changing miles to kilometres based on the Fibonacci sequence is correct to the nearest whole number.

22.2 The mass of a litre of water is 1 kg (1000 g). What will it be on the Moon?

22.3: Are these relationships transitive? a) 'is earlier than' applied to times of the day; and b) 'is half of' applied to lengths.

22.4: Measure the length of a sheet of A4 paper to the nearest millimetre. Give the answer: a) in millimetres; b) in centimetres; c) in decimetres; and d) in metres.

22.5: Which is the greater: a) half a pound or 250 grams; b) 2 pints or a litre; c) 6 feet or 2 metres; d) 50 miles or 100 kilometres; e) 4 ounces or 100 grams; f) 10 stone or 50 kilograms; and g) 9 miles to the litre or 35 miles to the gallon?

Summary of teaching points

1. Pupils should develop their skills and understanding of measurement through practical, purposeful activities.

2. Introduce new aspects of measurement through direct comparison and ordering.

3. Introduce the idea of measuring in units via non-standard units that are familiar and appropriately sized, and use these experiences to establish the need for a standard unit.

4. Refer to the things we use for weighing objects on a balance as 'masses' and use the language 'weighs the same as a mass of so many grams'. Then encourage pupils to say 'the mass is so many grams', whilst acknowledging that most people incorrectly say 'the weight is so many grams'.

5. With older pupils in the primary range you can discuss the effect of gravity and space travel on weight and the idea that mass does not change.

6. It is not necessary to do much work on solid volume, measured in cubic centimetres, in the primary age range.

7. But the measurement of liquid volume and capacity, in litres and millilitres, because of the scope for practical experience with water and various containers, is an important component of primary-school mathematics.

8. Restrict the range of metric units used for practical work in the primary school to metre, centimetre, millimetre, litre, millilitre, kilogram, gram. Reference may also be made to kilometre and decimetre.

9. Work on journeys and average speeds is most appropriately done in miles and miles per hour.

10. Make considerable use of estimation as a class activity, encouraging pupils to learn by heart the measurements of specific reference items.

11. Make collections and displays of packages, discussing which items are sold by mass or by volume, the units used, which are metric and which imperial.

12. Do not use formal subtraction algorithms for finding the length of time from one recorded time to the next; teach an *ad hoc* adding-on approach.

13. Do not use a circle to represent a day, because of the association with a 12-hour clock face.

14. Pupils should learn to choose and use appropriate measuring devices, discussing the idea of accuracy. Make explicit the notion that measurement is always to the nearest something.

15. Discuss imperial units still in everyday use. Give pupils practical experience that will enable them to become familiar with some useful equivalences between metric and imperial units.

23

Angle

Pupils should be taught to: know that angles are measured in degrees and that one whole turn is 360 degrees; recognize right angles, perpendicular and parallel lines; recognize angles as greater or less than a right angle or half-turn, estimate their size and order them; recognize that angles at a point total 360 degrees and that angles at a point on a straight line total 180 degrees; know that the sum of the angles of a triangle is 180 degrees; measure and draw acute, obtuse and right angles to the nearest degree.

In this chapter there are explanations of

- the dynamic and static views of angle;
- comparison and ordering of angles;
- the use of turns and fractions of a turn for measuring angle;
- degrees;
- acute, right, obtuse, straight, reflex angles; and
- the sum of the angles in a triangle, a quadrilateral, and so on.

What is an angle?

An angle is a measurement. When we talk about the angle between two lines we are not referring to the shape formed by the two lines, nor to the point where they meet, nor to the space between the lines, but to a particular kind of measurement.

There are two ways we can think of what it is that is being measured. First there is the *dynamic* view of angle: the angle between the lines is a measurement of the size of the *rotation* involved when you point along one line and then turn to point along the other. This is the most useful way of introducing the concept of angle to children, because it lends itself to practical experience, with the children themselves pointing in one direction and then turning themselves through various angles to point in other directions. Also, when it comes to measuring angles between lines drawn on paper, pupils can physically point something, such as a pencil or a finger, along one line and rotate about the intersection of the lines to point along the other line. We should note that there are always two angles involved when turning from one direction to another, depending on whether you choose to rotate clockwise or anticlockwise, as shown in Figure 23.1.

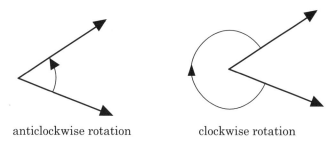

anticlockwise rotation   clockwise rotation

Figure 23.1   Angle as a measure of rotation

Second, there is the *static* view of angle. This is where we focus our attention on how pointed is the shape formed by the two lines. But the angle is still a measurement: we can think of it as a measurement of the difference in direction between the two lines. So, for example, in Figure 23.2, the angle marked in (a) is greater than that marked in (b), because the two lines in (b) are pointing in nearly the same direction, whereas the difference in the direction of the two lines in (a) is much greater. Thinking of angle as the difference in direction between two lines helps to link the static view of angle with the dynamic one of rotation, because the obvious way to measure the difference in two directions is to turn from one to the other and measure the amount of turn.

Figure 23.2   Angle as a measure of the difference in direction

Figure 23.2 illustrates that, like any aspect of measurement, the concept of angle enables us to make comparisons and to order (see Chapter 22). This can be dynamically, by physically doing the rotations involved (for example, with a pencil) and judging which is the greater rotation, which the smaller. It can also be experienced more statically, by cutting out one angle and placing it over another to determine which is the more pointed (the smaller angle). Figure 23.3 shows a set of angles, (a)–(f), ordered from smallest to largest.

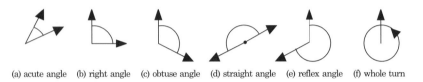

(a) acute angle   (b) right angle   (c) obtuse angle   (d) straight angle   (e) reflex angle   (f) whole turn

Figure 23.3   A set of angles in order from smallest (a) to largest (f)

The equivalent to making measurements of length, mass and capacity in non-standard units is to measure angle in turns and fractions of a turn, using the dynamic view. Figure 23.3(f) shows a whole turn, pointing in one direction and rotating until you point again in the same direction. Then, for example, if a pupil points North and then turns to point South they have moved through an angle that can be called a half-turn. Similarly, rotating from North, clockwise, to East is a quarter-turn. Figure 23.3(b) shows a quarter-turn from a horizontal position to a vertical position. This explains why a quarter-turn is also called a *right angle*: it is an *upright* angle. Figure 23.3(d) illustrates why a half-turn, formed by two lines pointing in opposite directions, is also called a *straight angle*.

The next stage of development is to introduce a standard unit for measuring angles. For primary-school use this unit is the degree, where 360 degrees (360°) is equal to a complete turn. Hence a right angle (quarter-turn) is 90° and a straight angle (half-turn) is 180°. There is evidence that this system of measuring angles in degrees based on 360 was used as far back as 2000 BC by the Babylonians, and it is thought that it may be related to the Babylonian year being 360 days. So we have here another example of a non-metric measurement in common use. There is actually a metric system for measuring angle, used in some European countries, in which '100 grades' is equal to a right angle, but this has never caught on in the UK. Interestingly, it is because 'centigrade' would then be one-hundredth of a grade, and therefore a measure of angle, that the 'degree centigrade' as a measure of temperature is now officially called the 'degree celsius', to avoid confusion.

The device used to measure angles in degrees is, of course, the *protractor*. I personally recommend the use of a 360° protractor, preferably marked with only one scale and with a pointer which can be rotated from one line of the angle being measured to the other, thus emphasising the dynamic view of angle. Even if there is not an actual pointer, pupils can still be encouraged to imagine the rotation always starting at zero on one line and rotating through 10°, 20°, 30° . . . to reach the other.

Can you remind me about acute, obtuse and reflex angles?

Mathematicians can never resist the temptation to put things into categories, thus giving them the opportunity to invent a new collection of terms. Angles are classified, in order of size, as: acute, right, obtuse, straight, reflex, as illustrated in Figure 23.3. An *acute* angle (a) is an angle less than a right angle. An *obtuse* angle (c) is an angle between a right angle and a straight angle. A *reflex* angle (e) is an angle greater than a straight angle, but less than a whole turn.

I remember that the three angles in a triangle add up to 180 degrees, but what about shapes with more than three sides?

A popular way of seeing this property of the angles of a triangle is to draw a triangle on paper, mark the angles, tear off the three corners and fit them together, as shown in Figure 23.4, to discover that together they form a straight angle, or two right angles (180°). The same thing can be done with the four angles of a quadrilateral (a shape with four straight sides), to discover that they fit together to make a whole turn, or four right angles (360°).

This illuminative experience uses the static view of angle. It is also possible to illustrate the same principle using the dynamic view, as

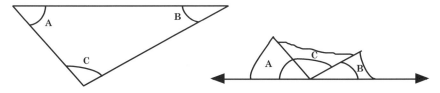

Figure 23.4   The three angles of a triangle fitted together to make a straight angle

shown in Figure 23.5, by taking an arrow (or, say, a pencil) for a walk round a triangle. Step 1 is to place an arrow (or the pencil) along one side of the triangle, for example on AC. Step 2 is to slide the arrow along until it reaches A, then rotate it through the angle at A. Now, for step 3, slide it up to B and rotate through that angle. Finally, step 4, slide it down to C and rotate through that angle. The arrow has now rotated through the sum of the three angles and is facing in the opposite direction to which it started! Hence the three angles together make a half-turn, or two right angles. Clearly this will work for any triangle, not just the one shown here.

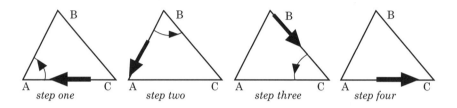

Figure 23.5   The three angles of a triangle together make a half-turn

The same procedure can then be applied to a four-sided figure (a quadrilateral), such as that shown in Figure 23.6. Now we find that the arrow does a complete rotation, finishing up pointing in the same direction as it started, so we conclude that the sum of the four angles in a four-sided figure is four right angles.

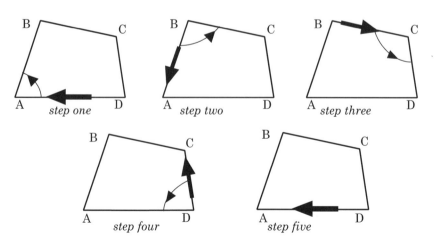

Figure 23.6   The four angles of a quadrilateral together make a whole turn

The delight of this activity is that it can easily be extended to five-sided figures, six sided, seven sided, and so on. The results can then be tabulated, using the approach given in Chapter 20, in order to formulate a sequential generalization and a global generalization. This is left as an exercise for the reader in question 23.2 below.

Self-assessment questions

23.1: Put these angles in order and classify them as acute, right, obtuse, straight or reflex: 89°, ⅛ of a turn, 150°, 90°, ¾ of a turn, 200°, 2 right angles, 95°.

23.2: Use the idea of taking an arrow round a shape, rotating through each of the angles in turn, to find the sum of the angles in: a) a five-sided figure (a pentagon); b) a six-sided figure (a hexagon); and c) a seven-sided figure (a heptagon). Give the answers in right angles, tabulate them and formulate both the sequential and the global generalizations. What would be the sum of the angles in a figure with 100 sides?

Summary of teaching points

1. Emphasize especially the dynamic view of angle, giving plenty of practical experience of rotating objects, themselves and pointers (such as fingers and pencils).
2. Include the important stages of developing a measurement concept when teaching angle: comparison, ordering and the use of non-standard units (turns and fractions of turns).
3. Get pupils to compare and order angles by cutting them out and placing them on top of each other.
4. I recommend the use of a 360° protractor for measuring angles in degrees. Emphasize the idea of rotation from zero when explaining to pupils how to use a protractor.
5. Use a transparent protractor on an overhead projector to demonstrate to pupils how to use this device for measuring angles.
6. When explaining about angles, do not always draw diagrams in which one of the lines is horizontal (see my example in the figures in this chapter!)
7. Pupils can cut out pictures from magazines, mark angles on them and display them in sets as acute, right, obtuse, straight and reflex.
8. Use both the static and the dynamic methods for discovering the sum of the angles in a triangle, a quadrilateral, and so on.

24

Transformations and Symmetry

Pupils should be taught to: recognize when shapes are identical; visualize and describe movements of shapes using appropriate language; transform objects in practical situations; transform images using ICT; visualize and predict the position of a shape following a rotation, reflection or translation; identify and draw two-dimensional shapes in different orientations on grids; recognize reflective symmetry in regular polygons.

In this chapter there are explanations of

- the fundamental ideas of transformation and equivalence;
- translation, reflection and rotation as types of congruence; and
- reflective and rotational symmetry for two-dimensional shapes.

What is a congruence?

To answer this question I will discuss the general ideas of *transformation* and *equivalence*, apply these to shapes and identify three types of transformation, *translations*, *rotations* and *reflections*, which, whilst changing shapes in some way or other, all produce *congruent* shapes. In general we call these transformations *congruences*.

Two fundamental questions when considering two mathematical entities are: 1) How are they the same? 2) How are they different? The first question directs our attention to what is called an *equivalence*, the second to a *transformation*. For example, in Chapter 14 we saw that we could *transform* a fraction such as ⅔ into an *equivalent* fraction such as ⁴⁄₆, by multiplying the top and bottom numbers by 2. The two fractions are, in a sense, different. For a start they use different top and bottom numbers; and two pieces of a pizza cut into three is not exactly the same situation in every respect as four pieces of a pizza cut into six. But you do get the same amount of pizza. So there is an important sense in which they *are* the same. A similar line of reasoning applied in Chapter 22, when discussing conservation of liquid volume. In the example shown in Figure 22.5, the water in the container is transformed in some way when it is poured into another container. It is a different 'shape', it has a different height, and so on. But something very important stays the same, namely, the volume of the water. Then if I draw a large diagram on the board and ask the class to copy it on to their paper, they all dutifully do this, even though none of them has a piece of paper anything like large enough to produce a diagram as big as mine. Their diagrams are different from mine, that is, different in size, whilst in many respects they might be the same as mine. Much of what we have to understand in mathematics comes down to recognizing the equivalences that exist within various transformations, which transformations preserve which equivalences, and how things can be different yet be the same. This way of thinking is central to developing an understanding of shape and space.

In a mathematics lesson Cathy was asked to draw on squared paper as many different shapes as possible which are made up of five square units. Figure 24.1 shows four of the shapes that she drew. Her teacher told her that they were all the same shape. Cathy insisted they were all different. Who was right? The answer is, of course, that they are both right. The shapes are all the same in some senses and all different in others.

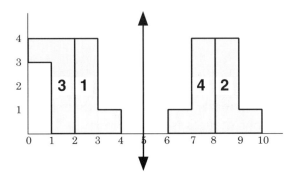

Figure 24.1   The same but different

First, consider how they are the same. All four shapes are made up of five square units; they have the same number of sides (six); each shape has one side of length four units, one side of length three units, one side of length two units and three sides of length one unit; each shape has five 90° angles and one 270° angle; and the sides and the angles are arranged in the same way in each of the shapes to make what we might recognize as a letter 'L'. Surely they are identical, the same in every respect? Well, they certainly are *congruent*. This word describes the relationship between two shapes which have sides of exactly the same length, angles of exactly the same size, with all the sides and angles arranged in exactly the same way, as in the four shapes shown in Figure 24.1. A practical definition would be that you could cut out one shape and fit it exactly over the other one. The pages in this book are congruent: as you can see, one page fits exactly over the next. The computer discs I am using whilst writing the book are all congruent: I can see them sitting on the desk at this moment in a neat pile, one placed exactly over the other, the bevelled corners and indentations along the edges matching perfectly.

So, how are the shapes in Figure 24.1 different? For example, how is shape 2 different from shape 1? Cathy's argument is that they are in different positions on the paper: shape 1 is here and shape 2 is over there, so they are not the same shape. Surely every time I draw the shape in a different position I have drawn a different shape, in a sense. So the shapes are different if you decide to take position into account. In order to do this we need a system of coordinates, as outlined in Chapter 21. The transformation that has been applied to shape 1 to produce shape 2 is called a *translation*. We saw in Chapter 21 that we can use the coordinate system to describe movements. So this translation can be specified by saying, for example, that to get from shape 1 to shape 2 you have to move 6 units in the x-direction and 0 units in the y-direction. Any movement of our shape like this, so many units in the x-direction and so many in the y-direction, is a translation.

If we now decide that, for the time being, we will not count translations as producing shapes which are 'different', what about shape 3? Is that different from shape 1? Cathy's idea is that shape 1 is an L-shape the right way up, but shape 3 is upside down, so they are different. So the shapes are different if you decide to take their orientation on the page into account. In order to take this into account we need the concept of direction, and, as we saw in Chapter 23, to describe a difference in direction we need the concept of angle. To transform shape 1 into shape 3 we can apply a *rotation*. To specify a rotation we have to indicate the point about which the rotation occurs and the angle through which the shape is rotated. If shape 1 is rotated through an angle of 180° (either clockwise or anticlockwise), about the middle of its left-hand side – the point with coordinates (2,2) – then it is transformed into shape 3. Imagine copying shape 1 on to tracing paper, placing a pin in the point (2,2) and rotating the tracing paper through 180°. The shape would land directly on top of shape 3. Any movement of our shape like this, turning through some angle about a given centre, is a rotation.

Now, if we decide that, for the time being, we will not count rotations or translations as producing shapes which are 'different', what about shape 4? Is that different from shape 1? Cathy's idea is that they are actually mirror images of each other and this makes them different. This difference can be made explicit by colouring the shapes, say, red, before cutting them out. Shapes 1, 2 and 3 can all be placed on top of each other and match exactly, with the red faces uppermost. But shape 4 only matches if we turn it over so that it is red face down. This surely makes it different from all the others! The transformation that has been applied now to shape 1 to produce shape 4 is a *reflection*. To specify a reflection all you have to do is to identify the mirror line. In the case of shapes 1 and 4 the mirror line is the vertical line passing through 5 on the *x*-axis, shown as a double-headed arrow in Figure 24.1. Each point in shape 1 is matched by a corresponding point in shape 4, the other side of the mirror line and the same distance from it. For example, the corner of the letter L with the reflex angle in shape 1 is 2 units to the left of the mirror line, but the corresponding point in shape 4 is 2 units to the right of the mirror line. Any transformation of our shape like this, obtained by producing a mirror image in any given mirror line, is a reflection.

What is reflective symmetry?

Sometimes when we reflect a shape in a particular mirror line it matches *itself* exactly, in the sense that the mirror image coincides precisely with the original shape. Shape A in Figure 24.2 is an example of this phenomenon. The mirror line is shown as a double-headed arrow. This divides the shape into two identical halves that are mirror images of each other. If we cut the shape out we could fold it along the mirror line and the two halves would match exactly. Another approach is to use the idea employed above of colouring the shape, cutting it out and turning it face down: we find that the shape turned face down could still fit exactly into the hole left in the paper. The shape is said to have *reflective symmetry* (sometimes called *line symmetry*) and the mirror line is called a *line of symmetry*. Shape D in Figure 24.2 also has reflective symmetry. There are actually four possible lines that divide this shape into ˙ halves with one half the mirror image of the other, althou these is shown in the diagram. Finding the other three lir try is an exercise for the reader (question 24.2). Again, noti coloured the shape, cut it out and turned it face down exactly into the hole left in the paper. Shape C does not have reflective symmetry. The colouring, cutting out and turning face down routine demonstrates this nicely, since it is clear that we would not then be able to fit the shape into the hole left in the paper.

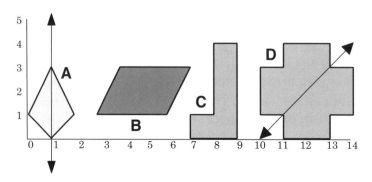

Figure 24.2   Are these shapes symmetrical?

Shape B (a parallelogram) is perhaps a surprise, because this too does *not* have reflective symmetry. If you think, for example, that one of the diagonals is a line of symmetry, copy the shape on to paper and use the colouring, cutting out and turning face-down procedure; or try folding it in half along the diagonal. But it does have a different kind of symmetry. To see this, trace the shape on to tracing paper and then rotate it around the centre point through a half-turn. The shape matches the original shape exactly. A shape that can be rotated on to itself like this is said to have *rotational symmetry*. The point about which we rotate it is called the *centre of rotational symmetry*.

Another practical way of exploring rotational symmetry is to cut out a shape carefully and see how many ways it can be fitted into the hole left in the paper, by rotation. For example, if we coloured shape B and cut it out, there would be two ways in which we could fit it into the hole left in the paper, by rotating it, without turning the shape face down. We therefore say that the shape has rotational symmetry of *order two*. Shape D also has rotational symmetry (see question 24.2 below). Shapes A and C do not have rotational symmetry. Well, not really. I suppose you could say that they have rotational symmetry of order one, since there is *one* way in which their cut-outs could fit into the hole left in the paper, without turning them face down. In this sense all two-dimensional shapes would have rotational symmetry of at least order one. Whilst recognizing this, it is usual to say that shapes ʾike A and C do not have rotational symmetry.

These ideas of reflective and rotational symmetry are fundamental to the creation of attractive designs and patterns, and are employed effectively in a number of cultural traditions, particularly the Islamic. Pupils can learn first to recognize these kinds of symmetry in the world around them, and gradually to learn to analyse them and to employ them in creating designs of their own.

Self-assessment questions

24.1: Describe the congruences that transform shape 2 in Figure 24.1 into: a) shape 1; b) shape 4; and c) shape 3.

24.2: In shape D in Figure 24.2, where are the other three lines of symmetry? What is the order of rotational symmetry of this shape?

24.3: Is it possible to draw a two-dimensional shape with exactly two lines of symmetry, where the lines of symmetry are not at right angles to each other?

24.4: Is it possible to draw a shape with exactly two lines of symmetry that does not have rotational symmetry?

Summary of teaching points

1. Use geometrical designs from different cultural traditions, such as Islamic patterns, to provide a rich experience of transformations and symmetry.

2. Use some of the numerous computer programs that are available to provide primary pupils with some fascinating opportunities to explore transformations and symmetry.

3. The most important emphasis for pupils' learning about shape and space in the primary school is the opportunity for lots of practical experience of colouring in shapes, cutting them out, folding them, turning them over, rotating them, looking at them in mirrors, fitting them together, making patterns, matching them, sorting them, classifying them, and so on. Our approach here can be much less structured than in other aspects of the mathematics curriculum.

4. Frequently use the two questions about transformation and equivalence to promote useful discussion in work with shapes: a) How are they the same? b) How are they different?

5. Use the tracing-paper approach to explore the ideas of rotation and rotational symmetry.

6. Use the colouring, cutting-out, turning face-down approach to explore the ideas of reflection and reflective symmetry.
7. An interesting project is to make a display of pictures cut from magazines that illustrate different aspects of symmetry.

25

Classifying Shapes

Pupils should be taught to: visualize and describe two-dimensional (2-D) and three-dimensional (3-D) shapes and the way they behave, making precise use of geometrical language, especially that of triangles, quadrilaterals, and prisms and pyramids of various kinds; make and draw with increasing accuracy 2-D and 3-D shapes and patterns; recognize the geometrical features of 2-D and 3-D shapes, including angles, faces, pairs of parallel lines and symmetry, and use these to classify shapes; visualize 3-D shapes from 2-D drawings.

In this chapter there are explanations of

- the importance of classification as a process for making sense of the shapes in the world around us;
- polygons, including the meaning of 'regular polygon';
- acute-angled, right-angled and obtuse-angled triangles;
- equilateral, isosceles and scalene triangles;
- parallelograms, rectangles, squares, rhombuses, and the relationships between them;
- tessellations;
- polyhedra, including the meaning of 'regular polyhedron';
- prisms and pyramids; and
- reflective symmetry applied to three-dimensional shapes.

Why are there so many technical terms to learn in geometry?

We need the special language of geometry in order to classify shapes into categories. Classification is an important intellectual process that helps us to make sense of our experiences. By coding information into categories we condense it and gain some control over it. Classification is at the heart of mathematics. The intellectual process involved is another example of the 'same but different' principle discussed in Chapter 24. We form categories in mathematics by recognizing attributes shared by various elements (such as numbers or shapes). These elements are then formed into a set. Although the elements in the set are different they have something the same about them. When it is a particularly interesting or significant set we give it a name. Because it is important that we should be able to determine definitely whether or not a particular element is in the set, the next stage of the process is often to formulate a precise definition.

For example, in Chapter 11 we recognized the attribute shared by these numbers, (2, 3, 5, 7, 11, 13, 17 . . .), that they had no factors apart from 1 and themselves. This led to putting them into a set and giving them a name, 'prime numbers'. Because of some uncertainty about whether or not the number 1 was prime, a definition was then produced, namely, that a prime number is a natural number that has precisely two factors. I suggested in Chapter 11 that awareness of various ways of classifying numbers contributes to a greater confidence with number. The same is true of shapes. Just as with numbers, we might recognize an attribute common to certain shapes (such as having three sides), form them into a category, give the set a name (for example, the set of triangles) and then, if necessary, make the classification more explicit with a precise definition. This process of classifying and naming leads to a greater confidence in handling shapes and a better awareness of the shapes that make up the world around us.

So, to participate in this important process of classification of shapes, we need first a whole batch of mathematical ideas related to the significant properties of shapes that are used to put them into various categories. This will include, for example, reference to whether the edges of the shape are straight, the number of sides and angles, whether various angles are equal or right-angled, and whether sides are equal in length or parallel. Second, we need to know the various terms used to name the sets, supported where necessary by a definition. My experience is that many primary teachers and student-teachers have a degree of uncertainty about some of these terms that undermines their confidence in teaching mathematics. For their sake the following material is provided for reference purposes.

What are the main classes of two-dimensional shapes?

The first classification of two-dimensional shapes we should note separates out those with only straight edges from those, such as circles, semi-circles and ellipses, which have curved edges. A two-dimensional closed shape made up entirely of straight edges is called a *polygon*. The straight edges are called *sides*. It's probably safest to restrict the use of the word 'side' to the straight edges of a polygon. It would not be appropriate, for example, to refer to the circumference of a circle as a 'side', so I'm a bit perplexed when a circle is referred to in some texts as a shape 'with one side'.

Polygons can then be further classified depending on the number of sides: *triangles* with three sides, *quadrilaterals* with four, *pentagons* with five, *hexagons* with six, *heptagons* with seven, *octagons* with eight, *nonagons* with nine, *decagons* with ten, and so on.

Then we can also categorize polygons into those that are *regular* and those that are not. A *regular polygon* is one in which all the sides are the same length and all the angles are the same size. For example, a regular octagon has eight equal sides and eight angles, each of which is equal to 135°. To work out the angles in a regular polygon, use the rule ($2n - 4$ right-angles) deduced in question 23.2 (Chapter 23) to determine the total of the angles in the polygon (for example, for an octagon the sum is $2 \times 8 - 4 = 12$ right angles, that is, 1080°), then divide this by the number of angles (for example, for the octagon, 1080° ÷ 8 = 135°). The word 'regular' is often misused when people talk about shapes, as though it were synonymous with 'symmetric' or even 'geometric'. For example, the rectangular shape of the cover of this book is *not* a regular shape, because two of the sides are longer than the other two – unless the publishers have decided to surprise me and produce a square book. I'm also a bit disappointed when every time you see an example of, say, a pentagon (or a hexagon) used in material for primary pupils it seems to be a regular one. This seems to me to confuse the distinction between a pentagon in general and a regular pentagon.

There is a fascinating way of forming the regular polygons, using the fact that the number of lines of symmetry increases as the number of sides increases. (For example, a regular triangle has three lines of symmetry, a regular quadrilateral has four, and so on.) You need two mirrors taped together, so that they can open out like the covers of a book. Draw a straight line on a sheet of paper and place the two mirrors, opened at 120° across the line, so that you can see the reflections in the mirrors. With care, you should be able to arrange the mirrors so that you can see a regular triangle in them. Then slowly close the two mirrors. As you do this the image will successively form each of the regular polygons. This is a delightful experience, not to be missed! Incidentally, as the number of sides increases the polygon approximates more and more closely to a circle. This is why mathematicians like to think of a circle as a regular polygon with an 'infinite' number of sides.

What are the different categories of triangles that I should know about?

There are basically two ways of categorizing triangles. The first is based on their angles, the second on their sides. Figure 25.1 shows examples of triangles categorized in these ways.

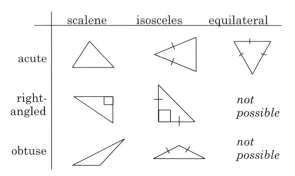

Figure 25.1   Categories of triangles

First, we can categorize a triangle as being *acute angled*, *right angled* or *obtuse angled*. (See Chapter 23 for the classification of angles.) An *acute-angled triangle* is one in which all three angles are acute, that is, less than 90°. A *right-angled triangle* is one in which one of the angles is a right angle; it is not possible, of course, to have two right angles since the sum of the three angles has to be 180°, and this would make the third angle zero! The right angles are indicated in the triangles in Figure 25.1 in the conventional fashion. An *obtuse-angled triangle* is one with an obtuse angle, that is, one angle greater than 90° and less than 180°; again it is only possible to have one such angle because of the sum of the three angles having to equal 180°. This condition also makes it impossible to have a triangle containing a reflex angle.

Second, looking at the sides, we can categorize triangles as being *equilateral*, *isosceles* or *scalene*. An *equilateral* (equal-sided) triangle is one in which all three sides are equal. Because of the rigid nature of triangles, the only possibility for an equilateral triangle is one in which the three angles are also equal (to 60°). So an equilateral triangle must be a regular triangle. This is only true of triangles. For example, you can have an equilateral octagon (with eight equal sides) in which the angles are not equal: just imagine joining eight equal strips of card with paper-fasteners and manipulating the structure into many different shapes, all of which are equilateral octagons but only one of which is a regular octagon.

An *isosceles* triangle is one with two sides equal. In Figure 25.1 the equal sides are those marked with a small dash. An isosceles triangle has a line of symmetry passing through the middle of the angle formed by the two equal sides. If the triangle is cut out and folded in half along this line of symmetry the two angles opposite the equal sides match each other. In this way we can discover practically that a triangle with two equal sides always has two equal angles.

Finally, a *scalene* triangle is one with no equal sides. Using these different categorizations it is then possible to determine seven different kinds of triangle, as shown in Figure 25.1.

What are the different categories of quadrilaterals that I should know about?

The most important set of quadrilaterals is the set of *parallelograms*, that is, those with two pairs of opposite sides parallel. Figure 25.2 shows some examples of parallelograms. Two lines drawn in a two-dimensional plane are said to be *parallel* if theoretically they would never meet if continued indefinitely. This describes the relationship between the opposite sides in each of the shapes drawn in Figure 25.2. In Chapter 24 we saw that not all parallelograms have reflective symmetry: in Figure 25.2, only the special parallelograms A, B and C, have reflective symmetry. But they do all have rotational symmetry of at least order two. This means that the opposite angles match on to each other, and the opposite sides match on to each other, when the shape is rotated through a half-turn. In other words, the opposite angles in a parallelogram are always equal and the opposite sides are always equal. There are then two main ways of classifying parallelograms. One of these is based on the angles, the other on the sides.

The most significant aspect of the angles of a parallelogram concerns whether or not they are right angled. If they are, as, for example, in shapes B and C in Figure 25.2, the shape is called a *rectangle*. Note that if

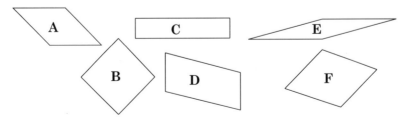

Figure 25.2   Examples of parallelograms

one angle in a parallelogram is a right angle, because opposite angles are equal and the four angles add up to four right angles, all the angles must be right angles. The rectangle is probably the most important four-sided shape from a practical perspective, simply because our artificial world is so much based on the rectangle. It is almost impossible to look anywhere and not see rectangles. Interestingly, however, there are children who grow up in rural areas of some African countries where their environment is based on the circle – they sit on circular stools in circular houses in circular villages – and this is often reflected in their relative confidence in handling the mathematics of circles and rectangles, compared with, say, British children.

Then, a *rhombus* is a parallelogram in which all four sides are equal, as, for example, in shapes A and B in Figure 25.2. A *square* (shape B) is therefore a rhombus that is also a rectangle, or a rectangle that is also a rhombus. It is, of course, a quadrilateral with all four sides equal and all four angles equal (to 90°), so 'square' is another name for a regular quadrilateral.

There is an important point about language to make here. A square is a rectangle (a special kind of rectangle) and a rectangle is a parallelogram (a special kind of parallelogram). Likewise, a square is a rhombus (a special kind of rhombus) and a rhombus is a parallelogram (a special kind of parallelogram). Sometimes one hears teachers talking about 'squares or rectangles', for example, as though they were different things, neglecting the fact that squares are a subset of rectangles. If you need to distinguish between rectangles that are squares and those that are not, then you can refer to *square rectangles* (such as B in Figure 25.2) and *oblong rectangles* (such as C). Figure 25.3 summarizes the relationships between different kinds of quadrilaterals, using an arrow to represent the phrase 'is a special kind of'.

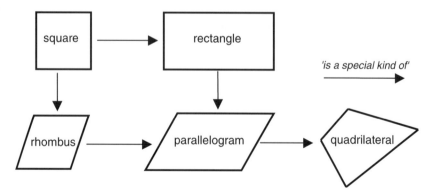

Figure 25.3   The relationships betweeen different kinds of quadrilaterals

What is a tessellation?

One further way of classifying two-dimensional shapes is to distinguish between those that *tessellate* and those that do not. A shape is said to tessellate if it can be used to make a tiling pattern, or a *tessellation*. This means that the shape can be used over and over again to cover a flat surface, the shapes fitting together without any gaps. In practical terms we are asking whether the shape can be used as a tile to cover the kitchen floor (without worrying about what happens when we reach the edges). The commonest shapes used for tiling are, of course, squares and other rectangles, which fit together so neatly without any gaps, as shown in Figure 25.4(a). This is no doubt part of the reason why the rectangle is such a popular shape in a technological world. Figure 25.4(b) demonstrates the remarkable fact that *any* triangle tessellates. If the three angles of the triangle are called A, B and C, then it is instructive to identify the six angles that come together at a point where six triangles meet in the tessellation, as shown. Because A, B and C add up to 180°, a straight angle, we find that they fit together at this point, neatly lying along straight lines. By repeating this arrangement in all directions the triangle can clearly be used to form a tessellation.

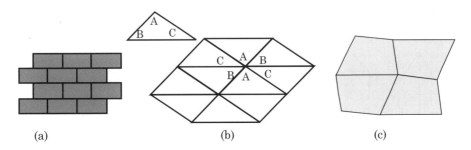

(a)   (b)   (c)

Figure 25.4   Tessellations

It is also true that *any* quadrilateral tessellates, as illustrated in Figure 25.4(c). Because the four angles add up to 360°, we can arrange for four quadrilaterals to meet at a point with the four different angles fitting together without any gaps. This pattern can then be continued indefinitely in all directions. Interestingly, apart from the equilateral triangle and the square, the only other regular polygon that tessellates is the regular hexagon, as seen in the familiar honeycomb pattern.

What are the main classes of three-dimensional shapes?

The first classification of three-dimensional shapes is to separate out those that have curved surfaces, such as a sphere (a perfectly round ball), a hemisphere (a sphere cut in half), a cylinder (like a baked-bean tin) and a cone (see the nearest motorway). A shape that is made up entirely of flat surfaces (also called *plane* surfaces) is called a *polyhedron* (plural: *polyhedra*). To describe a polyhedron we need to refer to the flat surfaces, which are called *faces* (not sides, incidentally), the lines where two faces meet, called *edges*, and the points where edges meet, called *vertices* (plural of *vertex*). The term 'face' should only be used for the flat surfaces of polyhedra. It is not appropriate, for example, to refer to a sphere 'as a shape with one face'. A sphere has one continuous, smooth surface – but it is not 'a face'.

As with polygons, the word *regular* is used to identify those polyhedra in which all the faces are the same shape, all the edges are the same length and all the angles between edges are equal. Whereas there is an infinite number of different kinds of regular polygons, there are, in fact, only five kinds of regular polyhedra. These are shown in Figure 25.5: a) the regular *tetrahedron* (four faces, each of which is an equilateral triangle); b) the regular *hexahedron* (usually called a *cube*; six faces, each of which is a square); c) the regular *octahedron* (eight faces, each of which is an equilateral triangle); d) the regular *dodecahedron* (twelve faces, each of which is a regular pentagon); and e) the regular *icosahedron* (twenty faces, each of which is an equilateral triangle).

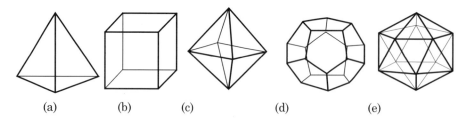

(a)   (b)   (c)   (d)   (e)

Figure 25.5   The regular polyhedra

These and other solid shapes can be constructed by drawing a two-dimensional *net*, such as those shown for the regular tetrahedron and cube in Figure 25.6, cutting these out, folding and sticking. It is advisable to incorporate some flaps for gluing in appropriate positions before cutting out. This is an excellent mathematical activity for primary-school pupils, in which a range of spatial concepts and practical skills come together.

A *prism* is a shape made up of two identical polygons at opposite ends, joined up by parallel lines. Figure 25.7 illustrates a) a triangular prism, b) a rectangular prism and c) a hexagonal prism. I like to think of prisms as being made from cheese: a polyhedron is a prism if you can slice the cheese along its length in a way in which each slice is identical. Note that they are all called prisms, although colloquially the word is often used to refer just to the triangular prism. Note also that another name for a rectangular prism is a *cuboid*: this is a three-dimensional shape in which all the faces are rectangles. A cube is, of course, a special kind of cuboid in which all the faces are squares. Note further that some 'sugar cubes' are cuboids but not cubes!

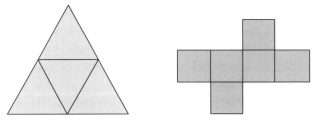

Figure 25.6   Nets for a regular tetrahedron and a cube

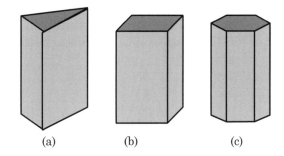

(a)   (b)   (c)

Figure 25.7   Some prisms

Another category of three-dimensional shapes to be mentioned here is the set called pyramids, illustrated in Figure 25.8. A *pyramid* is made up of a polygon forming the *base*, and then lines drawn from each of the vertices of this polygon to some point above, called the *apex*. The result of this is to form a series of triangular faces rising up from the edges of the base, meeting at the apex. Note that a) a triangular-based pyramid is actually a tetrahedron by another name, and that b) a square-based pyramid is the kind we associate with ancient Egypt.

To conclude this chapter I will make a brief mention of *reflective symmetry* as it is applied to three-dimensional shapes. In Chapter 24 we saw how some two-dimensional shapes have reflective symmetry, with a line

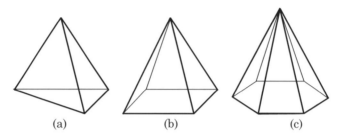

Figure 25.8   Pyramids

of symmetry dividing the shape into two matching halves, one a mirror image of the other. The same applies to three-dimensional shapes, except that it is now a *plane of symmetry* that divides the shape into the two halves. This is like taking a broad, flat knife and slicing right through the shape, producing two bits that are mirror images of each other, as illustrated with a cone in Figure 25.9. This cone, of course, has an infinite number of planes of symmetry, since any vertical slice through the apex of the cone can be used. All the three-dimensional shapes illustrated in the figures in this chapter have reflective symmetry. For example, the regular tetrahedron in Figure 25.5 has six planes of symmetry. Children can experience this idea by slicing various fruits in half, or by using solid shapes made out of Plasticene or similar moulding material.

Figure 25.9   A plane of symmetry

Self-assessment questions

25.1: Why is it not possible to have an equilateral, right-angled triangle or an equilateral, obtuse-angled triangle? (See Figure 25.1.)

25.2: What are the sizes of the three angles in a right-angled, isosceles triangle?

25.3: What is another name for: a) a rectangular rhombus; b) a regular quadrilateral; c) a triangle with rotational symmetry; d) a rectangular prism; and e) a triangular-based pyramid?

25.4: Which of the following shapes tessellate? a) A parallelogram; b) a regular pentagon; and c) a regular octagon.

25.5: How many planes of symmetry can you identify for a cube?

25.6: True or false? a) All parallelograms are rhombuses; b) all squares are rectangles; c) all cubes are cuboids; d) all squares are rhombuses; e) all pentagons have five equal sides; f) all isosceles triangles are acute-angled triangles.

Summary of teaching points

1. Pupils will develop geometric concepts, such as those discussed in this chapter, by experiences of classifying, using various attributes of shapes, informally in the first instance, looking for exemplars and non-exemplars, and discussing the relationships between shapes in terms of samenesses and differences.
2. The role of a definition in teaching is not to enable pupils to formulate a concept, but to sharpen it up once the concept has been formed informally through experience and discussion, and to deal with doubtful cases.
3. Give pupils opportunity to explore the properties of various shapes, including the different kinds of triangles and quadrilaterals, and regular and irregular shapes, by folding, tracing, matching, looking for reflective and rotational symmetries, and drawing out the implications of these.
4. Remember when talking about various special quadrilaterals that a square is a special kind of rectangle, and that a rectangle is a special kind of parallelogram.
5. Pupils can investigate which shapes tessellate and which do not, discovering, for example, that all triangles and all quadrilaterals do. They should use a plastic or card shape as a template, drawing round it in successive positions.
6. Construction of three-dimensional shapes from nets is an excellent practical activity drawing on a wide range of geometric concepts and practical skills.

26

Perimeter, Area and Volume

Pupils should be taught to: find perimeters of simple shapes; find areas of rectangles using the formula, understanding its connection with counting squares and how it extends this approach; calculate the perimeter and area of shapes composed of rectangles.

In this chapter there are explanations of

- the concepts of area and perimeter;
- the ideas of varying the area for a fixed perimeter, and varying the perimeter for a fixed area;
- a similar idea with volume and surface area;
- ways of investigating areas of parallelograms, triangles and trapeziums;
- the units used for measuring area and the relationships between them;
- the units used for measuring volume and the relationships between them;
- the number π and its relationship to the circumference and diameter of a circle;
- how to find the area of a circle.

How do you explain the ideas of perimeter and area so that pupils don't get them confused?

Area is a measure of the amount of two-dimensional space inside a boundary. The *perimeter* is the length of the boundary. I always use *fields* and *fences* to explain these ideas. The area is the size of the field and the perimeter is the amount of fencing around the edge. Pupils can draw pictures of various fields on squared paper, such as that shown in Figure 26.1. They can then count up the number of units of fencing around the edge, to determine the perimeter, which in this case is 18 units. Make sure that they count the units of fencing and not the squares around the edge, being especially careful going round corners not to miss out any units of fencing. To determine the area they can fill the field with 'sheep', using unit-cubes to represent sheep; the number of sheep they can get into the field is a measure of the area. This is, of course, the same as the number of square units inside the boundary, in this case 16 square units.

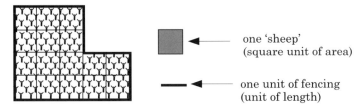

Figure 26.1   Fields and fences

What is the relationship between perimeter and area?

In general, there is no direct relationship between perimeter and area. This is something of a surprise for many people. It provides us with an interesting counter-example of the principle of conservation (see Chapter 22). When, for example, you rearrange the fencing around a field into a different shape, without changing the overall perimeter, the area is *not* conserved. For any given perimeter there is a range of possible areas. This makes an interesting investigation for pupils. Again it is usefully couched in terms of fields and fences. The first challenge is to find as many different fields as possible that can be enclosed within a given amount of fencing. Figure 26.2 shows a collection of shapes, drawn on squared paper, all of which represent fields made up from rearranging 12 units of fencing. They all have different areas! An important discovery is that the largest area is obtained with a square field. This is the best use of the farmer's fencing material. (If we were not restricted to the grid lines on squared paper the largest area would actually be provided by a circle: imagine the fencing to be totally flexible and push it out as far as you can in all directions in order to enclose the maximum area.)

The second challenge is the reverse problem: keep the area fixed and find the different perimeters. In other words, what amounts of fencing would be required to enclose differently shaped fields all with the same area? Figure 26.3 shows a collection of fields all with the same area, 16 square units. Once again, we find the square to be the superior solution, requiring the minimum amount of fencing for the given area.

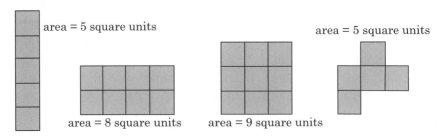

Figure 26.2   All these shapes have a perimeter of 12 units

If it is not possible actually to make a square, using only the grid lines drawn on the squared paper (for example, with a fixed perimeter of 14 units, or a fixed area of 48 square units), we still find that the shape that is 'nearest' to a square gives the best solution. (The more general result, getting away from squared paper, is that the minimum perimeter for a given area is provided by a circle.) It is interesting to note that in some ancient civilizations land was priced by counting the number of paces around the boundary, that is, by the perimeter. A shrewd operator in such an arrangement could make a good profit by buying square pieces of land and selling them off in long thin strips!

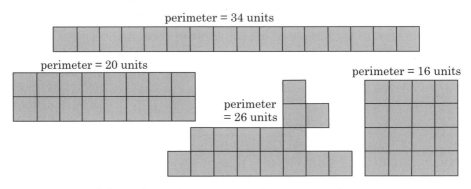

Figure 26.3   All these shapes have an area of 16 square units

There is an interesting parallel here with volume and surface area in solid shapes. Figure 26.4 illustrates two cuboids (see Chapter 25) with the same volume, 12 cubic units. They have been made by arranging 12 unit cubes in different ways. In cuboid (a) the total surface area (that is, the total number of square units on the six faces of the cuboid) is 32 square units, and in cuboid (b) it is 40 square units. This means that to cover (b) with paper you would need 40 square units of paper, but to cover (a) you would need only 32 square units. The fact that rearranging the volume changes the surface area actually explains why you some-times need less wrapping paper if you arrange the contents of your

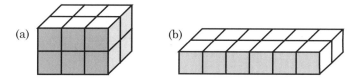

Figure 26.4   Two cuboids with the same volume, 12 cubic units

parcel in a different way. The closer you get to a cube (or more generally to a sphere) the smaller the surface area.

How can you find areas of shapes other than rectangles?

The rectangular fields in Figure 26.2 and 26.3 remind us of the simple rule for finding the area of a rectangle: that is, you just multiply together the lengths of the two sides. The reader is reminded that the visual image of a rectangular array is an important component of our understanding of the operation of multiplication, as has been discussed fully in Chapter 7 and exploited in developing a written method for multiplication calculations in Chapter 9. The units for measuring area are always *square units*. So, for example, a rectangle 3 cm by 4 cm has an area of 12 *square centimetres*. This is abbreviated to 12 cm², but should still be read as 12 *square centimetres*. If it is read as '12 centimetres squared' it could be confused with the area of a 12-cm square, which is, of course, 144 square centimetres!

More able pupils in primary schools might explore the areas of some other geometric shapes, so their teachers should be confident with the following material. For example, the area of a parallelogram is found by multiplying its height by the length of its base (any one of the sides can be called the base). Figure 26.5 shows how this can be demonstrated rather nicely, by transforming the parallelogram into a rectangle with

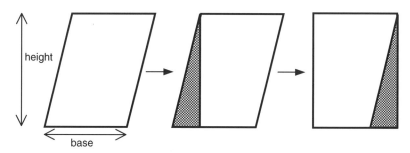

Figure 26.5   A parallelogram transformed into a rectangle with the same height and base

the same height and the same base. For example, if the parallelogram has height 3 cm and base 4 cm, it has an area of 12 cm².

This then gives us a way of finding the area of any triangle. As shown in Figure 26.6, if you make a copy of the triangle, and rotate it through 180°, the two triangles can be fitted together to form a parallelogram, with the same base and the same height as the original triangle. Since the area of the parallelogram is the base multiplied by the height, the area of the triangle is half the product of its base and height. For example, if the triangle has a height of 3 cm and a base of 4 cm, it has an area of 6 cm². Again, note that any one of the sides of the triangle can be taken as the base.

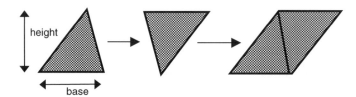

Figure 26.6   A triangle seen as half a parallelogram

Figure 26.7 shows a quadrilateral with just one pair of sides that are parallel. In Britain this is called a *trapezium*. This particular trapezium has a height of 3 cm and the parallel sides have lengths of 4 cm and 6 cm respectively. The area of a trapezium can be found by cutting it up into a parallelogram and a triangle, as shown in Figure 26.7. In this case we produce a parallelogram with height 3 cm and base 4 cm (area 12 cm²), and a triangle of height 3 cm and base 2 cm (area 3 cm²). So the area of the trapezium is 12 + 3 = 15 cm². Self-assessment question 26.7 at the end of this chapter provides the reader with an opportunity to generalize this approach and to formulate a rule for the area of a trapezium.

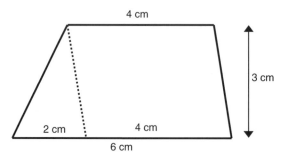

Figure 26.7   A trapezium transformed into a triangle and a parallelogram

What should I know about the relationships between units of area and between units of volume?

Students often get confused when changing between areas measured in square centimetres and square metres. This is because they fail to recognize that there are actually 10 000 cm² in 1 m². That does seem an awful lot, doesn't it? But there are 100 centimetres in 1 metre, and remember that a square metre can be made from 100 rows of 100 centimetre-squares, each with an area of 1 cm². So in Figure 26.8, if the large square represents a metre-square then it has an area of 1 m² or 10 000 cm². And the small square, representing a centimetre-square, has an area of 1 cm² or 0.0001 m². You really would need 10 000 of the small squares to build the large one! So converting areas between cm² and m² involves shifting the digits four places in relation to the decimal point. For example, 12 cm² = 0.0012 m², and 0.5 m² = 5000 cm². The potential for bewilderment is even greater in converting between square millimetres and square metres, since there are a million square millimetres in a square metre. Self-assessment question 26.8 gives the reader the chance to have a go at some of these conversions.

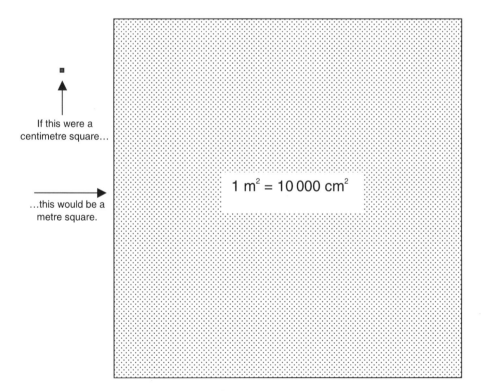

Figure 26.8   One square metre equals 10 000 square centimetres

So, what would be the area of a square of side 50 cm, expressed in square centimetres and in square metres? Using centimetres, the area is $50 \times 50 = 2500$ cm². Using metres, the area is $0.5 \times 0.5 = 0.25$ m². The reader should not be surprised at this result, because they should now recognize that 2500 cm² and 0.25 m² are the same area. We might also note that a square of side 50 cm would be only a quarter of the metre square represented in Figure 26.8, and ¼ expressed as a decimal is 0.25.

Volume is measured in cubic units. If, for example, the cuboid in Figure 26.4(a) was built from centimetre cubes we would give its volume as 12 cm³ (12 cubic centimetres). Note that this cuboid can be seen as 2 layers of 3 rows of 2 cubes, so the volume is given by $2 \times 3 \times 2$. In general, the volume of a cuboid is found by multiplying together the length, width and height. Now, a metre-cube is 100 layers of 100 rows of 100 centimetre cubes. So 1 m³ (a cubic metre) must be equal to $100 \times 100 \times 100 = 1\,000\,000$ cm³ (a million cubic centimetres). So converting volumes between cm³ and m³ involves shifting the digits six places in relation to the decimal point. For example, 12 cm³ = 0.000012 m³, and 0.5 m³ = 500 000 cm³.

If all this leads the reader to feel the need to brush up on their calculations with decimals, then they should now return to Chapter 15.

What is π?

A circle is the shape consisting of all the points at a fixed distance from a given point. The given point is called the *centre*. The distance from the centre to any point on the circle is called the *radius*. The distance from one point through the centre to the opposite point on the circle is called the *diameter*. Clearly the length of the diameter is twice the length of the radius. The perimeter of a circle is also called the *circumference* (see Figure 26.9).

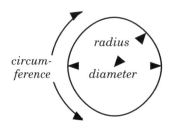

Figure 26.9 Terms used with circles

One of the most amazing facts in all mathematics relates to circles. If you measure the circumference of a circle and divide it by the length of the diameter you always get the same answer! This can be done in the classroom practically, using lots of differently sized circular objects, such as tin lids and crockery. To measure the diameter, place the circular object on a piece of paper between two blocks of wood, remove the object, mark the edges of the blocks on the paper and measure the distance between the marks. To measure the circumference, wrap some tape carefully around the object, mark where a complete circuit begins and ends, unwind the tape and measure the distance between the marks. Allowing for experimental error (which can be considerable with such crude approaches to measuring the diameter and the circumference) you should still find that in most cases the circumference divided by the diameter gives an answer of between about 3 and 3.3. Any results that are way out should be checked and measured again, if necessary. This result, that the circumference is always about three times the diameter, was clearly known in ancient civilizations and used in construction. It occurs in a number of places in the Bible; for example, in I Kings 7:23, we read of a construction, 'circular in shape, measuring ten cubits from rim to rim . . . taking a line of thirty cubits to measure around it.'

If we were able to measure more accurately, we might be able to determine that the ratio of the circumference to the diameter of a circle is about 3.14. This ratio is so important it is given a special symbol, the Greek letter π (pi). The value of π can be found theoretically to any number of decimal places. It begins like this: 3.14159265358979323846643 . . . and actually goes on for ever, without ever recurring (see Chapter 3). For practical purposes, rounding this to two decimal places, as 3.14, is sufficient!

Once we have this value we can find the circumference of a circle, given the diameter, by multiplying the diameter by π, using a calculator if necessary. For example, a circle with radius 5 cm has a diameter of 10 cm and therefore a circumference of approximately $10 \times 3.14 = 31.4$ cm. And we can find the diameter of a circle, given the circumference, by dividing the circumference by π. For example, a metre trundle-wheel is a circle with circumference of 100 cm, so the diameter will have to be approximately $100 \div 3.14 = 31.8$ cm. So the radius will have to be half this, namely 15.9 cm.

Finding the area of a circle is well beyond the scope of primary mathematics. But for completeness we might note here that the area of a circle is given by multiplying the radius by half the circumference. This remarkable result can be demonstrated delightfully by cutting up a circle into a number of *sectors*, as shown in Figure 26.10 and piecing them together to form something approximating to a rectangle. In Figure 26.10 I have cut the circle into eight pieces and then cut one of these in half, before reassembling them to form an approximate rectangle. Clearly, the more pieces you use in this procedure the closer the result will be to a rectangle. Readers should now convince themselves that the width of this rectangle is the radius of the circle and that the height is half the circumference. And the area of the rectangle is the width multiplied by the height . . . hence the area of the circle is the radius multiplied by half the circumference. For example, the area of a circular cake board with diameter 10 inches and circumference 31.4 inches will be the radius (5 inches) multiplied by half the circumference (15.7 inches), that is, 5 × 15.7 = 78.5 square inches.

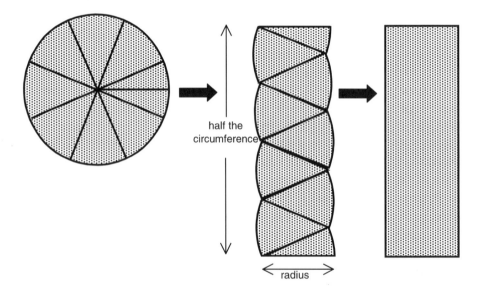

half the circumference

radius

Figure 26.10　Area of a circle = the radius × half the circumference

There is a common misunderstanding, perpetrated I fear by some mathematics teachers who should know better, that π is *equal* to ²²⁄₇ or 3¹⁄₇. This is not true. Three-and-one-seventh is an *approximation* for the value of π in the form of a rational number. As a decimal, 3¹⁄₇ is equal to 3.$\dot{1}$42857, that is, 3.142857142857 . . ., with the 142857 recurring for ever. Comparing this with the value of π given above, we can see that it is only correct to two decimal places anyway, and therefore no better an approximation than 3.14. In the days of calculators 3.14 is bound to be a more useful approximation for π than ²²⁄₇, which, along with quite a few of the things our teachers tell us at school, is probably best forgotten.

Self-assessment questions

26.1: Using just rectangular fields drawn on the grid lines on squared paper, what are the dimensions of the field that gives the maximum area for 20 units of fencing?

26.2: Using just rectangular fields drawn on the grid lines on squared paper, what are the dimensions of the field that gives the minimum length of fencing for an area of 48 square units?

26.3: How can a) 27 and b) 48 unit-cubes be arranged in the shape of a cuboid to produce the minimum surface area?

26.4: How much ribbon will I need to go once round a cake with diameter 25 cm?

26.5: Roughly what is the diameter of a circular running-track which is 400 metres in circumference?

26.6: Here's a neat method for drawing a parallelogram on squared paper. Draw a line 5 cm long along the bottom of a piece of cm-squared paper. From one end count up 3 units and then 2 units to the right and put a small cross. Do the same from the other end of the line. Join up the two crosses. Now join up the ends of the two 5-cm lines you have drawn. You should have a parallelogram. Use the method of Figure 26.5 and a pair of scissors to transform this into a rectangle. What was the area of the parallelogram? Try this with various lengths.

26.7: On squared paper draw a trapezium with height 10 cm and with the two parallel sides of lengths 12 cm and 8 cm. Cut this up into a triangle and a parallelogram, each with height 10 cm (see Figure 26.7) and hence find the area of the trapezium. Repeat this keeping the height and the 12 cm side fixed, but varying the length of the other side, for example, 6 cm, 9 cm, 10 cm, 11 cm, 14 cm. Think of each area as a multiple of 5. Can you now formulate a general rule for finding the area of a trapezium?

26.8: What is the area of a square of side 5 mm, expressed in square millimetres, in square centimetres and in square metres?

26.9: What would be the volume of a cube of side 5 cm? Give your answer in both cm^3 and m^3.

26.10: How many cuboids 5 cm by 4 cm by 10 cm would be needed to build a metre-cube?

Summary of teaching points

1. Use the illustration of fields and fences to explain area and perimeter and pose problems about area and perimeter in these terms.

2. Let pupils investigate the way in which a fixed perimeter can produce a range of different areas, and vice versa.

3. Pupils can be introduced to solid volume by rearranging various numbers of unit cubes in the shape of cuboids; use numbers with plenty of factors, such as 12 and 24. Older primary pupils could investigate the way the surface area changes.

4. Some more able pupils might explore areas of shapes such as parallelograms, triangles and trapeziums, using the methods of cutting and rearranging explained in this chapter.

5. Give pupils practical experience of measuring the diameters and circumferences of circular objects, leading to the discovery that the ratio is always about three, or three and a bit.

6. Introduce older pupils to π, using, for practical purposes, the value 3.14 as an approximation for this ratio.

27

Mathematical Reasoning

Pupils should be taught to: understand and investigate general statements; develop logical thinking and explain their reasoning.

In this chapter there are explanations of:

- the nature of mathematical conjectures;
- the language of generalizations;
- the role of counterexamples and special cases;
- hypotheses and inductive reasoning;
- explanation and proof;
- proof by deductive reasoning;
- proof by exhaustion; and
- axioms and theorems

What is a conjecture in mathematics?

The word *conjecture* is often used in the context of mathematical problem-solving and investigating. It refers to an assertion that something might be true, at the stage when there has not yet been produced the evidence necessary to decide whether or not it is true. A conjecture is usually followed therefore by some appropriate mathematical process of checking. This experience of conjecturing and checking is fundamental to reasoning mathematically.

For example, a pupil might make a conjecture that 91 is a prime number (see Chapter 11). To say this is a conjecture means that they don't know for sure at this stage that 91 is a prime number, but they have a hunch that it might be. After a little bit of exploration, dividing

91 in turn by 2, 3, 5 and then 7, they find that 7 divides into 91, 13 times, so 91 is not prime. So much for that conjecture.

Another pupil might be given a collection of containers and by examining them make a conjecture that the flower vase has the greatest capacity (see Chapter 22). To check this conjecture the pupil might carefully fill each of the other containers in turn with water and pour this into the empty flower vase. This might lead to the conclusion that the conjecture was correct.

What is a generalization?

Another pupil makes the conjecture that there are exactly four prime numbers less than 10. Checking leads to the confirmation of this conjecture, since 2, 3, 5 and 7 are all prime. The pupil then goes on to wonder if there are four prime numbers in every decade. (By *decade*, I mean 0–9, 10–19, 20–29, 30–39, and so on.) The pupil's thinking has moved from a specific case to the general. This is a *generalization*. However, the pupil should be advised that it is not good practice to generalize from a sample of one! (The reader is invited to check the validity of this generalization in self-assessment question 27.1 below.) So, a generalization is an assertion that something is true in a number of cases, or even in every case. In Chapter 20, we have discussed two particular kinds of generalizations, sequential and global, that often emerge in looking at patterns in numbers that have been tabulated. We also saw there the central role played by algebraic symbols in representing variables and enabling us to articulate generalizations. To make a generalization in words we will often use one or other of the following bits of language: always; every; any; all; if . . . then . . . .

It is also possible in English to imply 'always' without actually stating it. Here, for example, is a (true) generalization about multiples (see Chapter 11) stated in six different ways:

- Multiples of 6 are always multiples of 2.
- Every multiple of 6 is a multiple of 2.
- Any multiple of 6 is a multiple of 2.
- All multiples of 6 are multiples of 2.
- If a number is a multiple of 6 then it is a multiple of 2.
- A multiple of 6 must be a multiple of 2.

Note that the reverse statement of a true generalization is not necessarily true. For example, it is *not* true to say: if a number is a multiple of 2 then it is a multiple of 6.

What are counter-examples and special cases?

A *counter-example* is a specific case that demonstrates that a generalization is not valid. For example, to show the falsity of the generalization made at the end of the previous paragraph, we could use the number 14 as a counter-example. This would involve pointing out that 14 is a multiple of 2 (so it satisfies the 'if' bit of the statement), but it is not a multiple of 6 (so it fails the 'then' bit).

Sometimes a counter-example will lead us to modify our generalization rather than discarding it altogether. For example, a pupil might make the generalization that all prime numbers are odd. The teacher then points out that 2 is a counter-example, being a prime number that is even. However, this can be recognized as a *special case*. The generalization can therefore be modified, by excluding the special case, changing the set of numbers to which the generalization applies, as follows: all prime numbers greater than 2 are odd.

Often 0 or 1 will turn out to be special cases that need checking. For example, investigating fractions, we might notice that $\frac{1}{3} < \frac{1}{2}$, $\frac{1}{4} < \frac{1}{3}$, $\frac{1}{5} < \frac{1}{4}$, $\frac{1}{6} < \frac{1}{5}$, and so on, and generalize this to the statement that for any natural number n, $\frac{1}{n} < \frac{1}{(n-1)}$. However, we would have to exclude 1 from this generalization, because that would give us $\frac{1}{1} < \frac{1}{0}$, which is nonsense because $\frac{1}{0}$ is not a real number (division by zero is not possible). In another investigation, a pupil discovers that all square numbers have an odd number of factors. This is a correct generalization, apart from the special case of zero. The teachers asks, 'What about zero? Is that a square number? If so, how many factors does it have?' Well, 0 is technically a square number, since $0^2 = 0$. However, every natural number is a factor of zero! (Note that $0 \times 1 = 0$, $0 \times 2 = 0$, $0 \times 3 = 0$ and so on.) So, it is necessary to exclude zero as a special case in making the generalization, as follows: all square numbers greater than 0 have an odd number of factors.

What is a hypothesis?

The word *hypothesis* is usually used to refer to a generalization that is still a conjecture and which still has to be either proved to be true, or shown to be false by means of a counter-example. Often a hypothesis will emerge by a process of *inductive reasoning*, by looking at a number of specific instances that are seen to have something in common and then speculating that this will always be the case. In the example in Figure 20.3 in Chapter 20, by looking at the numbers in the columns in the table, we recognized that there was a 'left-to-right' rule for working out the number of children from the number of tables: multiply by 2 and add 4. This is a hypothesis, obtained by inductive reasoning. It always seems to be the case, and every example we check seems to work. But, however many cases we check, it is still only a hypothesis – until such time as we produce some kind of a *proof* that it must work in every case.

This is an important point, because sometimes a hypothesis may appear to be correct to begin with but then will let you down later. For example, someone might assert that all numbers that are 1 less or 1 more than a multiple of 6 are prime numbers. To start with this looks like a pretty good hypothesis: 5, 7, 11, 13, 17, 19, 23 are all prime. But the next number, 25, lets us down. In self-assessment question 11.11 in Chapter 11 we looked at Golbach's conjecture, which has been tested for millions and millions of even numbers and has never failed – but it has not yet been *proved*. Everyone believes it to be true, but until a proof is produced that it must work in every case it remains a hypothesis.

Hypotheses also turn up frequently in the context of probability and statistical data. For example, the assertion that a boy is more likely than a girl to have a digital watch would be a hypothesis that primary pupils might investigate, testing it by the collection and analysis of data from a sample of boys and girls. The evidence in this case would only lend support to the hypothesis, not prove it conclusively, of course.

What is the difference between an explanation and a proof?

Proof is a peculiarly mathematical way of reasoning. If a generalization is written in the form of a statement using the 'if . . . then . . .' language, a mathematical proof is a series of logical deductions that starts from the 'if . . .' bit and leads to the 'then . . .' bit. Proof therefore involves *deductive reasoning*. Here is a typical example of a formal mathematical proof: that all multiples of 6 are multiples of 2. First we write what we have to prove in the 'if . . . then . . .' version: if a natural number is a multiple of 6 then it is a multiple of 2. We then introduce some algebraic symbols to enable us to manipulate the mathematical concepts involved here. So, what we have to do is to construct a logical argument which starts with 'If a natural number N is a multiple of 6' and concludes with 'N is a multiple of 2'. Often the steps in the argument are connected by the symbol ⇒, meaning 'which implies'. So, here's the proof by deduction:

If a natural number N is a multiple of 6,
then $N = 6 \times k$, for some natural number k
$\Rightarrow N = (2 \times 3) \times k$

$\Rightarrow N = 2 \times (3 \times k)$, using the associative law of multiplication

$\Rightarrow N = 2 \times m$, where m is the natural number equal to $3 \times k$

$\Rightarrow N$ is a multiple of 2.

Clearly, primary pupils will not be able to handle proofs at this level of sophistication. They can, however, be encouraged to try to formulate explanations that might convince someone that their generalizations are valid. They can make an attempt to answer the question 'why?'. For example, having made the generalization above that all square numbers greater than zero have an odd number of factors, some primary pupils could offer an explanation as to why this must be so. Here's the basis of the argument. For all numbers other than squares, like 28, the factors can be linked in pairs: 1×28, 2×14, 4×7. These pairs are called co-factors. Because they come in pairs, the total number of factors must be even. But with a square number, like 36, as well as the pairs of co-factors (1×36, 2×18, 3×12, 4×9) there is an extra factor, in this case 6, because this is the number that is multiplied by itself to give 36. So the total number of factors must be odd. This is not a formal mathematical proof, but it is a convincing explanation.

Some hypotheses can be proved to be true by a method called *proof by exhaustion*. This is a method of proof that can be employed for a generalization that relates to only a finite number of cases. It might then be possible to check every single case, in other words, to exhaust all the possibilities. For example, in relation to Figure 26.3, in the previous chapter, we made the assertion that the 4×4 square was the shape with an area of 16 square units that had the smallest perimeter. This could be rephrased using the 'if . . . then . . .' format as a generalization, as follows: if a shape other than a square is constructed on a square grid from 16 square units then the perimeter will be greater than that of the square. Now we can actually prove this to be true, because the number of different shapes that can be made is finite. So we can exhaust all the possibilities by drawing all the possible shapes and checking that in every case the perimeter is larger that of the square.

What are axioms and theorems?

Some of the generalizations we use in mathematics are called *axioms*. An axiom is a statement that is taken to be true, usually because it is self-evidently true, but which cannot be proved as such. An axiom is one of the building blocks of mathematical reasoning. It is a statement that we have to accept as true, otherwise we would just not be able to get on and do any mathematics. Examples of axioms that we have discussed in this book would be the commutative, associative and distributive laws (see Chapters 4, 5 and 8). Another example would be the transitive property of the inequality 'greater than', discussed in Chapter 22: if $A > B$ and $B > C$, then $A > C$. These laws have been explained, examples of what they mean have been provided, and we have seen how they are used – but we have never questioned their truth or felt the need to prove them. These generalizations are not hypotheses up for discussion and investigation. They are axioms of mathematics.

Sometimes, when a generalization has been proved to be true it is given the status of a *theorem*. This is because it is likely to be useful in making other deductions or to prove other hypotheses. An example of a theorem that we have discussed in this book is Pythagoras's theorem (see Chapter 12). This has been proved (elsewhere) to be true, by deductive logic, and is therefore now available for us to use with complete confidence.

Self-assessment questions

27.1: Is the pupil's assertion that there are four prime numbers in every decade a correct generalization?

27.2: Which of these generalizations are true and which are false? If false, give a counter-example.

a) Any number greater than 5 is greater than 10.

b) A multiple of 6 must be a multiple of 3.

c) If a quadrilateral is a square then it is a rhombus.

d) Any quadrilateral with all sides equal is a square.

e) All parallelograms are quadrilaterals.

f) If a quadrilateral is a square then it is a parallelogram.

g) Every solid shape with six faces is a cuboid.

h) If a solid shape is a cuboid then it has six faces all of which are square.

i) If a solid shape has six faces all of which are square then it is a cuboid.

j) Every solid shape all of whose faces are equilateral triangles is a tetrahedron.

k) If $x > y$ and $z < y$ then $z < x$.

27.3: Prove by exhaustion the following: if a shape other than a square is constructed on a square grid from 4 square units, then the perimeter of the shape is greater than that of the square.

27.4: A pupil makes a chain of equilateral triangles, using match-sticks. The pupil finds that 3 matches are needed to make one triangle, 5 to make 2 triangles, 7 to make 3 triangles, and so on. Formulate a generalization.

Can you provide a convincing explanation why this must be so? What about zero triangles? Does this fit your generalization or is it a special case?

27.5: Write down three digits and write them down again, hence making a six-digit number (for example, 346 346). Use a calculator to check the hypothesis that all such numbers must be divisible by 7, 11 and 13. Why is this?

Summary of teaching points

1. Provide pupils with plenty of opportunity in problem-solving and investigating in mathematics to make conjectures and to decide how to check them.
2. Give pupils opportunity to formulate generalizations in words and in algebraic symbols.
3. In making general statements, encourage pupils to use the language: always, every, any, all, if . . . then . . ..
4. When a generalization has been tested, discuss with pupils whether the reverse statement is or is not true.
5. Make explicit to pupils the idea of a counterexample as a means of disproving a generalization.
6. Remind pupils to check special cases when they are making a general statement in mathematics.
7. Encourage older pupils to explain why something must be true, to formulate some kind of convincing argument.
8. Provide pupils with some examples of hypotheses that can be proved by exhaustion, by checking all the possibilities.
9. Remember that primary mathematics does not consist only of the content of Chapters 2–26 of this book, but also involves learning to reason in those ways that are distinctively mathematical that have been discussed in Chapter 27: conjecturing and checking, inductive reasoning to formulate hypotheses, generalizing, explaining and convincing, and deductive reasoning.

Answers to Self-assessment Questions

Particularly where the question asks for the invention of a sentence, a question, a method or a problem, the answers provided below are, of course, only examples of possible valid responses.

Chapter 2: Place value

2.1: CLXXXVIII, CCLXVII, CCC, DCXIII, DCC (188, 267, 300, 613, 700).
2.2: Four thousand one hundred (4099 + 1 = 4100).
2.3: a) $516 = (5 \times 10^2) + (1 \times 10^1) + 6$; b) $3060 = (3 \times 10^3) + (6 \times 10^1)$;
   c) $2\ 305\ 004 = (2 \times 10^6) + (3 \times 10^5) + (5 \times 10^3) + 4$.
2.4: 6 one-pound coins, 2 ten-penny coins, 4 one-penny coins.
2.5: 3.2 is 3 flats and 2 longs; 3.05 is 3 flats and 5 small cubes; 3.15 is 3 flats, one long and 5 small cubes; 3.10 is 3 flats and 1 long. In order: 3.05, 3.10, 3.15, 3.2.
2.6: 3.405 m, and 2.500 m (or 2.5 m or 2.50 m).
2.7: a) £0.25; b) 0.25 m; c) £0.07; d) 0.045 kg; e) 0.050 litres; f) 0.005 m.
2.8: 3.608 lies between 3 and 4; between 3.6 and 3.7; between 3.60 and 3.61; between 3.607 and 3.609.

Chapter 3: Mathematical modelling

3.1: Mathematical model is 4.95 + 5.90 + 9.95; mathematical solution, using a calculator, is 20.8; interpretation is that the total cost is £20.80.
3.2: Mathematical model is 27.90 ÷ 3; mathematical solution (calculator answer) is 9.3; this is an exact but slightly inappropriate answer, because of the convention of 2 figures after the point for money; interpretation is that each person pays £9.30.
3.3: Mathematical model is 39.70 ÷ 3; mathematical solution (calculator answer) is 13.233333; this is an answer that has been truncated; interpretation is that each person owes £13.23 and a little bit; two people pay £13.23, but one has to pay £13.24.

3.4: Mathematical model is 50 ÷ 0.32; mathematical solution (calculator answer) is 156.25; this is an exact but inappropriate answer; interpretation is that John can buy 156 bars of chocolate.

3.5: Mathematical model is 500 ÷ 35; mathematical solution (calculator answer) is 14.285714; this is an answer that has been truncated; interpretation is that it will take me 15 months to reach my target.

Chapter 4: Addition and subtraction structures

4.1: I buy two articles costing £5.95 and £6.99. What is the total cost?

4.2: My salary was £9750 and then I had a rise of £145. What was my new salary?

4.3: If the recipe requires 250 ml of water and 125 ml of milk, what is the total volume of liquid?

4.4: The class's morning consists of 15 minutes registration, 25 minutes assembly, 55 minutes mathematics, 20 minutes break, 65 minutes English. What is the total time?

4.5: 48 years; 2050 – 2002; this is an example of the inverse-of-addition structure.

4.6: 78 pages; 256 – 178; this is an example of the inverse-of-addition structure.

4.7: 27 years; 52 – 25; this is an example of the comparison structure.

4.8: 185 points; 750 – 565; this is an example of the inverse-of-addition structure.

4.9: The Australian Chardonnay is £3.95 and the Hungarian is £2.99. How much cheaper is the Hungarian?

4.10: The temperature in London is 25 °C, in Oslo it is –6 °C. What is the temperature difference between the two cities?

4.11: There are 250 pupils in a school. 159 have school lunches. How many do not?

4.12: I want to buy a computer costing £489, but have only £350. How much more do I need?

Chapter 5: Mental strategies for addition and subtraction

5.1: a) $67 - (20 - 8) = (67 - 20) + 8$; general rule: $a - (b - c) = (a - b) + c$.
b) $67 - (20 + 8) = (67 - 20) - 8$; general rule: $a - (b + c) = (a - b) - c$.

5.2: a) Pupil may have added, or done $2 - 0$ rather than $0 - 2$ in the tens column; b) any subtraction involving zero gives the answer zero! c) remembered decomposition recipe wrongly and written a little 9 instead of a little 1; d) 7 – 1 instead of 1 – 7 in units, and again mystified by zero in tens column; e) consistently taking the smaller from the larger; f) remembered decomposition recipe wrongly and written a little 9 instead of a little 1.

5.3: $500 + 200$ makes 700; $30 + 90$ makes 120, that's 820 in total so far; $8 + 4$ makes 12, add this to the 820, to get 832.

5.4: $423 + 98 = 423 + 100 - 2 = 523 - 2 = 521$.

5.5: $297 + 304 = $ double $300 - 3 + 4 = 601$.

5.6: $494 + 307 = 494 + 6 + 301 = 500 + 301 = 801$.

5.7: $26 + 77 = 25 + 75 + 1 + 2 = 100 + 3 = 103$.

5.8: $1000 - 458 = 1000 - 500 + 42 = 500 + 42 = 542$.

5.9: $819 - 519 = 300$, so $819 - 523 = 300 - 4 = 296$.

5.10: $732 - 389 = 11 + 300 + 32 = 343$.

5.11: a) $974 - 539 = 974 - 540 + 1 = 434 + 1 = 435$; b) $400 - 237 = 399 - 237 + 1 = 162 + 1 = 163$; c) $597 + 209 = 600 + 200 + 9 - 3 = 806$; d) counting back, $7000 - 6 = 6994$; e) counting on from 6998, $7000 - 6998 = 2$.

Chapter 6: Written methods for addition and subtraction

6.1: Put out 2 pound coins, 8 pennies; then 1 pound coin, 5 ten-pences and 6 pennies; then 9 ten-pences and 7 pennies; there are 21 pennies; exchange 20 of these for 2 tens, leaving 1 penny; there are now 16 tens; exchange 10 of these for 1 pound, leaving 6 tens; there are then 4 pounds; the total is 4 pounds, 6 tens and 1 penny, i.e. 461.

6.2: $800 + 130 + 14 = 944$

6.3: Put out 6 one-pound coins, 2 tens and 3 pence; take away 1 penny, leaving 2 pence; not enough ten-pences, so exchange 1 pound for 10 tens, giving 12 tens; take away 7 of these, leaving 5 tens; now take away 4 pounds; the result is 1 pound, 5 tens and 2 pence, i.e. 152.

6.4: $100 + 80 + 8 = 188$.

6.5: Put out 2 thousands and 6 units; not enough units to take away 8, no tens to exchange and no hundreds, so exchange 1 thousand for 10 hundreds, leaving 1 thousand; now exchange 1 hundred for 10 tens, leaving 9 hundreds; then exchange 1 ten for 10 units, leaving 9 tens and giving 16 units; can now take away 8 units, 3 tens and 4 hundreds; the result is 1 thousand, 5 hundreds, 6 tens and 8 units, i.e. 1568.

6.6: Add 2 to both numbers, to give $2008 - 440$; add 60 to both, to give $2068 - 500$; add 500 to both, to give $2568 - 1000$; answer, 1568.

Chapter 7: Multiplication and division structures

7.1: I bought 29 boxes of eggs with 12 eggs in each box . . . (29 lots of 12); there are 12 classes in the school with 29 children in each class . . . (12 lots of 29).

7.2: I bought 12 kg of potatoes at 25p per kilogram. What was the total cost?

7.3: The box can be seen as 4 rows of 6 yoghurts or 6 rows of 4 yoghurts.

7.4: If the length of the wing in the model is 16 cm, how long is the length of the wing on the actual aeroplane? ($16 \times 25 = 400$ cm).

7.5: $2827 \times 1.12 = 3166.24$; new monthly salary is £3166.24.

7.6: Scale factor is 20 ($300 \div 15$); an example of the ratio structure.

7.7: Price is 25p per pound-weight ($700 \div 28$); an example of the equal-sharing structure.

7.8: I can afford 8 CDs ($100 \div 12.50$); an example of the inverse-of-multiplication structure, using the idea of repeated subtraction.

7.9: I need 25 months ($300 \div 12$); this is an example of the inverse-of-multiplication structure, using the idea of repeated addition.

7.10: A packet of four chocolate bars costs 60p; how much per bar?

7.11: How many tapes costing £4 each can I afford if I have £60 to spend?

7.12: A teacher earns £1500 a month, a bank manager earns £4800. How many times greater is the bank manager's salary? ($4800 \div 1500 = 3.2$); the bank manager's salary is 3.2 times that of the teacher.

Chapter 8: Mental strategies for multiplication and division

8.1: $1 \times 2 \times 3 \times 4 \times 5 = 10 \times 12 = 120$.

8.2: In $288 \div 6 = 48$, 288 is the dividend, 6 is the divisor, 48 is the quotient.

8.3: 16 lots of 25 is easier to calculate than 25 lots of 16; $4 \times 25 = 100$, so $16 \times 25 = 400$.

8.4: $25 \times 24 = 25 \times (4 \times 6) = (25 \times 4) \times 6 = 100 \times 6 = 600$.

8.5: $25 \times (20 + 4) = (25 \times 20) + (25 \times 4) = 500 + 100 = 600$.

8.6: $22 \times (40 - 2) = (22 \times 40) - (22 \times 2) = 880 - 44 = 836$.

8.7: $4 \times 90 = 360$, $40 \times 9 = 360$, $40 \times 90 = 3600$, $4 \times 900 = 3600$, $400 \times 9 = 3600$, $40 \times 900 = 36\,000$, $400 \times 90 = 36\,000$, $400 \times 900 = 360\,000$.

8.8: $48 \times 25 = 12 \times 4 \times 25 = 12 \times 100 = 1200$.

8.9: $2 \times 103 = 206$; $4 \times 103 = 412$; $8 \times 103 = 824$; $16 \times 103 = 1648$; $206 + 824 + 1648 = 2678$.

8.10: $10 \times 103 = 1030$; $2 \times 103 = 206$; $1030 + 1030 + 206 + 206 + 206 = 2678$.

8.11: $154 \div 22$ is the same as $(88 + 66) \div 22$ which equals $(88 \div 22) + (66 \div 22)$; hence the answer is $4 + 3 = 7$; $154 \div 22$ is the same as $(220 - 66) \div 22$ which equals $(220 \div 22) - (66 \div 22)$; hence the answer is $10 - 3 = 7$.

8.12: $10 \times 21 = 210$; another 10×21 makes this up to 420; $2 \times 21 = 42$, which brings us to 462; 1 more 21 makes 483; answer is $10 + 10 + 2 + 1 = 23$.

8.13: $385 \div 55 = 770 \div 110$ (doubling both numbers) $= 7$.

Chapter 9: Written methods for multiplication and division

9.1: The four areas are 40×30, 40×7, 2×30 and 2×7, giving a total of $1200 + 280 + 60 + 14 = 1554$.

9.2: The six areas are 300×10, 300×7, 40×10, 40×7, 5×10 and 5×7, giving a total of $3000 + 2100 + 400 + 280 + 50 + 35 = 5865$.

9.3: From 126 take away 10 sevens (70), leaving 56, then 5 sevens (35), leaving 21, which is 3 sevens; answer is therefore $10 + 5 + 3$, i.e. 18.

9.4: From 851 take away 20 lots of 23 (460), leaving 391, then 10 more (230), leaving 161, then 5 more (115), leaving 46, which is 2×23; answer is therefore $20 + 10 + 5 + 2$, i.e. 37.

9.5: From 529 take away 50 lots of 8 (400), then 10 more (80), then 5 more (40), then 1 more (8), leaving a remainder of 1; answer is $50 + 10 + 5 + 1 = 66$, remainder 1.

Chapter 10: Remainders and rounding

10.1: The mathematical model is: 124×5.95 (or 5.95×124); the mathematical solution is 737.8; interpretation: the total cost of the order will be £737.80; to the nearest ten pounds, the total cost of the order will be about £740; to three significant figures, the total cost of the order will be about £738.

10.2: The mathematical model is: $365 \div 7$; the solution is 52 remainder 1; the answer to Jackie's problem is: there are 52 weeks in a year, plus one extra day; the remainder represent the one extra day; the calculator solution is 52.142857; this is an answer that has been truncated; the figures after the point represent a bit of a week.

10.3: a) 327 ÷ 40 = 8.175 (calculator), or 8 remainder 7. So 9 coaches are needed. We round *up* (otherwise we would have to leave 7 children behind); b) 500 ÷ 65 = 7.6923076 (calculator), or 7 remainder 45. So we can buy 7 cakes. We round *down* (and have 45p change for something else).

10.4: Calculator result is 131.88888; the average height is 132 cm to the nearest cm.

10.5: a) 3; b) 3.2; c) 3.16.

10.6: 205 books per shop; that's 205 × 17 = 3485 books altogether, so remainder is 3500 − 3485 = 15 books.

Chapter 11: Multiples, factors and primes

11.1: 3 × 37 = 111, 6 × 37 = 222, 9 × 37 = 333, 12 × 37 = 444, 15 × 37 = 555, 18 × 37 = 666, 21 × 37 = 777, 24 × 37 = 888, 27 × 37 = 999; pattern breaks down when 4-digit answers are achieved.

11.2: a) 47 × 9 = 423; sum of digits = 9; b) 172 × 9 = 1548; sum of digits = 18; sum of these digits = 9; c) 9 876 543 × 9 = 88 888 887; sum of digits = 63; sum of these digits = 9.

11.3: a) 2652 is a multiple of 2 (ends in even digit), 3 (sum of digits is multiple of 3), 4 (last two digits multiple of 4), 6 (multiple of 2 and 3); b) 6570 is a multiple of 2 (ends in even digit), 3 (sum of digits is multiple of 3), 5 (ends in 0), 6 (multiple of 2 and 3), 9 (digital root is 9); c) 2401 is a multiple of none of these (it is 7 × 7 × 7 × 7).

11.4: A three-digit number is a multiple of 11 if the sum of the two outside digits subtract the middle digit is either 0 (e.g. 561, 594, 330) or 11 (418, 979).

11.5: 24 (the lowest common multiple of 8 and 12).

11.6: a) Factors of 95 are 1, 5, 19, 95; b) factors of 96 are 1, 2, 3, 4, 6, 8, 12, 16, 24, 32, 48 and 96; c) factors of 97 are 1 and 97 (it is prime); clearly 96 is the most flexible.

11.7: Factors of 48 are 1, 2, 3, 4, 6, 8, 12, 16, 24, 48; factors of 80 are 1, 2, 4, 5, 8, 10, 16, 20, 40, 80; common factors are 1, 2, 4, 8, 16; could have 16 rows of 3 blue and 5 red, or 8 rows of 6 blue and 10 red, or 4 rows of 12 blue and 20 red, or 2 rows of 24 blue and 40 red, or 1 row of 48 blue and 80 red!

11.8: 71, 73, 79, 83, 89, 97 (*Note*: not 91, because this is 9 × 13).

11.9: 4403 = 7 × 17 × 37.

11.10: 5, 7, 11, 13, 17, 19, 23, 25, 29, 31, 35, 37, 41, 43, 47, 49, 53, 55, 59, 61; they are all prime except 25, 35, 49 and 55.

11.11: $4 = 2 + 2$, $6 = 3 + 3$, $8 = 3 + 5$, $10 = 3 + 7$, $12 = 5 + 7$, $14 = 7 + 7$, $16 = 3 + 13$, $18 = 5 + 13$, $20 = 7 + 13$, $22 = 11 + 11$, $24 = 7 + 17$, $26 = 3 + 23$, $28 = 5 + 23$, $30 = 13 + 17$.

11.12: The smallest answer is 2520.

Chapter 12: Squares, cubes and number shapes

12.1: 20 is a factor of 100; 21 is a triangle number; 22 is a multiple of 2 and 11; 23 is a prime number; 24 has eight factors; 25 is a square number; 26 is a multiple of 2 and 13; 27 is a cube number; 28 is a triangle number; 29 is a prime number.

12.2: 36 is both a triangle number and a square number.

12.3: The differences between successive square numbers are 3, 5, 7, 9, 11 . . ., the odd numbers; these are the numbers of dots added to each square in Figure 12.1(a) to make the next one in the sequence.

12.4: The answers should be the same. Whole numbers less than 100 that are both cubes and squares are 1 and 64.

12.5: a) 57; b) 17.

12.6: 14.14 m.

12.7: The cube root of 500 is between 7.93 and 7.94; so the length of the side of the cube should be about 7.9 cm (79 mm).

12.8: The answers are the square numbers: 4, 9, 16, 25, 36, and so on; two successive triangles of dots in Figure 14.4 can be fitted together to make a square number.

12.9: 20, 21 and 29 ($20^2 + 21^2 = 29^2$).

12.10: Approximately 14.14 cm.

12.11: a) $10 > \sqrt{50}$, b) $^3\sqrt{100} < 5$, c) $8 < \sqrt{70} < 9$.

12.12: $12 < \sqrt{150} < 13$.

Chapter 13: Integers: positive and negative

13.1: 472, 0 and –10 are integers.

13.2: The order is B (+3), A (–4), C (–5).

13.3: a) The temperature one winter's day is 4 °C; that night it falls by 12 degrees; what is the night-time temperature? (Answer –8); b) the temperature one winter's night is –6 °C; when it rises by 10 degrees what is the temperature? (Answer: 4).

13.4: a) If I am overdrawn by £5, how much must be paid into my account to make the balance £20? (Answer: 25); b) if I am overdrawn by £15, how much must be paid into my account so that I am only overdrawn by £10?

(Answer: 5); c) if I am overdrawn by £10 and spend a further £20, what is my new balance? (Answer: −30).

13.5: My basic calculator displays −42 with the negative sign at one end of the display and the 42 at the other; this is rather unsatisfactory.

13.6: The mathematical model is 458.64 − (−187.85) or 458.64 + 187.85; the cheque paid in was £646.49.

Chapter 14: Fractions

14.1: a) A bar of chocolate is cut into 5 equal pieces and I have 4 of them; b) $\frac{4}{5}$ of a class of 30 children is 24 children; c) share 4 pizzas equally between 5 people; d) if I earn £400 a week and you earn £500 a week, my earnings are $\frac{4}{5}$ of yours.

14.2: a) $\frac{1}{4} = \frac{2}{8} = \frac{3}{12}$; b) $\frac{1}{2} = \frac{2}{4} = \frac{3}{6} = \frac{4}{8} = \frac{6}{12}$; c) $\frac{3}{4} = \frac{6}{8} = \frac{9}{12}$; d) $\frac{4}{4} = \frac{8}{8} = \frac{12}{12} = \frac{6}{6} = \frac{3}{3} = \frac{2}{2} = 1$; e) $\frac{2}{12} = \frac{1}{6}$; f) $\frac{4}{12} = \frac{2}{6} = \frac{1}{3}$; g) $\frac{8}{12} = \frac{4}{6} = \frac{2}{3}$; h) $\frac{10}{12} = \frac{5}{6}$.

14.3: $\frac{3}{5}$ is $\frac{24}{40}$; $\frac{5}{8}$ is $\frac{25}{40}$; the latter is the larger.

14.4: $\frac{1}{6}$ ($\frac{2}{12}$), $\frac{1}{3}$ ($\frac{4}{12}$), $\frac{5}{12}$, $\frac{2}{3}$ ($\frac{8}{12}$), $\frac{3}{4}$ ($\frac{9}{12}$).

14.5: Compare by ratio the prices of two coffee-pots, pot A costing £15, pot B costing £25.

14.6: $\frac{9}{24}$ or $\frac{3}{8}$.

14.7: a) $\frac{1}{5}$ of £100 is £20, so $\frac{3}{5}$ is £60; b) £1562.50 (2500 ÷ 8 × 5).

14.8: They are all rational except $\sqrt{10}$.

14.9: $\sqrt{20}$ and $\sqrt[3]{9}$ are irrational (*Note*: $\sqrt{49} = 7$ and $\sqrt[3]{27} = 3$).

Chapter 15: Calculations with decimals

15.1: a) Mathematical solution is 6.90, total cost is £6.90; b) mathematical solution is 3.25, total length is 3.25 m; c) mathematical solution is 0.22, difference in height is 0.22 m or 22 cm; d) mathematical solution is 5.75, change is £5.75.

15.2: a) I have a 1.500-litre bottle of wine (one and a half litres) and pour out one glass of 0.125 litres (125 ml); how much is left? (Answer: 1.375 litres); b) what is the total mass (weight) of a bag of potatoes of 2.500 kg (two and a half kilograms) and a bag of onions of 1.120 kg? (Answer: 3.620 kg).

15.3: How much for 4 paperbacks costing £3.99 each? Answer: £15.96 (399 × 4 = (400 × 4) − 4 = 1596, so 3.99 × 4 = 15.96).

15.4: Divide a 4.40-m length of wood into 8 equal parts; each part is 0.55 m (55 cm) long. (Change the calculation to 440 cm divided by 8.)

15.5: a) 18.4; b) 18.4; c) 0.00184.

15.6: a) 18 (or 18.0); b) 18 (or 18.0); c) 0.0018 (or 0.00180).

15.7: 0.0001; find the area in square metres of a square of side 0.01 m (1 cm).

15.8: a) $2 \div 0.5 = 20 \div 5 = 4$; b) $5.5 \div 0.11 = 550 \div 11 = 50$.

15.9: a) 50; b) 0.0005; c) 0.005.

15.10: a) 0.17; b) 0.6; c) 0.35; d) 0.6666667 (approx); e) 0.1428571 (approx).

15.11: a) $9/100$; b) $79/100$; c) $15/100 = 3/20$.

15.12: Largest is 1.2×10^6, smallest is 2.4×10^5.

15.13: a) Answer should be about $3 \times 1 = 3$, so 2.66; b) answer should be about $10 \times 0.1 = 1$, so 0.964; c) answer should be about $28 \div 1 = 28$, so 31.

Chapter 16: Proportion and percentages

16.1: £12.

16.2: 25 °C.

16.3: Since one-third is about 33%, this is the greater reduction.

16.4: a) 13 out of 50 is the same proportion as 26 out of 100. So 26% achieve level 5 and 74% do not; b) 57 out of 300 is the same proportion as 19 out of 100. So 19% achieve level 5 and 81% do not; c) 24 out of 80 is the same proportion as 3 out of 10, or 30 out of 100. So 30% achieve level 5 and 70% do not; d) 26 out of 130 is the same proportion as 2 out of 10, or 20 out of 100. So 20% achieve level 5 and 80% do not.

16.5: English, about 42%; Italian, about 49%.

16.6: a) $3/20 = 15/100 = 15\%$; b) $65\% = 65/100 = 13/20$.

16.7: a) 10% of £120 is £12, so 30% is three times this, i.e. £36; b) 10% of £450 is £45; so 5% is £22.50; 1% is £4.50, so 2% is £9; so 17% is £45 + £22.50 + £9 = £76.50.

16.8: £271.04 (£275 × 1.12 × 0.88).

16.9: £150 (114% is £171 and we have to find 100%).

16.10: It makes no difference! In one case the calculation could be: 600 × 1.20 × 0.90; in the other it could be: 600 × 0.90 × 1.20; the results are the same, £648.

Chapter 17: Handling data

17.1: a) Which way of travelling to school is used by most children? How many fewer children walk than come by car? b) How many children have fewer than five writing implements? Which group has no children in it? c) How many have waist measurements in the range 60 to 64 cm, to the nearest centimetre? How many have waist measurements to the nearest centimetre that are greater than 89 cm?

17.2: a) Continuous; b) continuous; c) discrete; d) discrete, but should be grouped; e) discrete; f) discrete; g) continuous.

17.3: Examples (c) and (f), having a small number of possibilities, are best displayed in a pie chart. Example (g) is best displayed in a line graph, with the horizontal axis representing time.

17.4: Fifty-pence intervals will produce 10 groups: £0.00–£0.49, £0.50–£0.99, £1.00–£1.49, and so on.

17.5: a) 140 degrees; b) about 153 degrees (calculator answer: 152.72727).

Chapter 18: Comparing sets of data

18.1: Group A English, mean = 53.7, median = 53; Group B English, mean = 67.5, median = 71. Both averages support the view that Group B did better.

18.2: The mean for English for the two groups combined is 59.8 (1494 ÷ 25). This is less than the mean of the two separate means (the mean of 53.7 and 67.5 is 60.6). Because there are more pupils in Group A this mean has a greater weighting in the combined mean.

18.3: With 25 in the set the median is the thirteenth value when arranged in order; so for English, median = 56; for mathematics, median = 53. The range for English is 45 (90 – 45) and the range for mathematics is 72 (95 – 23).

18.4: For mathematics, John's mark (49) is less than the mean (53.6) and less than the median (56.5), but well above the bottom of the range.

18.5: The mode is 3. (There are 17 three-letter words, followed by 13 two-lettered and 12 four-lettered.)

18.6: P (about 68 cm per sec) had a greater average speed than Q (65 cm per sec).

18.7: Journey there takes 10 hours, journey back takes 8 hours. Total journey is 800 miles in 18 hours, so overall average speed is about 44.4 mph (800 ÷ 18).

18.8: Since the figure of 69% achieving level 2 or above falls between the fortieth percentile (72%) and the lower quartile (67%) it is fair to conclude that St Anne's is performing well below average compared to schools in this group. Because their percentage is less than the fortieth percentile, it means that more than 60% of schools in the group did better than St Anne's.

18.9: a) The diagram shows a marked difference in performance between the two groups, with group A showing considerably higher levels of achievement in reading. The boxes do not even overlap. This means that all the schools in the middle 50% of group A have a higher percentage of pupils gaining level 2 or above for reading than all the schools in the middle 50% of group E. b) About 90%. c) About 90%. d) About 67%. e) About 66%. f) Group E has a much greater range of achievement in reading: some schools have only 32% achieving level 2 or above for reading, whereas others get as many as 90% of their pupils achieving this level. For group A the range is from about 66% to 100%. g) The inter-quartile ranges are markedly different, showing that group E's performance is much more diverse: group A has an IQR of 13% (from 83% to 96%); group E has an IQR of 21% (from 56% to 77%).

Chapter 19: Probability

19.1: a) By experiment: finding the relative frequency of successful outcomes in a large number of trials; b) by collecting data from a large sample of people aged 50–59 years in England; c) using an argument based on symmetry, considering all the possible, equally likely outcomes.

19.2: 55% in the sample have less than 6 letters; so estimate of probability is 0.55.

19.3: a) $3/12 = 0.25$; b) $9/12 = 0.75$.

19.4: a) $12/36 = 0.33$ approximately; b) $9/36 = 0.25$; c) $20/36 = 0.56$ approximately.

19.5: Probability of scoring 1 is 0; probability of scoring less than 13 is 1.

19.6: They are independent but not mutually exclusive. Probability of black ace is $2/52 = 1/26 (= 1/13 \times 1/2)$.

19.7: The events are mutually exclusive but not independent. Probability of right way up or upside down is $0.35 + 0.20 = 0.55$. Probability of landing on a side is $1 - 0.55 = 0.45$.

19.8: These events are not independent (clearly being alive at 75 is dependent on being alive at 65!). Nor are they mutually exclusive (since both can happen to one person). The probability of both occurring is the probability of being alive at $75 = 0.5$.

Chapter 20: Algebra

20.1: $F = 3Y$. Criticism: using F and Y is misleading, since they look like abbreviations for a foot and a yard, instead of variables (e.g. the number of feet).

20.2: a) The total number of pieces of fruit bought; b) the cost of the apples in pence; c) the cost of the bananas; d) the total cost of the fruit. Criticism: using A and B is misleading, since they look like abbreviations for an apple and a banana; so $10A + 12B$ looks as though it means 10 apples and 12 bananas.

20.3: Jenny has 11 rides. Arithmetic steps: 12 divided by 2, add 5. Algebraic representation: $2(N − 5) = 12$.

20.4: a) 60; b) 10.

20.5: For Figure 20.2(c): a) add 5; b) 498; c) multiply by 5, subtract 2; d) $B = 5A − 2$. For Figure 20.2(d): a) subtract 1; b) 0; c) subtract from 100; d) $B = 100 − A$.

20.6: Side by side: a) add 2; b) 204; c) multiply by 2, add 4; d) $Y = 2X + 4$. End to end: a) add 4; b) 402; c) multiply by 4, add 2; d) $Y = 4X + 2$.

20.7: My number is 42; the equation is $X(2X + 3) = 3654$.

20.8: The first 10 triangle numbers are 1, 3, 6, 10, 15, 21, 28, 36, 45, 55. Their doubles are $2 = 1 \times 2$, $6 = 2 \times 3$, $12 = 3 \times 4$, $20 = 4 \times 5$, $30 = 5 \times 6$, $42 = 6 \times 7$, $56 = 7 \times 8$, $72 = 8 \times 9$, $90 = 9 \times 10$, $110 = 10 \times 11$. So the nth triangle number doubled is $n \times (n + 1)$. Hence the nth triangle number is $1/_2 n \times (n + 1)$. So the one-hundredth triangle number (which equals $1 + 2 + 3 + . . . + 100$) is $50 \times 101 = 5050$.

Chapter 21: Coordinates and linear relationships

21.1: The points are (1, 2), (1, 4), (2, 5), (4, 5), (5, 4), (5, 2), (4, 1) and (2, 1). Joined up in this order they form an octagon.

21.2: They are all linear relationships, producing straight-line graphs.

21.3: a) The total number of eggs; b) the equivalent number of francs; c) the top number in the fractions in the set.

21.4: The fourth vertex is (4, 5). The sum of the x-coordinates of two opposite vertices is the same as the sum of the x-coordinates for the other two opposite vertices. The same is true of the y-coordinates. The fourth vertex to go with (4, 4), (5, 8) and (13, 6) is therefore (12, 2), because $4 + 13 = 5 + 12$, and $4 + 6 = 8 + 2$.

21.5: A sequence of parallelograms is produced. The rules are exactly the same as those given for rectangles. The fourth vertex is (1, 3); if you join the points in a different order it could also be (1, −1) or (7, 5).

21.6: $2x + 1 = 6$ when $x = 2.5$.

21.7: Using the x-axis for weights in stones, the straight line graph should pass through (0, 0) and (11, 70). Then, for example, the point (10, 64) on this line (approximately) converts 10 stone to about 64 kg, and the point (9.4, 60) gives 9.4 stone as the approximate equivalent of 60 kg.

21.8: (a) 82 °F is approximately 28 °C; b) 16 °C is approximately 61 °F. These two conversions are very easy to remember!

Chapter 22: Measurement

22.1: It works as far as 55 miles, which is 89 km to the nearest km (88.5115). The next value, 89 miles, is 143 km to the nearest km (143.2277), rather than the Fibonacci number, 144.

22.2: It will still be 1 kg. It will weigh less, but the mass does not change.

22.3: a) Yes; if A is earlier than B and B is earlier than C, then A must be earlier than C; b) no; for example, 20 cm is half of 40 cm and 40 cm is half of 80 cm, but 20 cm is not half of 80 cm.

22.4: a) 297 mm; b) 29.7 cm; c) 2.97 dm; d) 0.297 m.

22.5: a) 250 g; b) 2 pints; c) 2 metres; d) 100 kilometres; e) 4 ounces; f) 10 stones; g) 9 miles to the litre.

Chapter 23: Angle

23.1: ⅛ of a turn (acute), 89° (acute), 90° (right), 95° (obtuse), 150° (obtuse), 2 right angles (straight), 200° (reflex), ¾ of a turn (reflex).

23.2: a) 6 right angles; b) 8 right angles; c) 10 right angles. The sequential rule is add two right angles. For a figure with N sides the global rule for the sum of the angles is $2N - 4$. When $N = 100$, the sum of the angles is 196 right angles.

Chapter 24: Transformations and symmetry

24.1: a) Translation, –6 units in x-direction, 0 units in y-direction; b) reflection in vertical line passing through (8, 0); c) rotation through half-turn about (5, 2), clockwise or anticlockwise.

24.2: a) A diagonal line passing through (11, 3) and (13, 1); b) a vertical line passing through (12, 2); c) a horizontal line passing through (12, 2). Order of rotational symmetry is four.

24.3: No.

24.4: No.

Chapter 25: Classifying shapes

25.1: Because all the angles in an equilateral triangle must be 60°.
25.2: 90°, 45° and 45°.
25.3: a) Square; b) square; c) equilateral triangle; d) cuboid; e) tetrahedron.
25.4: The parallelogram tessellates, as do all quadrilaterals.
25.5: Nine.
25.6: a) False; b) true; c) true; d) true; e) false; f) false.

Chapter 26: Perimeter, area and volume

26.1: The maximum area is given by the square field, 5 units by 5 units, i.e. 25 square units.
26.2: The minimum length of fencing is 28 units, for a field that is 6 units by 8 units.
26.3: a) As a cube with side 3 units; total surface area = 54 square units; b) as a cuboid, 4 units by 4 units by 3 units; total surface area = 80 square units (16 + 16 + 12 + 12 + 12 + 12).
26.4: About 78.5 cm (25 × 3.14); 80 cm to be on the safe side.
26.5: About 127 m (400 ÷ 3.14).
26.6: The area of the parallelogram is the same as that of a rectangle with base 5 units and height 3 units, i.e. 15 square units.
26.7: The area of the trapezium is 100 cm². The general rule is that the area is half the height multiplied by the sum of the parallel sides. E.g, for height 10cm, parallel sides 12 cm and 6 cm, the area is 5 × 18 = 90 cm²; for height 10 cm, parallel sides 12 cm and 9 cm, the area is 5 × 21 = 105 cm².
26.8: The area is 25 mm², or 0.25 cm², or 0.000025 m².
26.9: Volume is 125 cm³ or 0.000125 m³.
26.10: 20 × 25 × 10 = 5000 cuboids needed.

Chapter 27: Mathematical reasoning

27.1: Not correct. For example, there are only two prime numbers in the decade 20–29, i.e. 23 and 29.
27.2: a) False: a counter-example is 8; b) true; c) true; d) false: a counter-example is any non-square rhombus; e) true; f) true; g) false: a counter-example would be obtained by sticking together two regular tetrahedra; h) false: this book approximates to a cuboid but none of the faces is

square; i) true – it is also a cube, which is a cuboid; j) false: a counter-example would be a regular octahedron; k) true.

27.3: The square has a perimeter of 8 units. I can draw four other shapes. Checking these in turn, they all have perimeters of 10 units.

27.4: The number of matches is double the number of triangles, plus 1. Explanation: put down 1 match, then 2 further matches are needed to make a triangle and each subsequent triangle. Zero triangles does not require any matches, so this is a special case that does not fit the generalization.

27.5: This is because $7 \times 11 \times 13 = 1001$ and any six-digit number 'abcabc' is the three-digit number 'abc' multiplied by 1001.

Index